Contents

KU-346-078

Illuminate Publishing

WJEC GCSE
Health and Social Care,
and Childcare

Mark Walsh

Published in 2019 by Illuminate Publishing Ltd,
PO Box 1160, Cheltenham, Gloucestershire GL50 9RW

Orders: Please visit www.illuminatepublishing.com
or email sales@illuminatepublishing.com

British Library Cataloguing-in-Publication Data
A catalogue record of this book is available from the British Library.

ISBN 978-1-911208-95-2

Printed by Cambrian Printers, Aberystwyth

07.19

The publisher's policy is to use papers that are natural, renewable and recyclable products made from wood grown in sustainable forests. The logging and manufacturing processes are expected to conform to the environmental regulations in the country of origin.

Every effort has been made to contact copyright holders of material reproduced in this book. Great care has been taken by the author and publisher to ensure that either formal permission has been granted for the use of copyright material reproduced, or that copyright material has been used under the provision of fairdealing guidelines in the UK – specifically that it has been used sparingly, solely for the purpose of criticism and review, and has been properly acknowledged. If notified, the publisher will be pleased to rectify any errors or omissions at the earliest opportunity.

Editor: Helen Broadfield
Design and layout: Kamae Design
Cover design: Kamae Design
Cover photographs: (top) jax10289 / Shutterstock, (middle) Dave Clark Digital Photo / Shutterstock, (bottom) Miriam Doerr and Martin Frommherz / Shutterstock

Photo acknowledgements

p.1 (top) jax10289; p.1 (middle) Dave Clark Digital Photo; p.1 (bottom) Miriam Doerr Martin Frommherz; p.12 Rawpixel.com; p.13 Lia Koltyrina; p.14 Dundanim; p.15 (top) Suzanne Tucker; p.15 (middle) jennylipets; p.15 (bottom) Reprinted with permission of the World Health Organization from https://www.who.int/childgrowth/standards/cht_wfa_girls_p_0_6.pdf?ua=1; p.17 marilyn barbone; p.18 (top) GertjanVH; p.18 (bottom) Lordn; p.19 (top) dotshock; p.20 Halfpoint; p.21 SaferTim; p.23 (top) Monkey Business Images; p.23 (bottom) Monkey Business Images; p.24 Antonio Guillem; p.25 (top) Cresta Johnson; p.25 (bottom) Rawpixel.com; p.26 Speedkingz; p.27 (top) Chepko Ddanil Vitalevich; p.28 Emese; p.29 Eugenio Marongiu; p.30 wacpan; p.31 (top) Steve Bloom Images / Alamy Stock Photo; p.31 (bottom) Kateryna Kon; p.32 Africa Studio; p.34 Oleg Golovnev; p.35 (top) Skylines; p.35 (bottom) DGLimages; p.39 (top) Andreas Zerndl / Shutterstock.com; p.39 (bottom) Distinctive Images; p.40 Jack Frog; p.41 Alexa Zari; p.42 Tana888; p.43 (bottom) czitrox; p.44 (top) Roengrit Kongmuang; p.44 (bottom) Stephane Debove; p.45 MediaPictures.pl / Shutterstock.com; p.47 Asier Romero; p.48 WAYHOME studio; p.49 mavo; p.50 Avesun; p.51 Rawpixel.com; p.52 WAYHOME studio; p.53 (top) wavebreakmedia; p.54 (bottom) Monkey Business Images; p.55 Andrey_Popov; p.56 Belish; p.57 EL Comondear; p.58 Africa Studio; p.61 (top) Tyler Olson; p.62 George Rudy; p.66 Estrada Anton; p.67 Monkey Business Images; p.68 Mikhail Tchkheidze; p.70 fizkes; p.72 Monkey Business Images; p.73 Tiplyashina Evgeniya; p.76 Elena Shashkina; p.77 jax10289 / shutterstock.com; p.80 Intellectual Property Office © Crown copy7right 2018, www.publichealthnetwork.cymru/en/topics/policy/well-being-of-future-generations-wales-act-2015/; p.82 magda_shutterstock; p.83 Dragon Images; p.84 (top) Albina Glisic; p.84 (bottom) jax10289 / shutterstock.com; p.86 © NHS Wales, 2019, http://www.wales.nhs.uk/nhswalesaboutus/structure; p.87 Andrey Popov; p.88 Kzenon; p.89 Miriam Doerr Martin Frommherz; p.92 Africa Studio; p.93 Monkey Business Images; p.94 Phase4Studios; p.98 Alice Day; p.99 Nina Rys; p.100 Public Health Wales Observatory; p.102 palomadelosrios; p.103 Rawpixel.com; p.105 (top) Caftor; p.105 (bottom) NHS (Wales); p.106 (left) NHS (Wales); p.106 (right) © CCBC; p.107 Courtesy Cancer Research UK; p.108 majivecka; p.109 forma 82; p.111 (top) Lightspring p.111 (bottom) Oxford Media Library / Shutterstock.com; p.112 Image Point Fr; p.113 txking; p.115 bitt24; p.116 Iakov Filimonov; p.117 Rawpixel.com; p.118 NakoPhotography; p.119 finwal89; p.122 Jiri Miklo; p.123 (top) viaru; p.123 (bottom) muratart; p.124 Butterfly Hunter; p.125 Courtesy Drinkaware.co.uk; p.127 astarot; p.130 FXQuadro; p.131 William Perugini; p.132 YAKOBCHUK VIACHESLAV; p.134 Brian A Jackson; p.135 Rawpixel.com; p.136 Rawpixel.com; p.138 Lordn; p.139 kiwiofmischief; p.144 © Learned Society of Wales; p.145 Brian A Jackson; p.151 threeocksimages; p.152 (top) dvoevnore /Shutterstock.com; p.152 (bottom) Courtesy Wales NHS; p.154 Creative Commons; p.155 Intellectual Property Office © Crown copyright 2015; p.157 Rungruedee; p.158 CREATISTA; p.164 Nejron Photo; p.165 Albina Glisic; p.166 netzajamal; p.168 andrekoehn; p.169 bht2000; p.170 xtock; p.172 Paul Nash; p.175 esfera; p.178 JP WALLET; p.179 Monkey Business Images; p.183 Lisa F. Young; p.184 Africa Studio; p.187 Marcel Jancovi; p.188 FamVeld; p.195 Ivanskay Svetlana; p.196 (top) Axel Bueckert; p.196 (bottom) Rido; p.197 YIAKIOBCHUK VIACHESLAV; p.200 Eugenio Margonglu; p.201 (top) DGLimages; p.201 (bottom) rdonar; p.202 fizkes; p.203 googluz; p.204 Pressmaster; p.207 (top) Alextype; p.207 (bottom) Jne Valokuvaus; p.208 Photographee.eu; p.209 Zurijeta; p.210 fizkes; p.211 belushi; p.213 DarioZg / Shutterstock.com; p.215 Monkey Business Images

Introduction

How to use this book

This student book is designed to provide you with the detailed information and guidance for the WJEC GCSE in Health and Social Care, and Childcare whether you are studying for the single or double award. It introduces you to the theoretical frameworks underpinning the healthcare, social care and childcare sectors in Wales, which are essential for developing your understanding of the subject. You will find advice and guidance to help you prepare for the written examinations at the end of the course and for the practical, Non-Exam Assessments.

The WJEC GCSE Health and Social Care, and Childcare specification

The WJEC GCSE Health and Social Care, and Childcare course is designed to provide you with the knowledge, understanding and skills related to caring for and supporting individuals in Wales from birth to late adulthood. The specification will enable you to recognise that there are varying influences on growth, development, behaviour and well-being and that individuals using support services have individual abilities and physical, intellectual, emotional and social needs. The course aims to help you to understand how current service provision in Wales meets the needs of its population and how this might need to change throughout the 21st century in order to continue to meet those needs.

The WJEC GCSE in Health and Social Care, and Childcare can be studied as a single or double award and the structure is summarised below:

Single award

The single award comprises Units 1 and 2:

Unit	Assessment
1: Human growth, development and well-being 40% of single award qualification 20% of double award qualification	Written examination: 1 hour 30 minutes 80 marks
2: Promoting and maintaining health and well-being 60% of single award qualification 30% of double award qualification	Non-Exam Assessment: Approximately 25 hours 120 marks

Unit 2 is assessed through two tasks relating to a service provision (40%) and the promotion and maintenance of health and well-being (60%).

Double award

The double award comprises Units 1 and 2 **plus**:

Unit	Assessment
3: Health and social care, and childcare in the 21st century 20% of double award qualification	Written examination: 1 hour 30 minutes 80 marks
4: Promoting and supporting health and well-being to achieve positive outcomes 30% of double award qualification	Non-Exam Assessment: Approximately 25 hours 120 marks

Unit 4 is assessed through a task relating to meaningful activities suitable for a chosen target group.

Key features and structure of the book

The book is divided into four units which mirror the four units of the specification. The units are broken down into parts and then into topics to present the most important aspects of the specification content, including support for the components that will be assessed by Non-Exam Assessment. Each topic includes the following features:

Think about it

Key terms

Did you know?

Case study

Check your understanding

In addition to the above features in each topic, the book includes the following features:

- a graphical summary of the content at the end of each unit which helps to reinforce the concepts and knowledge

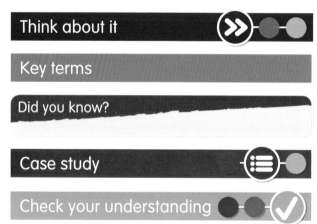

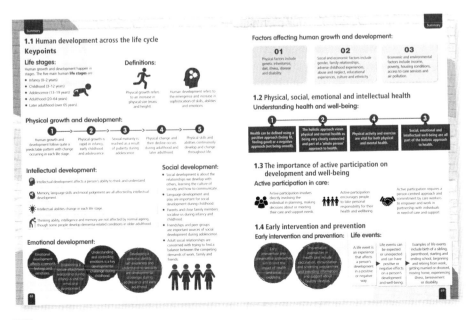

- a reference of the specific terminology appearing in the **Key terms** throughout the book.

Unit 1: You will learn about human development across the life cycle and the ways in which this can be affected. The unit also discusses ways in which individuals can take control of their health, well-being and any care they may need. Finally, you will look at methods of early intervention and prevention and how these may promote individuals' growth and development.

Unit 2: You will learn about the various health and social care, and childcare services available in Wales. The unit will examine how these services promote and maintain the health and well-being of the people living in Wales. The content of this unit will support you in completing your Non-Exam Assessment task for both the single and double award.

Unit 3: You will learn about the ethical issues affecting service provision in Wales. The unit will look at the challenges involved in providing and supporting a sustainable health and social care, and childcare system for Wales in the 21st century.

Unit 4: You will learn about the ways in which health and social care, and childcare services aim to provide support to individuals in Wales to achieve health and well-being. The unit also focuses on self-identity and the use of meaningful activities to support health, development and well-being. The content of this unit will support you in completing your Non-Exam Assessment task for the double award.

Non-Exam Assessment

If you are studying for the WJEC GCSE Health and Social Care, and Childcare **single award** you will need to complete two tasks for Unit 2 which will be assessed by your teacher. Task 1 is to write a report on local and national service provision within Wales to meet the needs of one of the following target groups: children, adolescents or adults. Within that service provision, you should investigate the roles of two key professionals and analyse the task. Task 2 is to write a report on the health promotion available to your chosen target group concerning a topic of your choice. You should also plan a health promotion campaign or activity surrounding this and analyse the task.

If you are studying for the WJEC GCSE Health and Social Care, and Childcare **double award**, in addition to your assessed work for Unit 2 as described above, you will need to complete one task for Unit 4 which will also be assessed by your teacher. You will need to choose a target group and write a report on your investigation work into their specific needs and the current service provision to meet those needs. You will analyse any local and national trends within Wales that may affect this provision. You will investigate meaningful activities to meet a particular need of your chosen target group and then plan and produce an activity. You will analyse and evaluate the task.

Examination practice and technique

This section will help you to prepare for the examination part of your course. Different people will find different revision and examination strategies helpful, so it is a good idea to try and think about the ways you learn and what works for you. For revising, you might find it helpful to make lists, draw pictures or even read your notes aloud and record them to listen back to at a later date.

Assessment

In the examination and Non-Exam Assessment elements of the course, you will be required to demonstrate three levels of knowledge and understanding.

Assessment objective	Specification detail	What this means in practice
AO1	**Demonstrate** knowledge and understanding of health and social care, and childcare concepts, values and issues.	You can describe and explain the key concepts, values and issues affecting the health and social care, and childcare sectors.
AO2	**Apply** knowledge and understanding of health and social care, and childcare concepts, values and issues in a variety of relevant contexts.	You can use your knowledge and understanding of the concepts, values and issues to examine a variety of areas within the health and social care, and childcare sectors and show their differences.
AO3	**Analyse** and **evaluate** health and social care, and childcare concepts, values and issues, making reasoned judgements and drawing conclusions.	You can consider how and when the concepts, values and issues in the health and social care, and childcare sectors may need to be applied differently and can then assess whether the care needs and support have been met.

How can I prepare for the exam?

Revision

The written examinations that you will take at the end of Units 1 and 3 (double award only) are a great opportunity for you to show what you can do. The examiner marking your work wants to give you as many marks as they can. They can only give you credit for what you write so it is very important to prepare well and know what is expected of you.

Revision planning

It is best to plan your revision – this puts you in control and is much more effective than random or last-minute revision. You should try to do the following:

- Review the unit specification and make a list of the subjects or topics that you could be examined on.

- Highlight the subjects or topics that need the most revision and prioritise time to cover these.

- Create a revision plan, divided up into revision blocks that cover the topics you need to know about and understand.

It is also very important to know when and where your exam will take place. Your teacher should let you know this well in advance of the exam. You should also ask your teacher to explain how the exam papers work and what you will need to do. Don't be the person who turns up at the wrong time or place, or the student who hasn't prepared for the exam!

Revision strategies

There are lots of different revision strategies to try. It is worth trying different techniques to discover what works well for you as well as what doesn't. As part of your revision you could try some of the following:

- Make summary notes in the run up to your exam – making summary notes of those summary notes just before the exam is a way of further reinforcing the key points.

- Turn notes into flashcards or create lists on sticky notes of ideas, key words or facts and stick them on your bedroom wall.

- Make mind maps or flow diagrams of key words and ideas linked to a topic – this helps to break up and summarise big topics into smaller, manageable and linked chunks that are easier to remember and recall.

- Revise with a friend who is supportive and will compare notes and share ideas – you could take turns and test each other.

- Use your phone to record your notes and listen to them on the way to school or college or when you need a break from reading and writing.

Students often find that it is best to revise for short blocks of time. For example, three 20-minute sessions with a short break in between is better than trying to revise for a continuous hour or more. Focusing on one topic for these three 20-minute blocks also works better than changing topic every 20 minutes.

Exam preparation

The best way to prepare for your Unit 1 and Unit 3 exams is to practise answering questions from past papers. This is the most realistic way of testing yourself before you sit the actual examination.

Sample assessment material and past papers for GCSE Health and Social Care, and Childcare can be found on the WJEC website. These are freely available for you and your teacher to download and use as part of your revision and exam preparation. You will need to obtain both the question paper and the mark scheme (the answer sheet). You may need your teacher to explain the mark scheme, especially the answers to longer, high-mark questions.

To make the most of past papers, there are some basic guidelines to follow:

- Set time limits when answering questions – as you have to in the real exam.

- Answer all the questions on a paper – as you have to in the real exam.

- Avoid using books or notes to look up or check answers – this isn't allowed in the exam itself.

- Make sure that you answer the question that is being asked – don't just write everything you know about a topic! The examiner can only give you credit for points that are relevant to the exam question.

- Check your answers against the mark scheme when you finish the paper – be honest and note any areas you need to revise more.

- Use your notes and this textbook to improve each answer, noting carefully what else you could say if this question came up in the real exam.

You might find that some questions are difficult or that you don't know how to answer a question. This is a good indicator that you need to revise these areas to improve your knowledge. Don't be tempted to skip these questions for others that are easier. Filling in the gaps in your knowledge and understanding now is the best way to improve your marks in the real exam.

Dealing with exam stress

Preparing for and taking GCSE exams is a stressful experience for many young people. You can do various things to manage, and minimise, the stress you experience at this point in your life. For example:

- Avoid late nights and make sure you get enough sleep.

- Eat regular, nutritionally balanced meals, avoiding junk food.

- Take regular exercise – physical activity can help you to relax and release feelings of stress.

- Make studying your priority – reduce or limit your other commitments until your exams are over and don't begin new clubs, hobbies or personal relationships that will compete for your time and attention.

- Develop a regular study routine – find suitable times and quiet places where you can concentrate on revision.

- Leave yourself enough time to revise – avoid putting off your revision until later and last minute 'cramming' as this will help to keep your anxiety levels down.

- Plan and take control of your revision – set yourself goals and objectives and reward yourself with a treat for achieving them.

- Revise in chunks of 15–20 minutes, taking a break between study chunks – staying up late and revising for hours without a break will make you more stressed.
- Slow, controlled breathing (inhale slowly through your nose, hold the breath for a second, then exhale slowly through your mouth) can reduce feelings of panic and help you to feel calmer.

Good luck with your exams! Planning revision, preparing summary notes and practising past papers will all help you to do your best.

1 Human Growth, Development and Well-being

This unit provides you with opportunities to gain knowledge and understanding of human development across the life cycle and the ways in which this may be affected; how individuals can take control of their care and health and well-being; and how early intervention (or action) and prevention can support the growth and development of individuals.

This unit consists of four main parts:

1.1 Human development across the life cycle

1.2 Physical, social, emotional and intellectual health

1.3 The importance of active participation on development and well-being

1.4 Early intervention and prevention to promote growth, development and well-being

Each part of the unit has been broken down into shorter topics. These topics will help you to understand your own growth and development as well as that of other people you may go on to work with or care for. This will help if you get a job as a health, social care or childcare worker after you have left school or college. It will also help if you have children or need to provide care for other members of your family at some point in your life. You also need to learn about human growth and development because there is an exam that you need to sit!

Assessment: 1.5 hour written examination

◄ Growth and development occurs across the different stages of the life cycle.

Part 1.1 Human development across the life cycle

Topic 1: Human growth and development

Topic 2: Understanding physical growth

Topic 3: Understanding physical development

Topic 4: Understanding intellectual development

Topic 5: Understanding emotional development

Topic 6: Understanding social development

Topic 7: Physical factors affecting growth, development and well-being

Topic 8: Social and economic factors affecting growth, development and well-being

Topic 9: Economic and environmental factors affecting growth, development and well-being

Part 1.2 Physical, social, emotional and intellectual health

Topic 10: Understanding health and well-being

Topic 11: Understanding social, emotional and intellectual health

Part 1.3 The importance of active participation on development and well-being

Topic 12: Active participation in care

Topic 13: Early intervention and prevention

Part 1.4 Early intervention and prevention to promote growth, development and well-being

Topic 14: Managing health conditions

Topic 15: Understanding life events

1.1 HUMAN DEVELOPMENT ACROSS THE LIFE CYCLE
1 Human growth and development

Think about it

1. List three ways a baby changes in the first two years of its life.
2. Which life stages do you think the people in the picture on the right are in at this point in their lives?
3. Describe three non-physical ways in which the baby in the picture on the right will change over the next five years.

▲ Human growth and development are continuous processes that happens to all people.

Life stages, growth and development

Just over 3 million people (3 113 200) were living in Wales in 2016. During this year, life began for 32 936 babies and ended for the 33 066 people who died (StatsWales, 2018 and Office for National Statistics, 2018). Studying human **physical growth** and development helps us understand the changes that happen to people between the beginning and end of their lives.

Human growth and development happen in stages. The five main **life stages** we will focus on are:

- infancy (0–2 years)
- childhood (3–12 years)
- adolescence (13–19 years)
- adulthood (20–64 years)
- later adulthood (over 65 years).

These life stages cover the whole of the human **life span**. On average, this is approximately 78 years for men and 82 years for women living in Wales today.

What is physical growth?

Physical growth involves changes in the human body. Typically, a person will experience a gradual increase in their height and weight as they move from infancy through childhood and into adolescence and early adulthood. At this point, when they are 'grown up', the person reaches physical **maturity** and will not grow any taller. They may still grow heavier, putting on weight, due to lifestyle and health factors.

What is human development?

As well as experiencing physical growth and change during each life stage, a person will also experience physical, intellectual, emotional and social (P.I.E.S) **development**. When a person develops, their skills, abilities and emotions change, becoming more sophisticated and complex at first and then declining as a result of ageing. Developmental change is a continuous, lifelong process which follows a pattern. This makes it possible to predict how a person will grow and develop, how they will change and when this will happen during their infancy, childhood and adolescence. This is summed up in the idea of **developmental norms**.

Key terms

Physical growth
An increase in physical size (mass and height).

Life stages
A stage, phase or period of the human life cycle.

Life span
The time between a person's birth and their death.

Maturity
The state of being fully developed or adult.

Development
The emergence (appearance) and increase in sophistication of skills, abilities and emotions.

Developmental norms
Standards by which the progress of a child's development can be measured.

Did you know?

A person will have reached their maximum height and completed most of their natural body-building processes by early adulthood.

Key term

Puberty
The process of physical change through which a child's body matures into an adult body capable of sexual reproduction.

► Examples of developmental norms.

Developmental norms

Developmental norms, or 'milestones', typically refer to the points in a person's life where particular changes are expected to happen. The average age at which a child walks, learns to talk, or reaches **puberty** would be a standard or developmental norm.

The table below outlines examples of age-linked developmental norms that occur in the human life cycle.

Age	Ability
3–4 months	Infants start on solid foods, develop better head control, can roll from side to side, reach for objects
6–9 months	Teething begins, learn to sit unaided, lift their heads and look around, use thumb and index finger to grasp objects
9–12 months	Infants can crawl, chew food, use their hands to explore, can walk holding onto parent or furniture ('cruising'), may say a few words, know their name and start to understand their parents' or caregivers' words
12–18 months	Toddlers learn to feed themselves, walk unaided, can understand simple requests – 'give it to me' – develop better memory and concentration
18–24 months	Toddlers can run, turn pages of a book, use simple sentences, have temper outbursts and can say their own name
10 years (girls) 12 years (boys)	Puberty begins
45–55 years (women)	Menopause occurs

Did you know?

A person is not abnormal if they achieve growth or development at slightly different times to the expected pattern. Growth and development can be different to the 'norm' for a variety of reasons.

Though human growth and development follow quite a predictable pattern, it is important not to think of this as an exact timetable that 'normal' people follow.

Case study

Andrea is 40 years old. She is the mother of Sally, aged two, and Lizzie, aged five. She has been married to Gareth, aged 44, for ten years. Maureen, who is 75 years old, is Andrea's mum and lives with the family in Pembrokeshire, west Wales. Gareth's parents, Elwyn, aged 79, and Anwen, aged 75, live in Llangefni, north Wales.

1. Which life stages are Sally and Lizzie in now?

2. Name the people who are in the later adulthood life stage.

3. How many people in the case study are in the adulthood life stage?

Check your understanding

1. What life stage is a four-year-old in?

2. What are 'developmental norms'?

3. Explain what the term P.I.E.S refers to when discussing human growth and development.

4. Alice is 12 months (one year) old. Which of the following milestones would she be expected to reach by now:
   a) Able to sit unaided.   **b)** Able to run.   **c)** Able to ask a question.

▲ Differing life stages.

2 Understanding physical growth

Think about it

1. List three ways in which Owen has changed physically during childhood.

2. Describe a different activity for each age shown in the photo that could help Owen to develop physically.

3. What kinds of physical changes is Owen likely to experience in his next life stage?

▲ Owen aged 3, 5, 7, 9 and 11 years.

Physical growth across the life cycle

Every person will experience physical growth and changes in their body in each life stage. What happens when we 'grow', and the pattern of human growth in each life stage, is our focus here.

Physical growth in infancy

Physical growth happens very quickly during infancy. As a result of rapid physical growth, infants quickly change from being small, light-weight, dependent babies into much larger, heavier and stronger 'toddlers' in the second year of their life.

An infant is first able to hold their head up without help before they are able to use their body to sit up. Following this, an infant is able to use their legs to crawl. An infant's bones gradually grow and get harder and their muscles get stronger in the same head-downwards, middle-outwards pattern during infancy. Within 18 months, many infants are quite robust, active 'toddlers'.

Key terms

Health Visitor
A qualified and registered nurse or midwife with additional training who assesses the health needs of individuals, children and their families.

Percentile chart
A way of monitoring and recording a child's growth by comparing it to a certain percentage of the population.

Did you know?

Physical change in a young infant's body occurs from the head downwards and from the middle of the body outwards.

3 months   6 months   7 months   9 months   12 months

◄ Physical change is rapid and quite dramatic during infancy.

A **Health Visitor** will usually monitor and measure an infant's physical growth in the first few years of their life. The Health Visitor will weigh the infant and measure the length of their body from the top of their head to their toes. These details are recorded on a **percentile chart** (see chart on the right). This allows the Health Visitor to compare the infant's growth pattern to average and expected patterns for all infants of the same age.

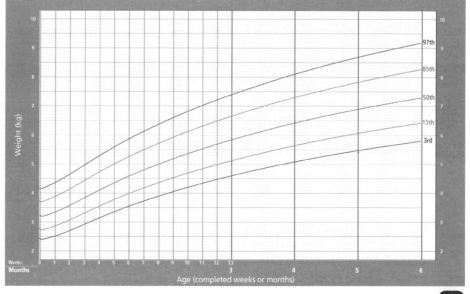

► A percentile chart for monitoring the growth of girls 0–6 months. Source: WHO

Growth spurt
A period of accelerated physical change that occurs in mid-childhood and during puberty.

Sexual maturity
The point at which a person is biologically capable of sexual reproduction.

Menopause
The ceasing of menstruation and loss of fertility in women.

▶ Physical changes in puberty.

Physical growth in childhood

A child's body changes noticeably in early childhood as they lose their baby shape and gradually develop the proportions of a small adult. Most children will experience a **growth spurt** in the middle part of childhood, though their rate of growth is slower in childhood than it was during infancy. It's harder to notice children's gradual physical changes until near the end of this life stage when puberty occurs.

Physical growth and change in adolescence

Puberty is the time when an adolescent's body undergoes rapid growth and physical change. As well as an individual growing taller and heavier, the process of puberty results in **sexual maturity** when they are physically capable of sexual reproduction. A person has usually also achieved their adult height and body shape by the end of puberty. The table outlines a range of physical changes that boys and girls experience during puberty.

Physical changes in boys	Physical changes in girls
Grow taller and heavier	Grow taller and heavier
Grow pubic, facial and underarm hair	Grow pubic and underarm hair
Penis and testes grow larger	Develop breasts
Shoulders and chest broaden and muscles develop	Hips broaden and shape changes
Voice 'breaks' or deepens	Menstruation (periods) start

Physical change in adulthood

Early adulthood is when people commonly think of themselves as being 'grown up'. A person's fitness and physical abilities peak in early adulthood and then slowly decline as they age. For example, in the second half of early adulthood, from about 30 to 45 years, the amount of fatty tissue in a person's body increases, they move more slowly and take longer to recover from their efforts. By the end of early adulthood, many people have also begun to lose their hair or go grey and will begin to see wrinkles developing around their eyes as their skin becomes less supple.

Physical change becomes more obvious during middle adulthood. From about 45 to 65 years of age a person is likely to experience some or all of the following physical changes:

- increasing and more obvious hair loss
- reduced muscle mass
- deteriorating eyesight
- appearance of wrinkles as the skin loses elasticity
- decline in fertility as sperm production diminishes (men)
- an increase in weight.

Menopause, or the ending of menstruation and the ability to produce children, is a physical change that occurs naturally in a woman's body during middle adulthood.

Physical change in later adulthood (65+)

The **normal ageing** process causes gradual changes in a person's physique and the way their body works. By later adulthood a person is likely to have:

- reduced heart and lung function
- reduced **mobility** due to muscle wastage, stiff joints and brittle bones
- reduced sensitivity to the cold, to taste and to smell
- some loss of hearing (quiet and high-pitched sounds)
- eyesight changes due to loss of elasticity in the lens of the eye
- weaker and more brittle bones (**osteoporosis**)
- loss of height as the spinal discs become thinner and posture becomes bent.

The effects of ageing mean that older people do have less strength and stamina than earlier in life. This doesn't mean that older people are inactive or disabled by these physical changes. In fact, being physically active helps many older people to remain in good physical health and stay fit.

Key terms

Normal ageing
Natural physical changes that happen over a person's life.

Mobility
The ability to move freely in a coordinated way.

Osteoporosis
A medical condition in which the bones become brittle.

Well-being
A state characterised by health, happiness and prosperity.

Case study

Alfie Jones is 53 years old. He lives in mid Wales with his wife Audrey (aged 47) and daughter, Janine (aged 19). Alfie is concerned about his health and **well-being**. He stopped playing football in his leisure time and put on 7 kilograms (15 pounds) in weight last year. Alfie has also started going bald and says he gets physically tired more easily than he used to. Audrey has told him he should stop smoking cigarettes as he has recently developed a bad cough and gets breathless when he mows the lawn at home. Alfie has also started wearing reading glasses at work as he can no longer read his computer screen or documents without them. He has now made an appointment with his GP (General Practitioner or family doctor) for an 'Over 50s Health Check' as he is worried that his health is failing.

1. What life stage are Alfie and Audrey in at this point in their lives?
2. Identify two physical changes that Alfie has experienced recently that are a part of normal ageing.
3. Which aspect of Alfie's recent physical health experience is not a part of normal ageing? Explain why he should see his GP about this.

▲ Alfie's health is now affected by the ageing process.

Check your understanding

1. What does the term 'physical growth' mean?
2. How does a percentile chart help a health visitor to assess a child's physical growth?
3. Explain what puberty is and how it changes boys' and girls' bodies.
4. What is the menopause and who does it affect?
5. Describe three physical changes that occur in later adulthood as a result of normal ageing processes.

3 Understanding physical development

▲ Hannah and Elin love to do **parkour** together.

Think about it

1. List three physical attributes that are needed to perform like Hannah and Elin in the picture on the left.
2. Give two reasons to explain why Hannah and Elin's age makes a difference to their athletic abilities.
3. Describe the physical abilities needed to perform well in your favourite sport.

Physical development across the life cycle

A person's physical skills and abilities are continuously changing and developing as they progress from one life stage to another. The basic physical abilities of infancy are soon replaced by greater abilities in childhood. By the time a person has reached adulthood, their physical skills and abilities are very sophisticated. In this section of the unit, we will focus on the way in which physical development occurs in each life stage.

Did you know?

A child will develop and improve their coordination and balance control by playing games where they skip, catch a ball or ride a bicycle.

Infancy and childhood

A person experiences a huge amount of physical development during infancy and childhood. This is partly because physical growth during infancy and childhood improves a child's strength, stamina and **dexterity**. This makes it possible for the child to use their body in new ways. As a result, a child's coordination, balance and physical movement all improve rapidly during their early years. Play and learning activities in the reception and lower infant classes of nurseries and primary schools help young children to practise and reinforce their **gross motor skills** and **fine motor skills**.

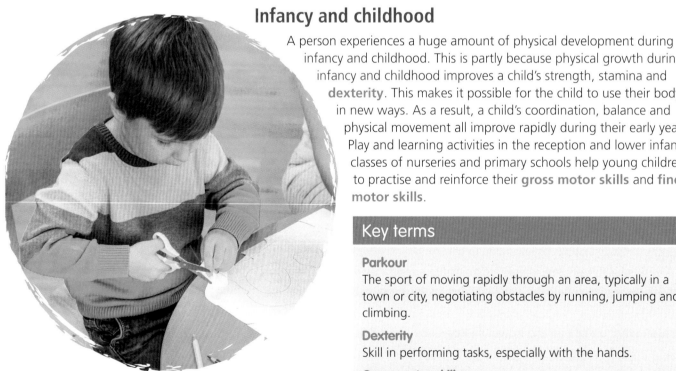

▲ A child needs to develop their fine motor skills in order to use scissors.

Key terms

Parkour
The sport of moving rapidly through an area, typically in a town or city, negotiating obstacles by running, jumping and climbing.

Dexterity
Skill in performing tasks, especially with the hands.

Gross motor skills
Whole body movements that depend on a person being able to control the large muscles in their arms and legs.

Fine motor skills
Movements of the hands, wrists, fingers, feet and toes that rely on control over smaller muscles.

Adolescence

Many basic physical skills have been mastered through learning and practice by the end of childhood. Despite this, adolescents generally have better physical skills and abilities than children. This is partly because adolescents are more physically mature than children but also because adolescents have had more time and opportunity to use and practise their fine and gross motor skills.

It's also important to know that physical development doesn't occur separately from intellectual, emotional and social development. An adolescent is likely to be a better tennis player, swimmer or footballer than when they were a child also because they now have more brain power and better emotional composure.

Adulthood

A person has generally stopped growing by the time they reach adulthood. This doesn't mean their physical development has stopped though.

Most people achieve their maximum physical performance during early adulthood. You may have noticed that athletes and sports professionals tend to be young adults.

It's also noticeable that athletes and professional sports people tend to get slower and gradually lose their ability to perform at the highest level as they reach their early thirties.

▲ Adolescents are able to use their bodies with greater skill and precision than children.

◄ Physique, fitness and physical ability slowly decline with age.

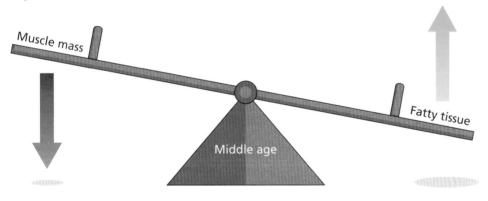

Did you know?

A lot of physical development occurs in early adulthood as people use and refine their physical potential and abilities.

By the end of early adulthood, a person's stamina, balance and coordination will have declined, affecting their physical skills and performance.

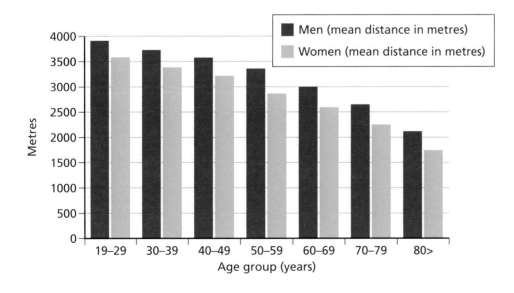

◄ The distance a person can swim in one hour declines with age.
Source: Based on statistics from Bongard, V., McDermott, A.Y., Dallal, G.E., & Schaefer, E.J. (2007).

Later adulthood

From middle age onwards, physical development is about adapting to the changes that are occurring in a person's ageing body. People tend to find new ways to do physical tasks and meet their everyday needs when their strength, stamina and physical skills decline and they lose the ability to function as they did earlier in life.

Many of the physical changes that occur in later adulthood, or old age, are part of the normal ageing process, although a person's physical abilities may also be affected by ill health and long-term conditions.

▲ Gross motor skills involve whole body movements.

Case study

Sam and Ceri's daughter, Ellen, is now a year old. She is able to pull herself up to a standing position and can walk while in the house if she holds on to furniture. She can sit unsupported on the floor and does this when playing with her toys. Sam and Ceri often take Ellen to the park in her pushchair. Ellen enjoys being pushed along as her parents jog around the park.

1. Identify one activity Ellen does where she uses gross motor skills.

2. How could Sam and Ceri encourage Ellen to develop her gross motor skills further?

3. What kind of toys or activities might help Ellen to develop her gross motor skills?

Check your understanding

1. What does the term physical development refer to?

2. Identify whether each of the following is an example of a gross or fine motor skill:
   a) kicking a football
   b) tying a shoelace
   c) sitting up unaided.

3. Outline two reasons to explain why a 15-year-old adolescent is likely to have better tennis playing skills than an 11-year-old child.

4. Explain how a person's physical skills and abilities change in later adulthood.

4 Understanding intellectual development

Think about it

1. How should we talk to babies? Should we use proper words like 'train' or baby-talk like 'choo-choo' instead?

2. Who taught you the difference between 'right' and 'wrong'?

3. What effect, if any, do you think old age has on the mental abilities of older people?

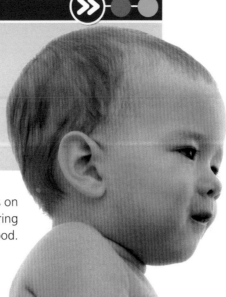

▶ Learning to talk relies on intellectual development during infancy and early childhood.

Intellectual development across the life cycle

Intellectual development affects a person's ability to think and understand. It changes their ability to make sense of situations, remember and recall things and use language. It also affects the way a person is able to make **moral judgements** about what is 'right' and 'wrong', 'good' and 'bad'.

Infancy

During infancy, we learn about ourselves and the world through our senses (touch, hearing, sight, smell and taste) and through physical activity. As well as handling, listening to and looking at new things, an infant will often put objects into their mouth as a way of investigating and trying to understand them.

One very important lesson that infants learn is that objects and people in the world continue to exist even when they can't be seen. This might seem obvious to you now, but it's not to a young baby.

Did you know?

An infant of eight months or less won't usually search for a toy that has been hidden or rolls out of sight because, to them, it no longer exists.

Did you know?

Intellectual development begins as soon as a baby is born and only stops when the person dies. A lot of basic intellectual development happens during infancy.

Key terms

Intellectual
Refers to a person's ability to think and understand ideas and information.

Moral judgement
The process of making decisions about the right course of action or an acceptable way to behave.

Learning to speak is a key part of intellectual development during infancy. A baby is born with the ability to communicate through crying, babbling and using facial expressions. Infants acquire a better understanding of the world around them quite quickly as they begin to explore their surroundings and interact with their main carers. By the time they are two years old most children can name familiar objects when they see them ('dog' or 'bus', for example) and will join a few simple words together ('go park' or 'shoes on', for example).

Childhood

Children become less reliant on physical learning (seeing, touching and holding things) to understand the world as they move into childhood.

Thinking about concepts is necessary for children to learn to read, write and tell the time, for example. Intellectual development during childhood results in huge improvements in a child's thinking and language abilities and in their **communication skills**. In early childhood, children ask lots of questions in an attempt to understand more about their environment and the society in which they live.

Learning the difference between 'right' and 'wrong' and 'good' and 'bad' is an important part of every child's intellectual development. Children learn to base their judgements about moral issues on rules they learn from authority figures, such as their parents and teachers. Children will generally obey rules that keep them from being punished or which lead to rewards. This lasts until late childhood or early adolescence, when making a moral judgement becomes a more sophisticated process.

Adolescence

Abstract thinking skills are a key feature of adolescents' intellectual development. This involves being able to think in a theoretical or hypothetical way. For example, mathematical equations involve abstract thinking as does thinking about what you would like to do in the future. Children do not usually have these thinking skills. This means they can't plan ahead or solve everyday life problems in the same way as adolescents. Abstract thinking is considered to be the final stage of thought development. However, a person's intellectual development is not completed in adolescence. This is because we gain and use experience during early, middle and later adulthood to improve our thinking, understanding and decision-making.

Adulthood

Adults are generally capable of abstract thought, have very good memory skills and can think very quickly. Acquiring new knowledge and skills is necessary during adulthood to cope with the challenges and changes that frequently occur in a person's personal or work life. People who want to progress in their jobs or be promoted will need to undertake some additional learning to achieve their goals. However, younger adults lack the experience of older people and therefore may not always make good decisions or have the same depth of knowledge.

Many middle-aged people also use hobbies, their social life or take evening classes or online courses to continue their intellectual development. Some people retrain for new careers or pursue new directions in their personal life during their middle age.

Did you know?

With childhood comes the ability to think about objects and concepts (such as numbers, letters and colours) that are not actually present.

Key terms

Communication skills
The ability to convey information and ideas to others.

Abstract thinking
The ability to think about objects, principles, and ideas that are not physically present.

Did you know?

A person typically achieves their highest career position during middle age when they are able to combine intellectual abilities developed during adolescence and early adulthood with experience gained throughout their adult working life.

Later adulthood

Older people keep and use their intellectual abilities in much the same ways as adults and middle-aged people. Both the young-old (60–75 years) and the old-old (75 years and over) need and enjoy intellectually stimulating activities in their lives. The speed at which older people are able to think and respond is generally reduced by ageing, but thinking ability and intelligence are not affected.

There are many negative ideas about older people's intellectual abilities. It is true that a minority of older people develop **dementia-related illnesses** and have memory problems – but the majority do not. People who develop dementia-related illnesses tend to have memory problems, especially in recalling recent information, and become confused more easily. These types of illnesses also result in the gradual loss of speech and other abilities that are controlled by the brain.

▲ Older people can develop and use their intellectual abilities in many different ways.

Case study

Harriet, aged five, has recently started primary school. She loves going to Ysgol Bryn Coch and has made several new friends already. Harriet's teacher reads stories to the class and encourages all pupils to take part in a range of practical activities. Harriet's favourite activities are painting and playing games in the kitchen corner.

1. List three things that you would expect Harriet to learn in her first year at Ysgol Bryn Coch.

2. Would you expect Harriet to be able to count to ten by the end of her first year at school? Give a reason for your answer.

3. Explain why Harriet's teacher tries to help her learn the difference between 'right' and 'wrong' when she is at school.

▲ Many different types of learning happen at primary school.

Check your understanding

1. Which life stage is a person usually in when they first learn the difference between 'right' and 'wrong'?

2. List three skills or abilities that rely on intellectual development during childhood.

3. Explain why the problem-solving skills of an adolescent are usually better than those of a child.

4. How are the intellectual skills of a person likely to change in later adulthood?

Key term

Dementia-related illnesses
Brain conditions that cause a gradual decrease in the ability to think and remember, which affect a person's daily functioning.

5 Understanding emotional development

Key terms

Emotions
A state of mind resulting from mood, relationships with others or the circumstances a person is in.

Self
A person's sense of 'who' they are.

Self-image
A mental picture a person has of themselves, their abilities and attributes compared to those of others.

Personal identity
A person's view of their qualities, beliefs, personality and sense of belonging.

Attachment relationship
A deep and lasting emotional bond that connects one person to another over time, such as a parent–child relationship.

Bonding
The formation of an emotionally close human relationship.

▼ **Emotions** are a natural part of being human.

Think about it

Erin describes herself as an 'emotional person'.

1. Make a list of five positive emotions and five negative emotions.

2. Describe how a person's behaviour can be affected by their emotions.

3. Explain what emotions may have caused Erin to react in the way she is in the picture above.

Emotional development across the life cycle

Emotional development affects a person's feelings or emotions. It involves:

- becoming aware of your '**self**'
- developing feelings about your 'self'
- working out how you feel towards other people
- developing a **self-image** and **personal identity**.

A person will develop and express emotions, such as love, happiness, sadness and anger, through the relationships and social situations they experience across the life cycle.

Infancy

Feeling loved, secure and cared for during infancy provides an important foundation for later emotional development. Infants should develop feelings of trust and security. This happens when an **attachment relationship** is made between an infant and their parents or main caregivers. The parental response to this emotional linking is known as **bonding**. Effective emotional development depends on the infant's needs being understood and met in a consistent way by their parents or caregivers.

Childhood

As we grow older, we learn to recognise, understand and take account of other people's feelings. The very early relationships we have with parents and close relatives, such as brothers, sisters and grandparents, play a vital role in this. The way that others treat us also affects our emotional development and sense of personal identity.

Learning to cope with our emotions and the feelings that others express towards us is one of the challenges of early childhood. Controlling anger, jealousy and frustration, and dealing with disapproval and criticism, can be difficult and may lead to tears, temper tantrums and **challenging behaviour** at times. A child's parents or caregivers, **siblings**, teachers and friends all help them to develop emotional control by offering love, acceptance and respect.

A child who feels encouraged and supported and who has good role models will develop self-control, **self-confidence** and a sense of independence more easily than a child who is criticised, discouraged and over-protected during early childhood.

Adolescence

Adolescence can be an emotionally difficult but eventful life stage. The hormonal changes of puberty can cause mood swings and intense emotions that may at times be difficult for the adolescent, as well as their family and friends, to cope with. Developing a clear personal identity, making supportive friendships and experiencing emotional support from peers and family members are all important concerns in this phase.

▲ Controlling anger and frustration is an important part of emotional development in childhood.

▲ Supportive friends are important for adolescent emotional development.

Adolescents often experiment with intimate personal relationships with members of the opposite or same sex. This kind of relationship provides an individual with opportunities to explore their **sexuality** and the positive and negative emotions that result from close relationships.

Adulthood and later adulthood

Adults are expected to be more emotionally stable, self-aware and mature than adolescents. This doesn't mean that adulthood is emotionally uneventful or that people don't experience emotional challenges or opportunities to develop. In fact, it is difficult to generalise about emotional development in early adulthood because people have such a broad range of experiences.

Achieving a stable and fulfilling personal relationship, perhaps also having children, is a life goal for many young adults. However, others choose to live their life without a partner and may not wish to have children either.

Key terms

Challenging behaviour
Behaviour that is seen as socially unacceptable and which challenges the coping ability of others (parents, teachers, care workers).

Sibling
A brother or sister.

Self-confidence
A feeling of trust that a person has in their abilities, qualities and judgement.

Sexuality
The ability to experience and express sexual feelings.

Did you know?

In this phase of emotional development, individuals tend to gain greater understanding of their own emotions as well as the thoughts, feelings and motives of others.

Listed below are some of the changes that people can experience during adulthood that may have important emotional consequences:

- marriage
- divorce or relationship breakdown
- parenthood
- increase in work responsibility
- death of parents.

I feel loved.

I feel supported.

I have achieved a lot so far in my life.

I regret things in my life.

I'm lonely.

I'm scared of growing old.

► Middle and later adulthood can be a period of varied emotions for different people.

▲ Adolescence can be an emotional time for both teenagers and parents.

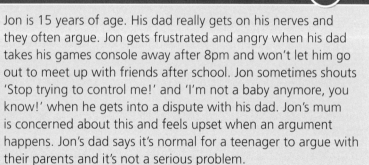

Case study

Jon is 15 years of age. His dad really gets on his nerves and they often argue. Jon gets frustrated and angry when his dad takes his games console away after 8pm and won't let him go out to meet up with friends after school. Jon sometimes shouts 'Stop trying to control me!' and 'I'm not a baby anymore, you know!' when he gets into a dispute with his dad. Jon's mum is concerned about this and feels upset when an argument happens. Jon's dad says it's normal for a teenager to argue with their parents and it's not a serious problem.

1. Is Jon's mum right to be concerned about the way he argues with his dad?

2. Give two reasons to explain why Jon is more likely to come into conflict with his dad during his current life stage.

3. Suggest three ways Jon could manage his frustration and avoid getting into arguments with his dad.

Check your understanding

1. What is an attachment relationship and why is it important for this to develop in early infancy?

2. List three different groups of people who can help a child to develop emotional control.

3. Explain how intimate person relationships help adolescents and adults to develop emotionally.

4. What kinds of life changes and challenges can affect the emotional development during adulthood and later adulthood?

6 Understanding social development

▶ Children seem to be born with a natural ability to play that is good for social development.

Social development across the life cycle

Social development is about the relationships we create with others, the relationship skills we develop and learning the **culture** of society. Parents and teachers have a key role in our early social development. They teach us:

- the acceptable ways of behaving
- how to relate to others in everyday situations
- the importance of making and keeping good relationships with others.

The process of helping a person to develop socially is known as **socialisation**. Parents or caregivers and close family members play a key part in an individual's **primary socialisation** during infancy and childhood. Friends, teachers and work colleagues then become important sources of secondary socialisation during adolescence and adulthood.

Infancy

An infant's social circle gradually expands as they form relationships with their siblings, other relatives and perhaps their neighbour's children. These relationships are strongly influenced by the communication skills an infant develops and is able to use during this life stage. At the same time, a developing child is increasingly able to look at the world from another person's point of view. This happens as the infant progresses to childhood and explores different styles of play.

Key terms

Culture
The way of life, especially the beliefs, customs and practices, of a particular group of people at a particular time.

Socialisation
The process of learning to behave in a way that is acceptable to society.

Primary socialisation
The first stage of socialisation when a child is taught by family members to interact, behave and talk in socially acceptable ways.

Did you know?

Most children can cooperate and appreciate the viewpoints and feelings of others in ways that infants cannot.

Childhood

Most children gradually increase their self-confidence, make friendships and become more independent at primary school. However, some children also find their first days at school emotionally difficult and distressing.

Cooperation and appreciating the feelings of others enables children to play together, joining in groups and team games. Friendships become very important and can also be emotionally intense during childhood.

▲ Children learn to play together in a more cooperative way during early childhood.

Key terms

Solo play
Children play independently, focusing on their own activity, without interacting with each other.

Parallel play
Children play independently in similar activities, alongside each other, without sharing or influencing each other's activity.

Associative play
Children take part in similar or identical activities as part of a group but there is no definite goal or organisation to their play.

Cooperative play
Organised play activity that has a goal and through which children interact.

Children's play changes from the **solo play** and **parallel play** of infancy to **associative play** and **cooperative play** during this life stage. Children are now able to choose their own friends and want their peers to like and approve of them. Successful social relationships among children are helped by:

- secure attachment in their early years

- mixing with other children, especially where this involves activities that require cooperation

- the personality of the child: friendly, supportive and optimistic children make friends more easily than children who are negative and aggressive.

Doing fun things with other people also uses the body and mind. Playing in a puddle, on a beach or in the school playground boosts a child's imagination and helps them to explore and understand the world, for example.

Most children develop a preference for same-sex friends and become very aware of and sensitive to differences between boys and girls.

Adolescence

The goal of adolescent social development is to achieve a distinctive sense of personal identity. Social relationships with close friends and **peer group** members become important influences and sources of advice and guidance in this quest. Adolescents often question and sometimes reject the values, beliefs and opinions of their parents and caregivers as part of this process. This can lead to conflict and difficulties in family relationships.

It is also common for adolescents to experiment with their clothes, appearance and behaviour to fit in with their peer group and find an identity for themselves. Wearing the right clothes, listening to the right music and being seen in the right places with the right people become important issues for many adolescents. This peer group pressure and the need to fit in can sometimes lead adolescents into activities and situations that they find difficult to resist or challenge, even when they know they should.

Adulthood

Leaving home to live independently is a major event in early adulthood. Greater independence requires new relationships. At the start of this life stage, young adults often make new friendships through work and social life and focus quite strongly on finding a partner. New responsibilities and an extension of the person's social circle may then result from marriage or cohabitation.

Each type of relationship in adulthood contributes to social development by giving the person a sense of connection and belonging to others.

Social development during middle age tends to revolve around people trying to achieve their position in society, their ambitions in life and making adjustments to some of their existing relationships.

During middle age people often find that they need to adjust their social relationships as their children leave home (the 'empty-nest syndrome'), their ageing parents become unwell or infirm and they retire from work. Changes in these social relationships often affect an individual's **self-concept** as well as their social roles.

Later adulthood

Social and emotional development takes on a new importance in later adulthood. For example, a person's relationships with their partner, family or caregivers and friends are all likely to change in this final life stage. An older person may:

- require more social support from others, particularly when their partner or friends die
- withdraw from a range of previous life roles (personal and work-related).

However, older people do continue to develop and change socially as they may:

- experience new social roles, such as becoming grandparents and retiring from work
- have more leisure time in which to build relationships with friends and family members.

Despite this, some older people experience **insecurity** and loneliness if their social contacts are reduced and they become isolated.

▲ Image and appearance are an important part of the adolescent search for identity.

Did you know?

Much of adulthood is concerned with trying to find a balance between the competing demands of work, family and friends.

Key terms

Peer group
A group of people about the same age, who see themselves (or are seen by others) as belonging together in some way.

Self-concept
The beliefs, ideas or mental image a person has about themselves, including their strengths, weaknesses and how others view them.

Insecurity
A lack of confidence, uncertainty or anxiety.

Case study

Tom (aged 32) and Lara (aged 30) Davies have been married for eight years. They live in a small town in mid Wales. Developing a close intimate relationship, getting married and having a child (Bobby, now 18 months old) has fundamentally altered their lives over the last five years. Tom is a social worker and Lara works in a primary school. The people they socialise with are either work colleagues or parents of other children at Bobby's nursery school. They would like to see their friends more often but find it difficult to find time to meet up because of work and family pressures. Tom and Lara are very committed to their role as parents and are also keen to develop their careers. They say that their current priority in life is bringing up Bobby to be happy and healthy.

1. Which life stage are Tom and Lara currently in?

2. Describe two key events that have affected Tom and Laura's social development in this life stage.

3. Explain how friendships influence social development during adulthood.

Check your understanding

1. What does the term social development refer to?

2. Give three examples of ways that parents socialise their children during infancy and childhood.

3. Explain how and why a person's friends play a key part in their social development during adolescence.

4. What kinds of events and changes affect a person's social development during later adulthood?

7 Physical factors affecting growth, development and well-being

Think about it

1. Identify three ways chimpanzees are similar to humans and three ways in which they differ.

2. Describe ways in which you share physical similarities with one or both of your parents.

3. Explain what it means to say that a disease or condition, such as **cystic fibrosis**, is 'genetically inherited'.

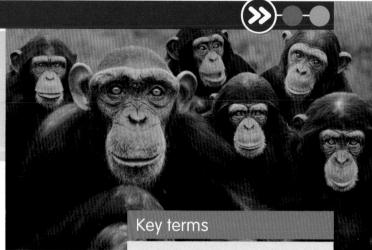

► Chimpanzees share 96 per cent of the same genes as humans.

Key terms

Cystic fibrosis
An inherited disorder that affects the cell membranes, causing the production of thick and sticky mucus in the lungs.

Genes
Small sections of DNA on a chromosome that are the basic units of heredity, and may be copied and passed on to the next generation.

Illness
A form of sickness affecting the person's body or mind.

Chromosomes
Chemical structures found in most living cells that carry genetic information in the form of genes.

Understanding physical factors

Human growth and development are influenced by a range of physical factors. Physical factors all relate to, and affect, the human body. Some factors, such as the **genes** that a person inherits, exist within the body and can't be changed or controlled. Other physical factors, such as diet, physical activity and some **illnesses**, are influenced by a person's lifestyle choices.

Genetic inheritance

The genes that we inherit from our parents control our physical growth, appearance and some of the abilities we develop. Each cell in the human body contains two sets of 23 **chromosomes**: one set from each parent.

Each chromosome can contain up to 4000 different genes. These are the 'instructions' that tell our body's cells how to grow. The genes that control how we

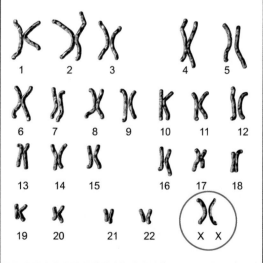

◄ Human chromosomes carry genetic instructions for growth. The 23rd chromosome determines a person's sex – XY for males and XX for females.

Did you know?

Genetic inheritance ensures you will grow and develop to look like one or both of your parents, as your body responds to the 'instructions' in your genes.

Key terms

Balanced diet
A diet consisting of a variety of different types of food and providing adequate amounts of the nutrients necessary for good health.

Hydration
The process of making your body absorb water or other liquid.

Nutrients
Substances found in food that are essential for growth and the maintenance of life. The five main nutrients are protein, carbohydrates, vitamins, minerals and fats.

Obese
Having excess body fat that may have a negative effect on health.

Did you know?

Being teased or bullied for being 'fat' may have a negative effect on a child's emotional development because it can lead to low self-esteem.

grow are a unique combination of our biological parents' genes. One consequence of this is that we can do very little to change the physical features and growth potential that we have. If both of your biological parents are over 1.8 metres tall, have large feet and are fast runners, you are likely to inherit these characteristics and abilities too. This also means that if your parents aren't tall, you are very unlikely to grow tall.

Genes and health

Genes also carry information that affects health and development throughout life. For example, a person's genes can be the cause of diseases that they develop during their lifetime. This is because the risk of getting conditions such as heart disease, cancers and strokes can be inherited. A person born into a family with a history of heart disease is at greater risk of developing this condition if either of their parents are carriers of a 'heart disease gene'. Whether the person goes on to develop heart disease will depend on many non-genetic factors too. Lifestyle, such as diet and exercise levels, for example, will be a key issue for a person in this position.

Diet, nutrition and hydration

Food is essential for life and a **balanced diet** and appropriate **hydration** form the basis of good physical health. This is true in all life stages. However, the amount and types of food required to meet a person's physical needs will depend on their age, physical build and gender, as well as how active they are.

Infancy

An infant of less than six months old can gain all the **nutrients** they require from breast milk or infant formula (specially-made powdered milk). However, as they become more active, they need to be weaned onto a balanced diet of solid foods to grow and develop appropriately.

Childhood

Children also need a balanced diet to maintain their physical growth and development and provide 'fuel' for their increasingly active lives. When a child consumes too much food, or an excessive amount of sugary or fatty food, they are likely to become overweight or even **obese**. This can harm the child's physical development as it may reduce their opportunities to exercise, limit mobility and hinder muscle development. Being overweight or obese can also lead to social and emotional problems for children.

An obese or overweight child may develop a negative self-image that reduces their self-confidence and their ability to make and maintain relationships with other children.

◀ Lack of physical activity and an unhealthy diet are the main causes of childhood obesity.

Adolescence

The onset of puberty during adolescence results in a physical growth spurt that has to be 'fuelled' by nutritionally balanced and regular meals. However, adolescents (particularly girls) may also become more conscious of how they look and possibly be less conscientious about eating balanced or regular meals. This sometimes results in the development of eating disorders such as anorexia nervosa and bulimia nervosa because the person fears 'being fat'. The consequences of eating disorders can be serious and may cause long-term physical damage.

Adulthood

An adult's nutritional and hydration needs will depend on how much energy they require for their work and everyday life. A person can safely consume more food if they have a physically demanding job or lifestyle that uses up a lot of energy. However, an adult's dietary needs may change if they become unwell, if they are pregnant or breastfeeding or if their level of physical activity changes for some reason. A person who does not have a balanced diet may develop health problems because they lack vital nutrients, such as **vitamins** and **minerals**. They may also become obese, develop heart disease or even type 2 diabetes if they consume too much fatty or sugary food and are not active enough to burn off the calories they have consumed.

Physical activity

Being physically active is important for physical growth and development in every life stage. Activity that exercises the different parts of the body is important in infancy and childhood because it builds up strength, stamina, suppleness and coordination. Failing to exercise may result in a person becoming unfit, overweight and even obese during any life stage. Lack of physical fitness, stiff joints, heart disease, osteoporosis, constipation and **strokes** may all be experienced by adults and older people who have not looked after their bodies well enough by taking regular physical exercise.

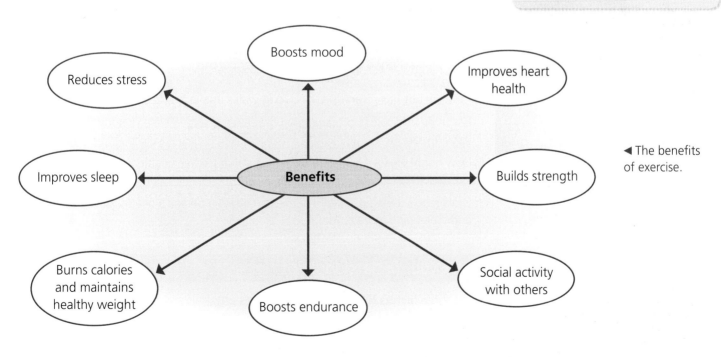

◄ The benefits of exercise.

Experience of illness, disease and disability

Many of the illnesses that we experience are short term and treatable. Coughs, colds and even broken limbs can all be cured with the right medicine and treatment and don't have any lasting impact on growth or development.

Some illnesses, **diseases** and conditions can have much more serious and long-term consequences on a person's health and development. See the following for some examples of these:

Genetic diseases	Infectious diseases	Degenerative conditions
Haemophilia, Down's syndrome, Cystic fibrosis	Tuberculosis, Meningitis, HIV	Alzheimer's disease, Multiple sclerosis, Arthritis
Lifelong conditions, cannot be cured	Can cause permanent damage and may even be fatal if left untreated	Worsen over time, tend to have impact in adulthood or later adulthood, can also affect social relationships, result in emotional distress and destroy intellectual abilities

▲ Many physical changes occur in later adulthood.

Case study

Helen Evans, aged 76, lives alone in a small village on the Welsh coast. She has experienced a number of changes in her physical appearance, abilities and health over the last 20 years. Her hair is now white and thinner and she has distinctive wrinkles around her eyes. She has experienced some hearing loss and has worn glasses for reading since her eyesight deteriorated when she was in her early fifties. Helen's GP has told her that she has experienced a slight decrease in height in the last few years and that her blood pressure is a bit too high. Helen experienced the menopause in her mid fifties and began hormone replacement therapy to counter some of the effects of this. She has constant aches, pains and stiffness in her joints but is still very active and a cheerful person. Helen tells people she has 'good genes', as both of her parents lived until they were 90 years old. She tries to stay active by walking to the local shop and around the village to see friends but has given up taking long walks as she has less stamina now.

1. List three effects of normal ageing that have changed Helen's body over the last 20 years.

2. How might Helen's genetic inheritance influence her health and well-being in later adulthood.

3. Explain how being physically active can affect a person's health, development and well-being in later adulthood.

Check your understanding

1. List three factors that influence a person's physical growth and development during the life cycle.

2. What are genes and how do they influence physical growth and development?

3. Explain what obesity is and describe two ways it can affect a person's development.

4. Give three reasons to explain why eating a balanced diet has a positive effect on human growth and development across the life span.

8 Social and economic factors affecting growth, development and well-being

▲ Social media provides a new way of forming and maintaining relationships.

Understanding social and emotional factors

Social and emotional factors are those things that influence our relationships, **attachments** and feelings about ourselves and other people in our lives. They have an important influence on a person's social and emotional development, particularly their sense of identity and **self-esteem**.

Gender

A person's sex refers to whether they are biologically male or female. **Gender**, on the other hand, refers to the behaviour society expects from men and women. In Western societies (such as Wales) girls are taught, or **socialised**, to express 'feminine' qualities such as being kind, caring and gentle. In contrast, boys are socialised to express 'masculine' characteristics such as being boisterous, aggressive and tough. Parents, schools, friends and the media all play a part in gender socialisation.

The gender expectations that we experience as we grow up influence how we think about ourselves and how we relate to others. We are now seeing challenges to the long-held idea that boys and men should experience better opportunities (especially in education and employment) than girls and women because they are the 'superior sex'. There are now laws promoting and protecting **equality** of opportunity and much greater awareness of the damaging effects of sexism and gender inequality. The #metoo movement and campaign for gender equality is an example of this.

Key terms

Attachment
An emotionally close, secure relationship with a parent or carer.

Self-esteem
Confidence in your own worth or abilities, closely linked to self-respect.

Gender
A term used to describe the social and cultural expectations of males and females.

Socialised
Behaving in a way that is expected, and acceptable, in one's own society.

Equality
Having equal status, rights and opportunities.

◄ A nursery teacher who doesn't fit the gender expectations of this work role.

Gender is still an important issue that affects personal development, but it isn't as powerful as it once was in affecting a person's opportunities and life chances. Girls and boys now have the same educational opportunities and there are similar numbers of men and women in employment. However, on average, men still earn more than women and still occupy more of the higher paid and most powerful jobs. Girls, on the other hand, currently get better results than boys in public examinations, such as GCSEs, and so may change this situation in the future.

Family relationships

Most people live as part of a family at some time in their life. The family carries out **primary socialisation**. This means that family members, especially parents, teach children the values, beliefs and skills that will prepare them for later life. The functions of the family and how they contribute to an individual's development are described as follows:

Key terms

Primary socialisation
The first stage of socialisation when a child is taught by family members to interact, behave and talk in socially acceptable ways.

Informal care
Care that is provided by family, friends and neighbours rather than by trained professionals.

Providing	Families provide informal education and socialisation for children. This teaches children attitudes, values and how to behave. Families also provide the physical resources needed for growth and intellectual development, such as food, toys and other stimulation.
Supporting	Families give emotional support from infancy through to adulthood. Early attachment and bonding are important sources of the stability and security we all need.
Protecting	Family members protect the health and well-being of other members by giving **informal care**, advice and guidance. Family relationships are often very deep and have a lifelong influence on human development.

Whatever type of family we live in, our physical, intellectual, emotional and social development will be strongly influenced by other family members.

Relationships

We first learn how to behave and relate to others through family relationships during infancy. As we move through the life stages, relationships can play different roles:

Early childhood	Friendships are formed with other children
Adolescence	Friendships help create an identity separate from parents
Adulthood	Friendships form the basis of social lives outside of the family
Later adulthood	Friendships are a source of companionship and connection to the past

Throughout life, friendships play a role in helping people to feel they belong, are wanted and liked by others, and that there are people they can turn to for support. However, the other side of childhood and adolescent relationships, such as bullying and rejection by peers, can have a negative effect on an individual's self-esteem and identity.

Intimate personal and sexual relationships are occasionally a feature of late adolescence but are a normal part of adulthood. For many teenagers their first intimate relationship is an intense emotional experience rather than a sexual one. Intimate relationships that are more emotionally and physically involved may occur in late adolescence but are more likely to occur when a person has greater emotional maturity and a stronger sense of personal identity as a young adult.

During adulthood people typically search for a partner. They may experience emotionally and physically intimate relationships with one or more individuals before they form a longer-term relationship, usually with just one person. Engaging in sexual activity as part of an intimate relationship with a partner expresses both a physical and emotional need for most adults. Sexual relationships with more than one person and extramarital affairs may damage an individual's existing relationship and personal development and cause emotional distress to an existing partner. Adults who find themselves in emotionally controlling or sexually abusive relationships may also experience significant emotional distress, physical injury, or low self-esteem until they find a way of ending the relationship or stopping the abuse.

Adverse childhood experiences (ACEs)

Infancy and childhood are very important stages of human development in which the basic foundations for later development are laid down. Adverse childhood experiences (ACEs) can harm a child's brain development, change the way they respond to **stress** and cause long-term damage to their health. Examples of ACEs include:

- physical, sexual and verbal abuse
- physical and emotional neglect
- being bullied by a parent, another adult or a peer
- living in an unsafe neighbourhood
- exposure to parental mental illness, addiction or imprisonment
- witnessing domestic abuse of a parent, sibling
- loss of a parent due to separation, divorce or **bereavement**.

The **trauma** of experiencing an ACE, and the toxic stress that follows, is associated with the later development of long-term physical and mental health problems, violent behaviours and addictions. These in turn are likely to have a negative effect on a person's ability to make and sustain personal relationships and achieve their educational and work potential.

Abuse and neglect

Young people, vulnerable adults, older people and people with **disabilities** who do not receive protection and **safeguarding** from parents, other adults and care workers may experience abuse, neglect and ill treatment that damages their personal development. Abuse and neglect are most commonly perpetrated by parents on children, by one partner on another and by carers on vulnerable people who are unwell, frail or who have developmental problems.

The different forms of abuse that members of vulnerable groups may experience include:

- physical abuse
- sexual abuse
- emotional and psychological abuse
- financial exploitation
- neglect.

Abuse and neglect can damage personal development in a range of ways (see right) but are particularly damaging to an individual's social and emotional development.

Key terms

Stress
Physical or mental tension caused by threats, difficulties or challenges to a person's coping skills.

Bereavement
The feeling of loss and grief following the death of a loved one.

Trauma
A deeply distressing or disturbing experience.

Disabilities
Impairments of physical, mental or sensory functions that affect a person's abilities or activities.

Safeguarding
Protecting children and vulnerable adults from abuse or neglect and educating those around them to recognise the signs and dangers.

▼ Effects of abuse and neglect.

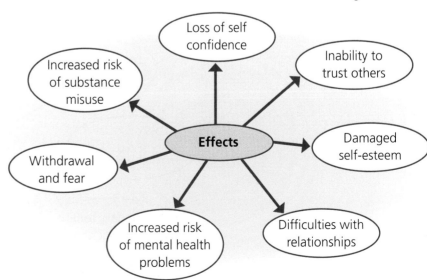

Educational experiences

Most children go to school between the ages of 5 and 16 years to receive their formal education in Wales and the United Kingdom generally. Children and young people in Wales now have to spend a minimum of 12 years in primary and secondary education. Education promotes intellectual development because it is about learning. Intellectual development happens when a person increases their knowledge and thinking skills. However, education also has a powerful effect on a person's social and emotional development. Educational experiences are part of what is known as secondary socialisation. That is, friends, peers and teachers influence the attitudes, values and ways in which a child or young person behaves. This builds on the primary socialisation that has already occurred within the family.

Some people learn a lot at school, succeed at exams and see education as a positive influence on their development. However, not everybody enjoys school and not everybody succeeds. Failure and bad experiences at school can lead some people to develop a negative self-image and low self-esteem.

► The benefits of a good education.

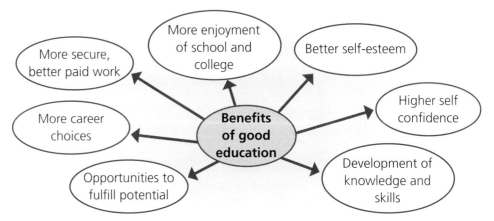

Employment

Employment is part of secondary socialisation because a person's values, beliefs and attitudes are often influenced by employers and work colleagues. Work is also an opportunity to develop new skills and extend physical, intellectual and social abilities. People often develop strong friendships at work, especially if they stay in the same job for a long time. As well as learning the social skills of cooperating with and supporting others, work-based relationships can lead to emotional development where colleagues care about each other and have a shared sense of belonging to a friendship group.

► Unemployment and loss.

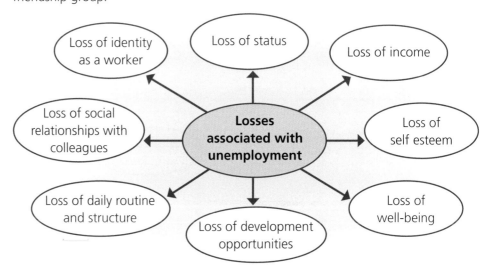

A lack of employment can also affect an individual's development because it is a stressful experience. People who become unemployed may feel angry about what they have lost, anxious about their future and can suffer a sense of rejection that affects their self-esteem and self-concept. The loss of income that unemployment brings may also mean that a person can no longer participate in social and leisure activities with friends, such as going to the cinema, the pub or on holiday. Over time this could affect social relationships and may even exclude the unemployed person from a friendship group.

▲ The population of Wales is becoming increasingly diverse.

▼ Religion, culture and ethnicity are often inseparable parts of a person's identity.

Cultural and ethnic (racial) diversity

Wales is a country with a growing and increasingly diverse population. This means that a range of different social, cultural, language, ability, ethnic and religious groups exist within its population.

Ethnicity can be an important feature of a person's identity, particularly where religion plays a part. It may affect personal development because it leads the individual to seek out and take part in special community activities or social groups. It may also be a label (for example, 'Asian', 'Black', 'Welsh', 'Muslim' or 'Jewish') that influences how other people treat and respond to the person. This can have a powerful effect on personal development.

Being exposed to different views, ideas and perspectives is one of the advantages of living in a diverse society.

Diverse communities are also often innovative and find new ways of living and working together. Tolerance and acceptance of difference is also likely to reduce prejudice, stereotyping and discrimination against members of minority communities.

Key term

Ethnicity
People with the same ethnicity have a shared way of life or culture, a common geographical origin, a similar skin colour or a common language or religion.

Did you know?

Cultural difference and diversity provide different communities with opportunities to experience and learn from each other's way of life.

Key terms

Diversity
A range of different and varied things.

However, cultural and racial **diversity** can also bring difficulties and challenges where tensions and conflict develop between different cultural and racial groups in a community. This can be due to a lack of integration of one group into the broader community, a clash of values and lifestyles, or the belief that a cultural group's sense of identity is being changed or lost because of the influences of diversity.

Case study

Ffion, Nia and Eleri are all 32 years of age. They have known each other since they started primary school together when they were five years old. They are all now married, have two children each and live in different parts of Wales. Living apart from each other hasn't got in the way of their friendship. All three communicate regularly, sending text messages a couple of times a week and speaking quite frequently on the phone. Ffion still lives in Caernarfon where the three friends grew up. When Nia and Eleri visit their families at Christmas and in the summer, they also arrange to go out for a meal or have a barbeque at Ffion's house. The three women discuss quite personal feelings and seek advice from each other when they have problems to deal with. They trust each other and believe they have a genuine friendship that they can rely on no matter what happens.

1. Which aspects of the three women's personal development is likely to have been affected by their friendship?

2. Explain how Ffion, Nia and Eleri's friendship is likely to affect their emotional well-being.

3. Using the information provided, identify possible reasons why the friendship between the three women has been so long-lasting and successful.

Check your understanding

1. List two social or emotional factors that can have a positive influence and two social or emotional factors that can have a negative effect on human development.

2. Describe the role a person's family can play in their development across the human life cycle.

3. Identify three ways abuse and neglect can damage a person's development during childhood or adolescence.

4. How can cultural and ethnic diversity have a positive effect on the development of people living in a diverse community?

9 Economic and environmental factors affecting growth, development and well-being

◄ How is having money linked to health, development and well-being?

Think about it

1. How much money do you think a family of four needs each month to live on?

2. Make a list of three features of 'good housing' and three features of 'bad housing' conditions.

3. Why is pollution bad for health?

Economic factors

Human growth and development can be affected by a range of money-related or **economic** factors. At the most basic level, having enough money to be able to afford a healthy diet, a warm, safe home and other basic necessities of everyday life has a direct effect on health and well-being. Indirectly, economic factors also influence the kinds of development opportunities a person can enjoy in each life stage.

Income

Income is the money that a household or individual receives. People receive money through working, pension payments, welfare benefits and other sources such as investments. The amount of income an individual and their family have, and the things they spend it on, can have a big impact on their personal development because it affects their quality of life. People with sufficient income are likely to have better educational and leisure opportunities and are likely to live in better circumstances than people who have a low income and who may be in poverty. Having better opportunities and no money-related stress puts some individuals and families in a position to make the most of their abilities and potential. The reverse is the case for poorer people.

Key terms

Economic
Money-related.

Income
The money a person receives usually from work.

Material possessions and poverty

People who have a very low income and fewer material possessions are likely to be living in **poverty**. They are also more likely to suffer ill health and have their opportunities for personal development restricted. The following quotation explains this:

'Poverty means staying at home, often being bored, not seeing friends, not going to the cinema, not going out for a drink and not being able to take the children out for a trip or a treat or a holiday. It means coping with the stresses of managing on very little money, often for months or even years. It means having to withstand the onslaught of society's pressure to consume…Above all, poverty takes away the building blocks to create the tools for the future – your "life chances". It steals away the opportunity to have a life unmarked by sickness, a decent education, a secure home and a long retirement. It stops people being able to plan ahead. It stops people being able to take control of their lives.' (Oppenheim and Harker (1996))

Because of the existence of welfare benefits it is rare for people in the United Kingdom not to have enough income for essential food, clothing and housing. Despite this, there are still situations in which some people fall through the welfare benefits 'safety net' and live for periods of time in **absolute poverty**. This means that they find themselves without the basic means to pay for essential items such as food, clothing and housing.

Far more people in the United Kingdom live in **relative poverty**. This means that a person is poor when compared to most other people in society.

Many people living in poverty experience **social exclusion**. Children who are born into families experiencing poverty may find this difficult to escape from. Poverty and social exclusion have such a powerful effect on personal development and life chances that people are often held back by the disadvantages and lack of opportunities that result from social exclusion.

▲ Some people find themselves living in absolute poverty.

Did you know?

People living in relative poverty often don't have access to the same services and can't afford the same material possessions as others in their local community.

Key terms

Absolute poverty
Lacking the minimum amount of income needed to meet basic living needs for food, shelter or housing.

Relative poverty
Having a household income that is 50 per cent less than the median (average) income.

Social exclusion
Being isolated and lacking the rights, benefits and resources normally available to members of society.

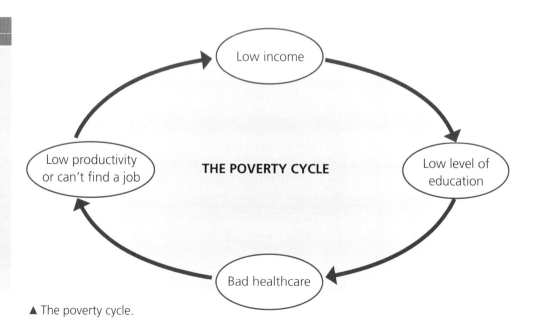

▲ The poverty cycle.

Environmental factors

A person's physical growth as well as other aspects of their development can be directly and indirectly affected by the physical conditions, or environment, in which they live.

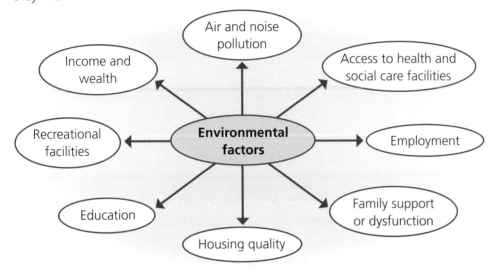

◄ Environmental factors affecting human development.

Housing conditions

The quality of a person's housing is important because it can affect their physical health and development as well as their mental health. Overcrowded, neglected properties provide the kinds of conditions that can lead to **respiratory disorders** and infectious diseases such as **bronchitis** and tuberculosis. Small, cramped housing can also have a damaging effect on the growth and physical development of babies, children and young people, who need enough space to play and be active.

The type and standard of housing that people live in is related to their income. People with low incomes are less able to afford a good standard of housing and are also less able to maintain and heat it adequately, for example.

Availability of health and social care, and childcare services

Access to good health and welfare services is likely to improve a person's life chances, as they will be able to obtain services that meet their needs. This may be particularly important for people who have **chronic health problems**, for women when they are pregnant and for older people who make more use of health and welfare services as they age.

The 'postcode lottery' faced by some people, particularly those living in rural areas, means that some people may not have an equal and fair chance of receiving health and welfare services when they require them. Specialist care for children or for people with cancer, for example, is not equally available throughout the United Kingdom. People living in more remote rural areas may also find they have to travel long distances to access both general healthcare and more specialist services.

▲ The quality of a person's housing can affect their health and development in a number of ways.

Key term

Postcode lottery
The idea that access to health, social care and childcare services is affected by where a person lives.

Air pollution

Physical growth and development can be directly affected by the presence of pollution in the atmosphere. Carbon monoxide and other harmful gas emissions from vehicles, ships and factories are particularly damaging to a person's respiratory system. Babies and children can have their growth potential restricted, although people at all stages of life can have their physical health damaged by the effects of poor air quality. Noise pollution from vehicles, aircraft and busy crowded environments can damage a person's hearing and their psychological well-being. Unwanted noise is also associated with high stress levels, sleep disturbances and high blood pressure. Noise pollution is worst in built-up, urban environments.

◄ Air pollution has a direct effect on physical health, causing many respiratory disorders.

Case study

Hayley is 19 years old. She lives with her boyfriend Ed in a caravan on the farm where they work. Hayley doesn't like living in the caravan because the cattle are noisy at night and she says it is damp, cramped and cold. Hayley and Ed spend long hours working, from 5am until 9pm most evenings. They receive a low wage and free use of the caravan. Hayley has difficulty sleeping, often gets chest infections and has a wheezy cough. Ed encourages her to see the GP but this is seven miles away and she has no way of getting there other than by walking. She is also worried that if she takes time off, she won't get paid. Ed and Hayley would like to move as they think their living conditions are unhealthy.

▲ Where you live can affect your health.

1. Identify two ways in which Hayley and Ed's living conditions may be harmful to their health and development.

2. What economic factors are affecting Hayley and Ed's ability to improve their living conditions?

3. Describe two positive effects of living and working on the farm on Hayley's health and well-being and two negative effects.

Check your understanding

1. List two examples of economic factors and two examples of environmental factors that affect growth and development.

2. Describe how poverty can affect an individual's development, health and well-being.

3. Explain what a 'postcode lottery' is and how this can impact a person's health.

4. Explain the link between one or more types of pollution and physical ill health.

1.2 PHYSICAL, SOCIAL, EMOTIONAL AND INTELLECTUAL HEALTH
10 Understanding health and well-being

◀ A physical disability isn't a barrier to healthy exercise.

Think about it

1. List three activities that you think are 'healthy' and three that you think of as 'unhealthy'.

2. Compare your lists of healthy and unhealthy activities with another learner, explaining why you made each choice.

3. What do you do in your everyday life to try and be 'healthy'?

Experiencing health and well-being

This topic enables you to gain knowledge and understanding of what physical health and good mental health involve and the ways in which they are closely connected.

Physical health and well-being

Are you physically 'healthy' at this point in your life? This leads to another question: how do you define what 'being healthy' is? There isn't a right or wrong answer because there are different ways to define what 'being healthy' involves. The table below outlines a few of these ways.

◀ Approaches to health.

Type of approach	What does this involve?
Positive approach	Being healthy involves having positive personal qualities and abilities. Being physically fit, the correct weight for their height and feeling happy might be evidence that a person is healthy.
Negative approach	Being healthy involves not being sick or ill. A person who is free from disease, illness and pain is 'well' or 'healthy' and might say 'I'm okay, there's nothing wrong with me,'

You probably already know about, and regularly use, both the approaches to health described in the table. The times when you see your GP because you think you might be unwell or think there is something wrong with your 'health', are an example of how you might use a negative approach to health. But I'm also hoping that you do try to keep fit by playing sports and taking regular exercise, try to eat a balanced diet and that you have friends and a social life that you feel happy with. If so, you are also using a positive approach to being healthy by trying to look after yourself and doing things that are good for you.

Mental health and well-being

'Mental health', like physical health, is something that people can define and experience in different ways. It is about the way a person can deal with their feelings and thoughts. Using a negative approach to mental health, a person would be 'mentally healthy' if they were not experiencing distressing feelings or disordered thinking. Most of the time, this is the majority of people. Using a positive approach, a person would be 'mentally healthy' if they possessed certain mental qualities or characteristics. For example, a person who is mentally healthy:

- feels good about themselves
- can think positively
- can enjoy things
- can do their (school) work
- can deal with common setbacks, such as a flat phone battery or a bad test score
- feels comfortable interacting with other people.

Being mentally healthy is now recognised as a key part of overall or **holistic** health. An individual's physical, emotional, social and intellectual development are all best supported by good mental health. The state of a person's mental health will affect their ability to deal with emotions, stress, how they socialise with others and their ability to make decisions, whatever their age.

Well-being and holistic health

The term '**well-being**' refers to the way people feel about themselves. If people feel 'good' (positive) about themselves and are happy with life they will have a high level of well-being, and vice versa. As individuals, we are the best judges of our personal sense of physical, mental, intellectual and social well-being.

This holistic or 'whole person' approach to health encourages us to focus on our:

- physical (bodily) health and well-being
- intellectual (thinking and learning) well-being
- social (relationship) well-being
- emotional (feelings) well-being.

Now that we know what 'being healthy' involves, the big question is how can we achieve it? Research has shown that people say 'being healthy' is just as likely to make them feel happy as winning lots of money. Fortunately, 'being healthy' depends more on the choices you make and what you do with your time than on pure luck. In particular, being physically active really boosts a person's chances of being physically and mentally healthy.

Key terms

Holistic
Focusing on the whole person, physically, intellectually, emotionally and socially.

Well-being
A state characterised by health, happiness and prosperity.

Did you know?

The World Health Organisation says that health is 'a state of complete physical, mental and social well-being, not merely the absence of disease or infirmity' (WHO, 1946).

The health benefits of physical activity

Physical activity and exercise play a key part in being both physically and mentally healthy. Undertaking an appropriate amount and type of exercise is important for physical growth and development in every life stage.

Failing to exercise may result in health issues during any life stage. More positively, being physically active right up into later adulthood is good for the body in various ways, as seen in the table below.

Regular exercise	No exercise
Encourages stamina	General lack of fitness
Supports increasing coordination	Excess weight, even obesity
Helps with overall suppleness	Stiff joints
Builds up strength	Heart disease
	Weak bones
	Constipation
	Stroke

◄ What a difference exercise can make.

Exercise isn't just about physical health and development though. It has important mental health benefits and can also be a good way of meeting a person's emotional and social needs. These links between a person's body and mind work in both directions. For example, physical activity reduces a person's feelings of stress. Reduced stress is associated with lower blood pressure, better sleep and having more energy.

▼ The benefits of exercise to mental health.

It helps me to manage and reduce any stress.

It allows me to connect to people.

It has led to me making new friends.

My self-esteem and mood are always improved afterwards.

Case study

Dev, 22 years old, has started cycling to college and going to the gym with his friend Brett, also aged 22. Dev hasn't done any regular physical exercise since he left school five years ago. He says he feels unfit, overweight and unhealthy. He admires how fit and healthy his friend Brett is. Dev says 'I'm not "sick" or anything like that, but I'm not healthy either. I want to be healthier.' Brett doesn't drink alcohol, goes to the gym four evenings a week to do weight training and cycles three miles to college every day. He didn't have any days off sick from college last year and says 'I'm healthy. I feel good, happy, fit and strong right now.'

1. Is Dev using a positive or negative approach to define 'health'?

2. List three behaviours that contribute to Brett being 'healthy'.

3. Explain how Dev's health would benefit from increasing his levels of physical activity.

▶ How healthy am I?

Check your understanding

1. List three ways of defining health.

2. Describe how a positive definition can be used to define health and well-being.

3. Explain what mental health and well-being refers to.

4. What are the health and well-being benefits of physical activity? Refer to both physical and mental health benefits in your answer.

11 Understanding social, emotional and intellectual health

11 Understanding social, emotional and intellectual health

Think about it

1. How important is sleep to your health and well-being?
2. What makes you feel happiest and most content with your life?
3. List three ways in which you stimulate your brain or use your intelligence in everyday life.

Supporting social, emotional and intellectual health

The holistic definition of health used by the World Health Organisation (1946) says that health is 'a state of complete physical, mental and social well-being, not merely the absence of disease or infirmity'. In this section of the unit we are going to focus on social, emotional and intellectual health and examples of tools and processes that can be used to become and stay socially, emotionally and intellectually healthy.

▲ Yoga has health and well-being benefits for both the mind and body.

Social health and well-being

Social health and well-being are concerned with the relationships we have with otherswell-being and help to protect us from feelings of loneliness, isolation and low self-esteem.

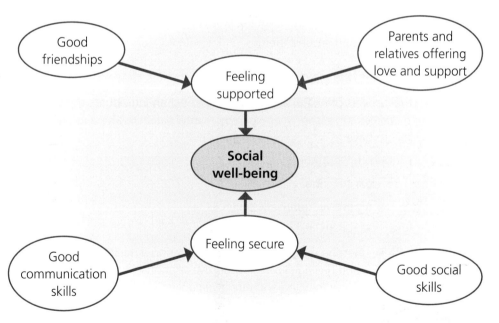

◄ Factors contributing to social well-being.

People don't always find themselves living in families that are loving and supportive. Life can also have its ups and downs as friendships and close personal relationships end or break down. Ill health and disability can sometimes result in people losing contact with friends and former work colleagues too. In these different situations, a person may find their social support network is insufficient. Being stressed, unsupported and isolated also reduces a person's **resilience** or ability to adapt to the challenges, social disadvantages and adverse conditions that they may be facing.

Key term

Resilience
The ability to adapt to and deal with a crisis or difficulty and return to normal afterwards again.

A person in this situation can strengthen their resilience and boost their social well-being by:

- building up their social network
- developing their problem-solving skills
- improving their communication and social skills
- setting themselves achievable well-being goals for the future.

Emotional health and well-being

A person's emotional health and well-being is linked to their 'inner life' – their feelings about themselves and other people. Living a healthy lifestyle is likely to have a positive impact on an individual's emotional well-being. This is likely to include:

- greater levels of happiness
- improved mood
- improved self-confidence and self-esteem
- a positive self-image
- reduced stress
- improved personal relationships.

Positive social relationships, including friendships, feeling in control of (school) work and personal life and having supportive, trusting relationships with those close to you are all ways of achieving a sense of emotional well-being.

Exercise, feeling listened to and using relaxation techniques to reduce stress can help to improve poor emotional well-being. One example of this is **mindfulness**. This is an integrative, mind–body based approach that can help individuals better manage their thoughts, feelings and mental health. It involves paying more attention to the present moment so that the person is aware and in control of their own thoughts and feelings and the world around them.

Key term

Mindfulness
Maintaining a moment-by-moment awareness of our thoughts, feelings, bodily sensations and surrounding environment, through a gentle, nurturing focus.

Did you know?

Poor emotional well-being is closely linked to being stressed and can lead to mental health problems.

Intellectual health and well-being

The intellectual aspects of health and well-being affect an individual's thinking and learning abilities. A person who experiences intellectual health and well-being is likely to have:

- good concentration
- clear thinking
- a positive, optimistic outlook
- the ability to learn.

Getting enough sleep and rest, eating a healthy, balanced diet and having secure, supportive relationships all contribute to clear thinking and effective concentration. It's also important to have interesting and challenging (school) work, stimulating hobbies and interests and opportunities to develop, explore and express your ideas.

◀ Mindfulness on the beach might involve noticing the colours of the sky, listening to the sound of the waves and feeling the breeze on your face.

Improving intellectual health and well-being

People who can perform at a high level, in their job or sport for example, often say that they need to be 'in the zone' to achieve their best work. This seems to be a hyper-focused, almost spiritual, state of mind where anything feels possible. Maybe this has happened to you? Time collapses. Sound falls away. Words flow easily and naturally. Suddenly you look up. Your homework or assignment is done! The big question is how can you get into 'the zone' to achieve this sense of intellectual or mental well-being? The answer is to feel inspired but not overwhelmed. It's also necessary to have the right attitude and positive self-belief.

Growth mind-set

Having a **growth mind-set** helps to boost your intellectual well-being. This involves the belief that you can learn and improve your intellectual abilities and well-being if you understand that effort makes you smarter and stronger intellectually. Putting in extra time and effort and believing that you can improve is what really leads to higher achievement and a better sense of intellectual well-being.

Key term

Growth mind-set
The belief that skills and abilities can be improved, and that their development is the purpose of the work you do.

▲ People with a growth mind-set don't fear failure – they try again and believe in themselves.

```
My growth
mind-set means...
```
→ I cope well with challenges and transitions in life.

→ I have a greater ability to control and apply my thinking.

→ I am more determined.

→ I am more able to view the efforts and achievements of others more positively.

◀ Characteristics of those with a growth mind-set.

Key term

Symptom
A physical or mental indicator of a condition or disease.

There is also evidence suggesting mental health benefits as those with a growth mind-set have been found to be less aggressive, with higher self-esteem and have fewer **symptoms** associated with depression and anxiety.

Case study

Gareth is sitting in a café, explaining to his friend Chris that he no longer wants to be a delivery driver. He has decided that he is a very different person now compared with when he started the job five years ago. Gareth told Chris he is bored and frustrated with driving a van and wants to become a nurse. Chris laughed at him at first but is now listening to Gareth's explanation. Gareth goes to college three evenings a week after work to study an Access to Nursing course. He is finding some of this difficult but believes that he will succeed if he puts the time and effort in over the next six months. Chris can see that his friend is very determined and encourages him to 'go for it'. As they leave the café, Chris is wondering what he can do to reduce his stress levels and make his own life better.

1. What evidence is there that Gareth has a growth mind-set and how might he benefit from this?

2. How might the friendship between Gareth and Chris affect their social and emotional well-being?

4. What strategies could Chris use to improve his own emotional well-being?

Check your understanding

1. What does 'social well-being' refer to?

2. How can a healthy lifestyle and supportive relationships affect a person's emotional well-being?

4. Explain what a growth mind-set is and how it can affect a person's well-being.

6. Explain what mindfulness involves and why people use mindfulness techniques.

1.3 THE IMPORTANCE OF ACTIVE PARTICIPATION ON DEVELOPMENT AND WELL-BEING
12 Active participation in care

Think about it

1. Give three medical reasons why Roz, right, may need to use a wheelchair in her everyday life.

2. What daily living and personal care needs would you want assistance with, and what would you want to do for yourself, if you were unable to stand or walk unaided like Roz?

3. Explain why it is better to say that Roz is a 'wheelchair user' rather than 'wheelchair bound'.

Understanding active participation

Have you ever been admitted to hospital or needed help and support when you were ill? Did the doctors, nurses and other healthcare staff, or the people caring for you when you were ill, ask you how they could help or what kind of assistance you would find helpful? Hopefully they did, but it's quite possible that this didn't happen.

This doesn't mean that the staff didn't care about you or weren't bothered about your care needs. There is a good chance that they assumed they knew what these were without asking you though. Until recently, the wishes, preferences and **active participation** of the users of care services weren't a priority for many care workers. This has now changed.

▲ Roz has been a wheelchair user since being involved in a car accident four years ago.

Key term

Active participation
Direct, influential involvement in planning, making decisions about or meeting care and support needs.

▼ Active participation is based on a partnership between the individual and the care worker.

▶ Comparing passive and active approaches to care.

Key term

Social care
Social work, personal care, protection or social support services to children or adults in need or at risk.

Childcare
Services that safeguard or promote the development of children.

Health, **social care** and **childcare** workers are now trained to encourage active participation in care. This involves treating people who need care and support as active partners in their own care and support. As a result, users of care services should no longer be seen as passive recipients of care. Active participation also recognises that each person should:

- be consulted about their care needs, wishes and preferences
- have the right to make their own choices
- be as independent as possible in everyday life.

The importance of active participation in care and support becomes clearer when this approach is compared to the, now out-dated, passive or dependent approach to care, as shown in the table below.

Passive, dependent approach	Active, independent approach
Individuals are seen as dependent on professionals/experts for care and support.	Individuals are seen as independent, with choices and rights.
Professionals don't share information and make important care-related decisions for individuals, often without consulting them.	Individuals expect to be consulted, want information about their options and are able to make their own decisions.
People receiving care lose individuality and identity as they become 'patients' or 'clients' of the care worker or service.	Individual identity is supported as each person's wishes, preferences and beliefs are acknowledged.
Care and support focus on what the person can't do for themselves.	Care and support are based on an individual's strengths and what they can do independently.
Individuals are referred to the services that are available.	Services to meet the individual's particular needs are sought and adapted to create a 'best fit' for the person.

How does active participation work in practice?

Active participation in care can cover a range of areas. It may include individuals having control of day-to-day decisions about what to wear, what to eat and how they want to spend their time. It may also support individuals being consulted and included in decisions about how services are run or which care services should be provided.

Taking personal responsibility for health, care and support

An individual should take as much responsibility for their health and well-being as they can to be an active participant in their own care and support. Rather than relying on care workers and care services to 'look after' them, the person should be encouraged and supported to:

- choose a healthy lifestyle
- be as independent as possible
- minimise **risks** to their health and well-being.

Did you know?

An individual must have some real influence over decisions and activities that affect them for genuine active participation to occur.

Key term

Risk
Exposure to danger, harm or loss.

Taking personal responsibility for living a healthy life will reduce the person's use of expensive care resources and ensure that care workers are able to prioritise people in greatest need of service. In the long term, if more people in Wales take personal responsibility for their health and well-being, care organisations will be able to offer services that are more **sustainable** and which reach those most in need.

What if a person can't make their own decisions?

Children, people living with dementia and people who have learning disabilities may be unable to make independent decisions about their care and support. This doesn't mean that they can't take an active role in expressing or meeting their own care needs. In some situations, a child's parents or an adult's partner or next-of-kin can act as their **advocate** to speak on their behalf and represent their best interests. It may also be possible for care workers to use alternative, non-verbal means of communication to find out about a person's wishes and preferences as part of the care planning process.

How can care workers promote active participation?

One of the most effective ways of promoting active participation in care is to use a **person-centred approach** to care practice. This involves focusing care and support on the needs of the person rather than the needs of the service or the preferences of the care worker. Today, most people who need care or support aren't happy just to sit back and let care workers do what they think is best. People have their own views on what's best for them and their own priorities in life. In response, care workers have to be flexible to meet their needs. The emphasis is on 'doing things with' the individual rather than 'doing things for (or to)' them.

Care workers who support active participation need to know a lot about the people they work with. Finding out about an individual's personal history, their likes, dislikes, abilities and wishes is the starting point. Care workers also need to continually look for ways of engaging and including each person in meeting their needs and wishes. This is different from trying to make the individual fit into existing or available services or making decisions about care or support on their behalf.

Did you know?

It is important to get to know anyone you are caring for and to encourage and enable them to use their strengths and existing self-care skills to look after themselves as much as they are able.

Key terms

Sustainable
Able to be supported, maintained or kept going over time (for example, a service).

Advocate
A person who supports, promotes the best interests of or speaks on behalf of another person.

Person-centred approach
An holistic approach that puts the needs of the individual first.

◄ Physical disability isn't a barrier to active participation in everyday life.

Did you know?

A person-centred approach puts the focus on the individual, their wishes and their abilities, and on using these to maximise the person's independence.

The benefits of active participation

Active participation provides a number of benefits to people with care and support needs. These include:

- greater control over decisions about their lives, including their care and support
- increased opportunities for:
  - learning and development of important skills and knowledge
  - education and employment
  - social contact and interpersonal relationships
  - participating as independently as possible in everyday activities that are important to them
- improved feeling of **self-worth** and confidence
- reduced vulnerability and scope for abuse by others
- improved physical and mental health, and resilience.

▲ Using aids and forms of help, such as assistance dogs, enables people with long-term conditions to participate actively in everyday life.

Individuals with long-term conditions and disabilities are most likely to benefit from active participation and personal assistance (rather than care) to help them meet their health and support needs. Active participation benefits these individuals as it enables them to achieve their potential and improve their life experience, rather than making them a passive recipient of care or support.

Potential barriers to active participation

Active participation in care and support is now encouraged in the Welsh care system. However, it doesn't always happen in practice.

Key term

Self-worth
An individual's sense of their own value or worth as a person.

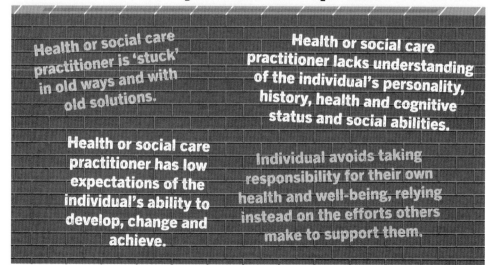

Active participation

Health or social care practitioner is 'stuck' in old ways and with old solutions.

Health or social care practitioner lacks understanding of the individual's personality, history, health and cognitive status and social abilities.

Health or social care practitioner has low expectations of the individual's ability to develop, change and achieve.

Individual avoids taking responsibility for their own health and well-being, relying instead on the efforts others make to support them.

▲ Which barriers might prevent the implementation of an active participation approach?

Changing attitudes is key to reducing barriers to active participation. Improving society's attitudes to, and expectations of, people with long-term conditions and disabilities is an important part of this.

Case study

Brian, aged 78, was recently admitted to hospital after falling and breaking his left arm at home. He has some difficulties with his memory but is still able to live in his own home with the help of carers who visit twice each day. When he was at home, Brian was able to wash and dress himself without help and looked forward to the carers visiting at meal times. They chatted to him and warmed some food for his lunch or dinner. Since being in hospital, Brian's daughter Julia has noticed that her dad now seems less capable of meeting his own personal care needs. The last time she visited early on a Saturday morning, she saw a nurse giving Brian a shave and telling him to put on a t-shirt afterwards. The nurse explained that it was quicker to do this than to wait for Brian to get washed and dressed himself. When Julia asked her dad whether he still washed and dressed himself, he said 'No, I can't now. They do it for me don't they?'

1. Is Brian an active or passive recipient of care?

2. What could the nurses and care workers looking after Brian do to promote and support active participation?

3. Describe how Brian would benefit from being an active participant in his own care.

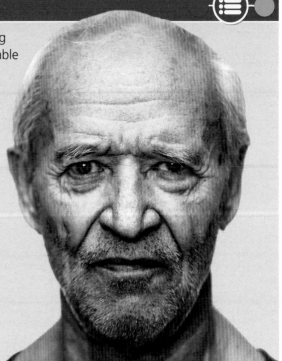

▲ Brian needs support and encouragement to maintain his self-care skills.

Check your understanding

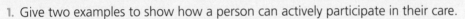

1. Give two examples to show how a person can actively participate in their care.

2. Describe how a person can take personal responsibility for their health and well-being.

3. Explain why active participation benefits the person receiving care or support.

4. Outline three barriers to active participation in care.

13 Early intervention and prevention

► Dani, a newly qualified nurse, is about to receive the BCG Booster vaccine to immunise her against tuberculosis.

Think about it

1. List all the **vaccinations** that you can remember having, or which you know you have had.

2. Give two reasons why it is important for people working in healthcare, social care or childcare jobs to have up-to-date vaccinations.

3. Describe two illness prevention services that are available in your local area.

Key terms

Vaccinations
Treatment with a vaccine to produce immunity against a particular infectious disease, virus or tropical disease.

Chronic condition
A long-term, constantly recurring and incurable condition.

Did you know?

Healthcare workers have been telling people for a long time that prevention is always better than cure.

Understanding early intervention and prevention

Here are a few questions that you should think about and answer as honestly as you can:

- How long do you think you will live?

- How long do you want to live unaffected by an illness or **chronic condition**?

- What can you do to live a longer, healthier life?

My answer to the first two questions would be the same: as long as possible. To give ourselves the opportunity to live a long and healthy life, we all need to be able to answer the last question. But, what can you do?

It is possible to prevent, or at least reduce your risk of developing, many life-limiting and life-altering conditions including cancers, heart disease, diabetes and chronic respiratory diseases, by making and practising healthy lifestyle choices. People who are relatively fit and healthy in middle-age and later adulthood haven't usually achieved their good health by chance or accident. Many people who do have chronic health problems in middle and older adulthood could probably have reduced their suffering and difficulties by doing a few things differently earlier in life.

The aims of early intervention and prevention

Early **intervention** and preventative health services aim to prevent people from becoming ill and offer early treatment and support to limit the impact if they do. It isn't possible to guarantee that a person won't develop a particular condition, like diabetes or heart disease, at some point in their life. It is possible and a very good idea to reduce the risk of this happening though. So, in basic terms:

Prevention service	Early intervention service
Tries to influence health behaviour and lifestyle choices in a positive way before a person has any symptoms or conditions.	Aims to provide treatment, support or assistance to limit the impact of health or social problems so they don't get any worse.

Effective early intervention and prevention services help to reduce the pressure on the National Health Service (NHS) and other care services. They also ensure that people can live longer, healthier lives.

Taking personal responsibility for health

Taking personal responsibility for your health and making healthy choices is the equivalent of investing early for the rewards of a healthier, longer life. It is something everyone can, and should, do.

Key terms

Interventions
Actions or activities designed to improve health and well-being.

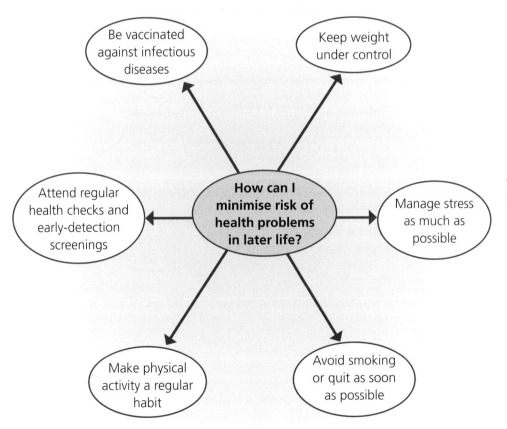

◀ Lifestyle choices can help to minimise health problems in later life.

How can GPs and primary care staff help?

Healthcare practitioners, such as GPs, provide a range of illness prevention services including:

- Vaccinations against infectious diseases such as polio, diphtheria and measles; against viruses, such as influenza (flu), that affect many older people; and against tropical diseases, such as malaria, that can affect overseas travellers visiting areas where the virus is present.

- Advice and information services to help people change their unhealthy behaviour and live healthier lives. GPs, for example, provide advice about stopping smoking and ways of losing weight.

- Classes where health workers teach people ways of improving their health. For example, relaxation, Pilates and yoga for people who are stressed, or opportunities for people to meet and talk about their problems.

The general health of the population of Wales is much better now than it was at the beginning of the 20th century. A very high proportion of children survive early childhood, and both men and women now live much longer lives. Infectious diseases such as tuberculosis, pneumonia and diphtheria were major causes of death and disability at the start of the 20th century. This is no longer the case.

▶ The widespread use of screening and vaccination has been important in improving the health of the population of Wales.

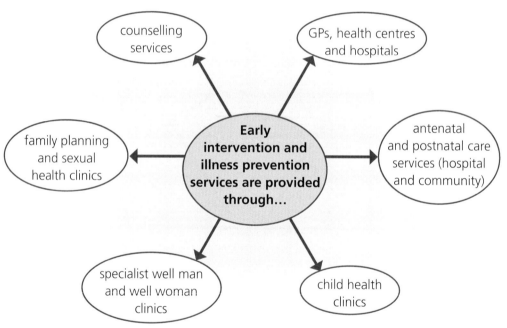

The Welsh government has developed and support a number of early intervention and prevention programmes. These have the aim of supporting disadvantaged children's health and development at an early stage in their lives. They include *Flying Start*, *Talk Childcare* and the *Active Offer*.

Key term

Screening
A strategy used with a population to identify the possible presence of as yet unidentified disease in those without signs or symptoms.

Screening programmes

Screening is a way of monitoring health. It is used to detect disease in people who have no obvious signs or symptoms of that disease. The aim is to identify disease early enough to treat people and hopefully prevent them becoming more unwell. Common screening tests for adults include blood pressure measurement, blood cholesterol tests, cervical smears, bowel cancer screening and mammograms for breast cancer.

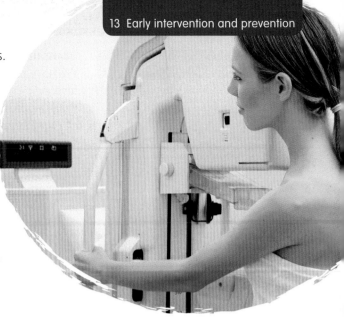

Screening programmes are provided in hospital and community settings. Mobile services such as the NHS Breast Screening and Breast Test Wales programmes are examples of community-based screening services.

Immunisation programmes

Vaccination is an illness prevention strategy. It involves giving a person a vaccine (usually, but not always, by injection) that produces **immunity** to a disease. Vaccinations are the most medically- and cost-effective way of preventing infectious diseases. Babies and young children are given a number of vaccines as part of an immunisation programme in infancy and early childhood to protect them from infectious diseases. Older people (65+ years) and those with chronic heart and respiratory diseases are also encouraged to have an influenza vaccination (flu jab) each year.

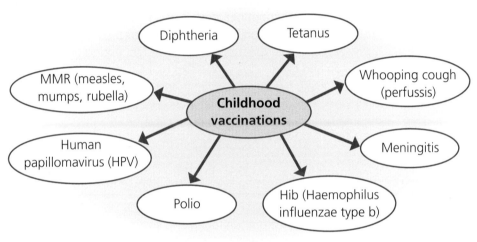

▲ Some common childhood vaccinations.

▲ The mammogram is a specialist type of scan used to screen for the signs and symptoms of breast cancer.

Key terms

Immunity
Protection against an infectious disease.

Sexually transmitted infection
An infection transmitted through the exchange of semen, blood or other bodily fluids during sex.

Substance misuse
A term to describe illegal or unauthorised drug abuse or excessive use of alcohol that is damaging to health.

Government guidelines and initiatives

A range of government guidelines have been produced to promote the health and well-being of individuals in Wales. These include guidelines relating to:

- diet, including the Eatwell Guide
- **sexually transmitted infections** (STIs)
- alcohol and **substance misuse**
- smoking
- healthy living.

The latest version of the Welsh Government's guidelines on each of these health topics can be accessed online (https://gov.wales). The guidelines on a specific issue provide healthy lifestyle information and advice as well as information that encourages appropriate use of services.

Key term

Consultation
A meeting with a doctor or another health professional to diagnose and discuss health problems or treatments.

Community involvement and support

We have seen that early intervention and prevention of ill health is both a personal responsibility and something that the health, social care and childcare services of Wales address. In addition, community involvement and support is another way of promoting healthy lifestyles and providing support for people when they don't have other options. Networks of friends, faith groups and community organisations provide low-cost, often free, forms of support from advice and guidance, to information-giving and counselling services to toy, clothing and food banks.

▲ Gill is trying to change her lifestyle and health behaviour.

Case study

Gill is 30 years old. She has been trying to get pregnant since marrying Phil two years ago. Gill recently made an appointment with her GP hoping that there might be a quick and simple solution to the problem. Dr Evans said he would need to carry out some tests to assess Gill's current state of physical health. He also talked to Gill about her lifestyle and health behaviour. At the end of the **consultation**, Dr Evans encouraged Gill to eat a more nutritious, balanced diet, to lose some weight and to enrol in relaxation and Pilates classes. He said that Gill should also monitor her own health for the next three months to see if the changes she made had any effect. He reminded her that being in good physical health would help her to conceive.

1. What aspects of Gill's physical health would you expect Dr Evans to check?

2. How could Gill monitor her own health over the next three months?

3. What kind of health monitoring and screening services are available to young women like Gill in your local area?

Check your understanding

1. List four ways a person could take responsibility for their own health and development.

2. Explain what screening involves, giving an example of a screening programme carried out in Wales.

3. Describe the way in which immunisations work to protect a person's health.

4. Identify four different organisations or services that provide early intervention and prevention services in Wales.

1.4 EARLY INTERVENTION AND PREVENTION TO PROMOTE GROWTH, DEVELOPMENT AND WELL-BEING
14 Managing health conditions

Think about it

1. Give three examples of short-term health conditions and three examples of long-term health conditions.

2. Describe your last 'illness' and the way in which it was treated.

3. Explain what makes people decide to go to the doctor or hospital when they become ill.

Understanding short- and long-term conditions

Healthcare workers make a distinction between minor, short-term illnesses and more serious or **disabling** long-term conditions. In most cases, short-term conditions are not serious and will improve quickly. However, in some cases, the **acute** or sudden onset of **symptoms** can be an indicator of a more serious problem that requires immediate treatment.

Short-term conditions

It is common for people to experience minor health problems, such as coughs, colds and sore throats, especially during the winter. This is when healthcare services are under most pressure as people go to their GP (family doctor) or even their local hospital, to try and obtain treatment. Doing this can be inappropriate if the condition will get better on its own through basic home treatment.

Taking responsibility for looking after your own health allows healthcare services to focus on those most in need. This isn't always possible though, as there are some conditions that do require medical attention to identify the cause and treat the symptoms. These conditions can include food poisoning, rashes, fever, coughs and colds, chickenpox and measles infections.

Key terms

Disabling
Limiting a person's movements, senses or activities.

Acute
Severe, lasting a short time.

Symptom
A physical or mental indicator of a condition or disease.

▼ Preventing and managing short-term conditions.

Condition	Symptoms	What to do?
Food poisoning	Feeling sick; diarrhoea; vomiting; stomach cramps; high temperature 38°C or above; feeling unwell, tired or having aches and chills.	• Rarely serious. • Usually better within a week with self-care or help from family members. • Washing hands before and after handling raw foods, using clean food preparation areas and equipment, storing food correctly and serving at correct temperatures all reduce risk of food poisoning. • GP or hospital should assess the person if symptoms persist unchanged after two days or are extreme.
Skin rash	Skin rashes in babies and children should be referred to a GP as they may be a symptom of another condition. Some of these, such as meningitis, are serious. Others, such as hives, cradle cap and ringworm, are not harmful and are easily treated.	• Most rashes go away on their own. • If a child or adult also feels unwell and the rash persists, see a GP to find out the cause and obtain treatment (usually a cream). • Regular and effective personal hygiene and good nutrition reduce the risk of developing fungal skin rashes.
Fever	A fever is a high temperature of 38°C or more. There are many causes in both children and adults. Fever is the body's natural response to fighting infections. It can also be a symptom of more serious conditions such as meningitis.	• Babies and children with a fever and a rash should be seen by a GP or hospital doctor. • Plenty of fluids should be given to avoid dehydration, food if the person wants it, resting at home and taking small amounts of paracetamol or ibuprofen are also ways of self-managing fever in adults. • A GP or hospital doctor should be consulted if fever persists or does not respond to self-care.
Coughs and colds	Most coughs go away in about three weeks. A persistent cough, a very bad hacking cough, a cough with chest pain, swollen, painful neck glands or which produces bloody phlegm should be seen by a doctor/GP.	• Self-care including staying warm, rest and drinking plenty of fluids will all help recovery. • A GP or hospital doctor should be consulted if the cough persists or has other physical symptoms that don't respond to self-care.
Chickenpox	The symptoms of this childhood infection include very itchy spots on the skin, a high temperature, aches and pains, loss of appetite and feeling generally unwell.	• Adults, newborn babies and pregnant women with chickenpox should all be seen urgently by a GP. • Drinking plenty of fluids, wearing loose clothing and using cooling gels or creams can all help to ease the symptoms. • Infected people should stay away from nursery, school or work for five days after spots appear. • A vaccine can be given if there is a risk to others (for example, a pregnant parent) from a chickenpox infection.
Measles	Most people are vaccinated to protect them from measles. Cold-like symptoms, sore, red eyes, a fever, small greyish-white spots inside the cheeks and a red-brown blotchy rash beginning on the head–neck area but spreading to other parts of the body are the main indicators of this viral infection.	• An urgent appointment should be made by phone with a GP if a person develops symptoms of measles. Turning up unannounced risks spreading measles to other people. • Vaccination with the MMR (measles, mumps and rubella) vaccine is the best way to prevent infection in yourself and others. • Drinking plenty of water, resting, staying away from others and closing the curtains to reduce light sensitivity all help with self-care.

Long-term conditions

Long-term conditions involve ongoing health problems that tend to require additional care and support for an individual to maintain their health and well-being. This can include regular contact with health services or other care workers, frequent check-ups or support from family members or the community.

▼ Long-term conditions requiring additional care and support.

Condition	Causes	Additional care and support needs
Obesity	A person who is very overweight, with lots of body fat and a body mass index of 30+ is obese. It is generally caused by eating too many calories and not taking enough exercise. In rare cases a medical condition can also cause obesity. In most cases obesity is preventable and can be reversed.	• Weight, blood pressure and heart monitoring by medical staff. • Motivational weight loss programmes, diet planning and monitoring. • Exercise programmes and support from specialists, family and friends. • Mobility assistance.
Type 2 diabetes	This condition occurs where the body doesn't produce enough insulin or the body's cells don't react to insulin. As a result, the person's blood sugar levels are too high. Type 2 diabetes is preventable and can be reversed through changes to diet and exercise.	• Blood sugar monitoring. • Medication prescription and management. • Dietary and exercise advice and support. • Regular physical health and eye tests.
Heart disease	Heart disease occurs when the blood supply to a person's heart is interrupted or blocked by a build-up of fatty substances in the arteries. Smoking, poor diet, lack of exercise and high blood pressure increase heart disease risk. Heart disease is a condition that is preventable in many cases and can be reduced though treatment and lifestyle changes.	• Blood pressure checks and heart function tests. • Medication prescription and management. • Medical advice on diet and exercise. • Motivation and support from family to improve diet and exercise levels.
Arthritis	This condition causes pain and inflammation in a person's joints. Other symptoms include reduced movement of the joints, weakness and muscle wasting and warm, red skin over the affected joint.	• Medical advice on diet and exercise. • Medication prescription and management of anti-inflammatory drugs. • Occupational therapy assessment and provision of aids to assist with daily living activities. • Adaptions to the home to enable independence.
Dementia	This refers to a range of conditions that affect the brain and which gradually get worse over time. They cause memory, thinking and self-care problems.	• Cognitive and memory tests to monitor changes in functioning. • Support and assistance from family or carers to manage self-care and daily living activities. • Support to safely manage daily activities and travel.
Cancer	Cancer is the term given to a condition where cells in a specific part of the body grow and reproduce uncontrollably. Cancerous cells can invade and destroy surrounding health tissues, including organs.	• Medication, chemotherapy or radiotherapy to treat disease. • Assistance with daily living activities when unwell. • Counselling and support to adapt to ongoing treatment and changes in condition.

An individual who has a long-term condition also has the usual range of physical and mental health needs too. They may require additional care and support because they have one or more long-term conditions that can be disabling. Additional medical treatment, check-ups and ongoing support may be required to cope with the demands of everyday life. It is not always possible to prevent or avoid long-term conditions from developing, although living an active healthy lifestyle does reduce the risk of developing obesity, type 2 diabetes and heart disease, for example.

Case study

Rachel, aged 22, felt sick as soon as she arrived home last night. She'd been to a craft fair at her local community centre and bought a chicken burger to eat while she was there. Rachel didn't finish the burger as one of her friends pointed out that the meat looked very pink in the middle. She has had stomach cramps, is feeling sick and has a high temperature. Her boyfriend is worried and says he will take her to the local accident and emergency department for treatment.

1. Why do you think that Rachel is feeling sick at this time?

2. Does Rachel have a short- or long-term health problem?

3. What do you think is the most appropriate way of treating Rachel's symptoms?

◀ Rachel was feeling very unwell.

Check your understanding

1. Give three examples of long-term conditions that result in additional care and support needs.

2. What is the most appropriate treatment for a persistent cough?

3. Explain why it is not appropriate to see a GP or go to hospital immediately if you develop a bad cold or have food poisoning.

4. Describe an example of a long-term condition that is disabling.

15 Understanding life events

Think about it

1. Which aspect of your personal development (P.I.E.S) was most affected when you started secondary school?

2. Make a list of life events that you expect to experience over the next ten years.

3. How could the experience of a sudden and unexpected serious illness have both a positive and negative effect on an individual's personal development?

▶ Kian is always ready to learn and has felt more self-confident since starting secondary school.

Life events, health and well-being

A life event is an experience that affects a person's development in a positive or negative way.

Expected life events	Unexpected life events
Starting school, getting married, retiring from work	Sudden illness or injury, **redundancy**, **bereavement**
<ul><li>predictable</li><li>act as milestones in personal development</li><li>often mark a transition from one life stage to another</li></ul>	<ul><li>unpredictable</li><li>often associated with loss</li><li>positive change can occur afterwards however (for example, illness or disability results in a person giving up work and spending more time with partner)</li></ul>

◀ There are two types of life event.

Key terms

Redundancy
The loss of a job because an employer no longer needs a person to do it.

Bereavement
The feeling of loss and grief following the death of a loved one.

Sibling
A brother or sister.

Self-concept
The beliefs, ideas or mental image a person has about themselves, including their strengths, weaknesses and how others view them.

Birth (of a sibling or own child)

The birth of a child is a significant life event for every member of a family. New relationships are formed and existing relationships, with parents and **siblings**, change with the arrival of a new baby. Children can sometimes have mixed feelings about this though. It can provide an opportunity for a child to develop their **self-concept** as an older brother or sister. However, some children can also resent the loss of attention and find themselves competing with their baby brother or sister for parental affection.

Parenthood

Becoming a parent is usually seen as a positive change, although it can also be seen as a point at which a person 'lost' their individual freedom and sense of identity. New parents are faced with a challenging situation because they must adapt their own roles and relationship to cope with the needs of their dependent child. This can feel overwhelming, particularly if a person has only limited experience of babies and young children. Many people cope by drawing on their own experiences of childhood and by relying on their parents and other relatives to provide practical and emotional support.

Parenthood can also be a major test of the new parents' relationship, as both find themselves under increasing pressure. Some people can offer their partner the practical and emotional support needed to cope with this and strengthen their relationship when they become parents. These people are also likely to adapt better to the change in self-concept that occurs when they become a 'mum' or 'dad'. Other people find that they are unable or unwilling to offer support or adapt their self-concept and experience relationship difficulties, and even the breakdown of their marriage or partnership, as a result.

For many, the birth of a child is a positive emotional milestone that results in them changing their lifestyle and life goals to be the best possible parent they can be. However, for others, parenthood can be an unwelcome burden that triggers major stress and mental health difficulties. It can lead some to neglect or abuse their child because they cannot cope with the pressures and demands that parenthood places on them.

▼ Becoming a parent is a life event that has a big effect on personal development.

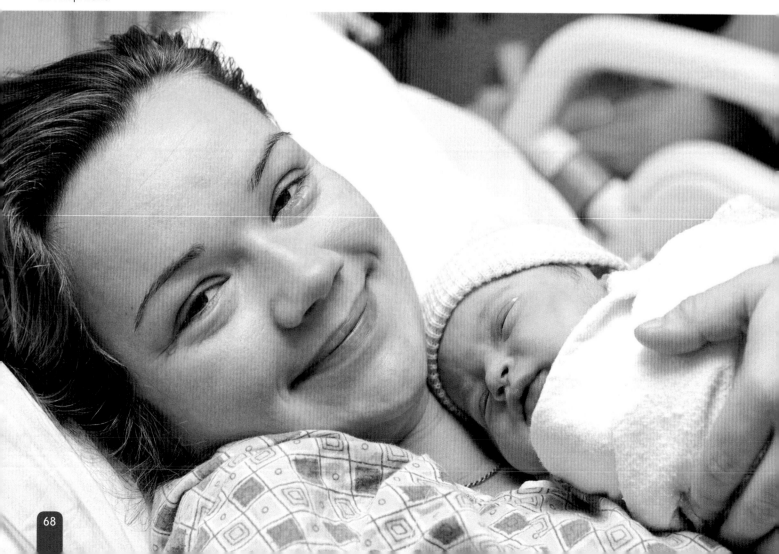

Education-related life events

The time we spend in education has a major impact on our personal development.

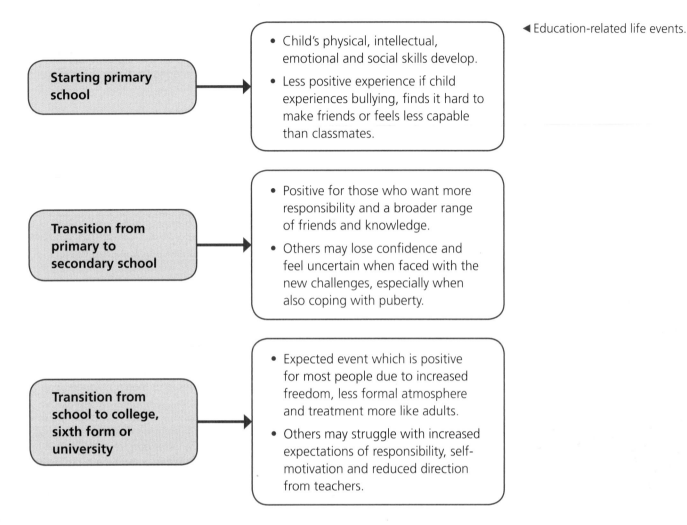

Starting primary school
- Child's physical, intellectual, emotional and social skills develop.
- Less positive experience if child experiences bullying, finds it hard to make friends or feels less capable than classmates.

Transition from primary to secondary school
- Positive for those who want more responsibility and a broader range of friends and knowledge.
- Others may lose confidence and feel uncertain when faced with the new challenges, especially when also coping with puberty.

Transition from school to college, sixth form or university
- Expected event which is positive for most people due to increased freedom, less formal atmosphere and treatment more like adults.
- Others may struggle with increased expectations of responsibility, self-motivation and reduced direction from teachers.

◀ Education-related life events.

Employment-related life events

A number of work-related transitions can impact a person's life, affecting their work status, their sense of identity, as well as their relationships with other people.

Starting work

Starting work is a predictable life event for most people. It is a point at which young people are required to behave more independently as workers, without the support of parents and teachers. A person's friendship circle can increase as they make new friendships with co-workers and there is often a boost in intellectual development as people undertake training courses in a specific area of work. This can affect a person's self-concept and their self-esteem as their area of work become part of their identity and a source of pride ('I am a nurse').

Retirement

When people reach the state pension age, they usually retire from work. Retirement is a major predictable change that a person needs to adjust to. Retirement also alters a person's social status and has an impact on their relationships and financial situation. People who have been very committed to their work, and whose work provided their social life, can struggle to cope with having non-work time to fill and the loss of contact with work friends. Retirement can also be the beginning of financial hardship for some older people. By contrast, people who have planned for their retirement, who have other interests and friendships and enough income can use retirement to pursue new opportunities, enjoy hobbies and spend more time with friends and family. For these people retirement is welcomed as a positive life event.

Redundancy

Redundancy happens when an employer decides that a job is no longer required and ends the contract of employment of the person who does that job. It is different from dismissal or sacking, as people who are made redundant lose their jobs through no fault of their own. Despite this, being made 'redundant' can have a significant effect on a person's self-esteem and emotional well-being.

Redundancy may be expected or unexpected. In either case, it can have a major impact on a person's well-being and lifestyle, as the loss of salary can lead to financial problems and emotional insecurity. Redundancy can also break up friendships and leave people feeling as though they lack a clear life role. There can also be a positive outcome to redundancy for some people. The loss of a job may motivate them to learn new skills, to start a small business or to change their lifestyle in a way that leads to them feeling happier and more satisfied in the long term.

Unemployment

Unemployment occurs when a person is unable to find work or get a job. This can have a very negative impact on a person's self-esteem, cause ongoing financial problems, and damage a person's emotional well-being and mental health. The feelings of hopelessness, a lack of purpose and low **self-confidence** can lead some people to use harmful substances such as alcohol, tobacco and illegal drugs as a way of coping with the negative feelings that result from long-term unemployment.

Marriage and civil partnership

Marrying or forming a civil partnership is a life event that most people think about in a positive way. Hundreds of thousands of people commit themselves to a relationship by getting married or by forming a civil partnership each year. This commitment can involve big changes in personal relationships and behaviour for the couple and for their close relatives and friends.

▶ Couples who marry or become civil partners aim to establish a deep emotional and psychological commitment to each other.

Marriages and civil partnerships also alter family relationships. For example, in-laws become part of a wider family network and relationships between original family members may weaken because of the practicalities of a son or daughter moving away to live with their new partner. This can cause a sense of loss for the parents of the new couple and for the couple themselves as they move away from their birth family to begin a family of their own.

Divorce

People do not marry intending to get divorced, but divorce is now quite common throughout the United Kingdom. Despite this, divorce is an unexpected life event that often has a major emotional impact (anxiety, grief and depression, for example) on the couple involved and on other members of their family, especially children.

Marriage breakdown and the process of going through a divorce usually have major financial and practical consequences too. Separation will probably mean having to find different accommodation and independent sources of income. Where the couple has children, the impact of their divorce will be felt by the children because of new living arrangements, changing relationships and sometimes the need to adapt to step-parents. Although divorce can have a negative impact on the lives of those affected, it may still be preferable to being in a stressful and unhappy relationship.

Bereavement

Bereavement is the term given to the deep feelings of loss that a person experiences when someone close, such as a partner, relative or friend, dies. Bereavement can cause a major change in a person's life, affecting their social and emotional development as well as impacting on their self-concept.

Sometimes a person's death may be expected and prepared for because of old age or because they have a terminal illness. In other cases, a person's death can be sudden and unexpected. Even when a person's death is expected because of illness, the sense of loss that follows can be very hard to accept and the powerful emotions of disbelief, sadness, anger and guilt that can follow may be very difficult to deal with. Bereavement can be even more traumatic and psychologically difficult when a person's death occurs suddenly or dramatically because of an accident, serious injury or suicide, for example.

> **Did you know?**
>
> A sense of bereavement can cause both short- and long-term problems in accepting and adjusting to the loss of the person concerned.

Serious illness, accidents and acquired disability

Accidents and illness can affect a person's development at any stage of their life. Where an accident or illness is serious it may cause either a temporary problem that the person can recover fully from or have a permanent effect on the person. For example, accidents and some types of illness can result in a disability, such as the loss of a person's sight or hearing or the loss of a limb. People who experience serious illnesses, such as heart attacks, multiple sclerosis or cancer, may find they are no longer able to carry out their usual daily routines, and they may lose their independence.

A person who acquires a disability in this way will need to adapt their skills and lifestyle to cope with the everyday situations that they face. Serious illness, accidents and acquired disabilities may also result in psychological stress, change a person's self-concept and affect their personal relationships. Friends, family and colleagues will need to adjust their relationship with the person to take account of the affected person's new situation.

▲ Moving home can be a very stressful as well as a very exciting life event.

Moving home

Home is usually a place we associate with safety, security and stability. Moving home can be unsettling as it involves a break with the past and perhaps with friends, neighbours and the security of familiar surroundings. The practical demands of organising the removal of possessions, the financial cost of moving, and perhaps buying a house or flat, add to the emotional strain associated with this life event.

A person may relocate their life from one place to another for a variety of reasons. An adult may move to be near relatives, to live with their partner or to take up work or educational opportunities. In these instances, the choice to move is likely to have a positive effect on personal development.

Where a person is unable, for whatever reason, to stay in the place they would like to live, relocation may have a disruptive and negative effect on their personal development. This can happen, for example, when an older person moves from their own home to a care home. A fundamental change in self-concept can occur in this situation as the older person loses their independence and their social and emotional connections with friends, neighbours and the community more generally.

Case study

Lowri is now a devoted mother and very proud parent of two-year-old twins Catrin and Cian. She finds caring for them very tiring but also sees it as the best thing that has happened to her. Rhys, her partner, does his best to provide practical help when he is at home. He is also very proud of his new role as a dad but says that his relationship with Lowri is sometimes strained by the pressures of caring for their children. Lowri and Rhys spend almost all their time with their children and see a lot less of their friends and family. Rhys hopes that this will change as their children get older because he misses his friends. Lowri says that she finds it hard to remember what her life was like before she had children. Sometimes she worries that she will get stuck being 'just a mum'.

1. Which aspects of Rhys and Lowri's personal development have been affected by parenthood?

2. In what ways has motherhood affected Lowri's self-concept?

3. What concerns do Rhys and Lowri have about the effect parenthood might be having on their personal development or relationships?

▲ Having children is a major life-changing event.

Check your understanding

1. List five different life events.

2. Describe how one specific life event could have both a positive and/or negative impact on an individual's personal development.

3. Explain how a work-related life event could have an impact on a person's social and emotional development.

4. Which aspects of development and well-being can be affected by bereavement?

1.1 Human development across the life cycle
Keypoints

Life stages:

Human growth and development happen in stages. The five main human **life stages** are:

- Infancy (0–2 years)
- Childhood (3–12 years)
- Adolescence (13–19 years)
- Adulthood (20–64 years)
- Later adulthood (over 65 years).

Definitions:

Physical growth refers to an increase in physical size (mass and height).

Human development refers to the emergence and increase in sophistication of skills, abilities and emotions.

Physical growth and development:

1 Human growth and development follow quite a predictable pattern with change occurring in each life stage.

→ **2** Physical growth is rapid in infancy, early childhood and adolescence.

→ **3** Sexual maturity is reached as a result of puberty during adolescence.

→ **4** Physical change and then decline occurs during adulthood and later adulthood.

→ **5** Physical skills and abilities continuously develop and change throughout life.

Intellectual development:

 Intellectual development affects a person's ability to think and understand.

 Memory, language skills and moral judgement are all affected by intellectual development.

 Intellectual abilities change in each life stage.

 Thinking ability, intelligence and memory are not affected by normal ageing, though some people develop dementia-related conditions in older adulthood.

Social development:

- Social development is about the relationships we develop with others, learning the culture of society and how to communicate.
- Language development and play are important for social development during childhood.
- Parents and close family members socialise us during infancy and childhood.
- Friendships and peer groups are important sources of social development during adolescence.
- Adult social relationships are concerned with trying to find a balance between the competing demands of work, family and friends.

Emotional development:

Emotional development affects a person's feelings and emotions.

Establishing a secure attachment relationship during infancy is vital for emotional development.

Understanding and controlling emotions is a key developmental challenge during childhood.

Developing a personal identity, self-awareness and understanding sexuality are developmental challenges during adolescence and early adulthood.

Factors affecting human growth and development:

01
Physical factors include genetic inheritance, diet, illness, disease and disability.

02
Social and economic factors include gender, family relationships, adverse childhood experiences, abuse and neglect, educational experiences, culture and ethnicity.

03
Economic and environmental factors include income, poverty, housing conditions, access to care services and air pollution.

1.2 Physical, social, emotional and intellectual health

Understanding health and well-being:

1 Health can be defined using a positive approach (being fit, feeling good) or a negative approach (not being unwell).

2 The holistic approach views physical and mental health as being very closely connected and part of a 'whole person' approach to health.

4 Physical activity and exercise are vital for both physical and mental health.

3 Social, emotional and intellectual well-being are all part of the holistic approach to health.

1.3 The importance of active participation on development and well-being

Active participation in care:

 Active participation involves directly involving the individual in planning, making decisions about or meeting their care and support needs.

 Active participation encourages people to take personal responsibility for their health and well-being.

 Active participation requires a person-centred approach and commitment by care workers to empower and work in partnership with individuals in need of care and support.

1.4 Early intervention and prevention

Early intervention and prevention:

Early intervention and preventative approaches aim to limit the impact of health and social problems.

Preventative approaches in health care include vaccination, immunisation and screening programmes and providing information and support about healthy lifestyles.

Life events:

A life event is an experience that affects a person's development in a positive or negative way.

▶ Life events can be expected or unexpected and can have positive or negative effects on a person's development and well-being.

▶ Examples of life events include birth of a sibling, parenthood, starting and ending school, beginning and retiring from work, getting married or divorced, moving home, experiencing illness, bereavement or disability.

2 Promoting and Maintaining Health and Well-being

This unit provides you with opportunities to gain knowledge and understanding of the range of health and social care, and childcare services provided in Wales and how these services promote and maintain the health and well-being of the nation.

This unit consists of three main parts:

2.1 Health and social care, and childcare provision in Wales to promote and support health and well-being

2.2 Public health and health promotion across the life cycle

2.3 Factors affecting health and well-being across the life cycle

Each part of the unit has been broken down into shorter topics. These topics will help you to understand how services are organised and how they aim to benefit different groups in Welsh society. As well as focusing on services, you will also explore public health issues and factors that affect health and well-being across the life cycle. Understanding how and why ill health occurs at a population and personal level should help you to see the importance of providing a range of effective health, social care and childcare services in Wales.

Assessment: A Non-Exam Assessment (NEA) that is composed of two tasks set by WJEC.

Part 2.1 Health and social care, and childcare provision in Wales to promote and support health and well-being

Topic 1: Care provision in Wales

Topic 2: Care sectors and healthcare provision in Wales

Topic 3: Social care and childcare provision in Wales

Topic 4: Working in health, social care and childcare

Part 2.2 Public health and health promotion across the life cycle

Topic 5: Public health in Wales

Topic 6: Health promotion in Wales

Part 2.3 Factors affecting health and well-being across the life cycle

Topic 7: Indicators of health and well-being

Topic 8: Influences on health and well-being

Topic 9: Risks to health and well-being

Topic 10: Lifestyle risks to health and well-being

◀ Exercise plays a key role in ensuring health and well-being.

2.1 HEALTH AND SOCIAL CARE, AND CHILDCARE PROVISION IN WALES TO PROMOTE AND SUPPORT HEALTH AND WELL-BEING

1 Care provision in Wales

◄ NHS Wales is an example of a national healthcare organisation.

Think about it

1. List three examples of *local* care services that you or your family have used in your part of Wales.

2. Identify whether these are healthcare, social care or childcare services.

3. How good are the services you have identified? How do you know this?

Care laws and systems in Wales

Health, social care and childcare service provision in Wales is affected by a range of laws. The organisations and practitioners who provide care services must work within these laws. The section that follows focuses on the way laws and regulation affect the provision of care services.

Setting standards for care services

All health and social care and childcare services in Wales are guided and regulated by national **regulatory bodies**. Their main task is to set standards of care and then monitor and inspect organisations providing care to ensure they are meeting these standards. The main regulatory bodies are:

- Healthcare Inspectorate Wales (HIW)
- Care Inspectorate Wales (CIW)
- Estyn.

Healthcare Inspectorate Wales (HIW)

The role of HIW is to regulate and inspect NHS services and **independent healthcare providers** in Wales against a range of standards, policies, guidance and regulations to highlight areas requiring improvement. Regulation involves applying rules to an issue or applying the law. The main aim of HIW's work is to ensure that the people of Wales receive good quality healthcare services from NHS Wales and other independent healthcare providers.

Key terms

Regulatory body
An independent organisation, such as the Nursing and Midwifery Council, that makes rules and sets standards for a profession such as registered nursing.

Independent healthcare provider
A non-government organisation or private practitioner.

HIW carry out **inspections** of healthcare services throughout Wales to check whether a provider is meeting healthcare standards, complying with regulations and meeting legal and professional standards. Part of the inspection involves speaking to people about their experiences of receiving care from the provider being inspected. HIW then produces a report that is made public through the HIW website (www. hiw.org.uk). HIW can tell providers to make improvements to their services and continues to monitor information received from the public, staff members and other organisations about the provider.

Care Inspectorate Wales (CIW)

CIW is the independent regulator of social care and childcare in Wales. The role of CIW is to register, inspect and take action to improve the quality and safety of services for the well-being of the people of Wales. These services include:

- **local authority** social services
- care homes (for children or adults)
- domiciliary support services (home care and support)
- adult placement schemes
- childminders
- children's day care
- independent fostering agencies
- voluntary adoption agencies and adoption support services
- residential family centre services.

CIW performs a very similar regulatory and inspection role to HIW but in relation to social care and childcare providers. It decides who can provide these services, inspect them and ensure they meet all the legal and regulatory requirements. Inspection reports and any recommendations made as a result of inspection are published on the CIW website (https://careinspectorate.wales/).

Estyn

Estyn is an independent body funded by the Welsh government to set standards for education and inspect education providers in Wales. Estyn carries out inspections and produces reports relating to all types of education and training providers in Wales, other than universities. These include:

- nursery schools and settings that are maintained by, or receive **funding** from, local authorities
- schools
- pupil referral units
- further education providers
- independent specialist colleges
- adult community learning
- local government education services
- teacher education and training
- Welsh for adults
- work-based learning
- learning in the justice sector.

Estyn provides advice and guidance on quality, standards and best practice in education in Wales, and works with other regulatory bodies to ensure that education service providers are **accountable** on the quality and standards of education and training to service users and the public generally (https://www.estyn.gov.wales/).

Key terms

Inspection
Looking at or examining something carefully.

Local authority
An organisation that is officially responsible for public services and facilities in a particular area.

Funding
Finance or money to pay for services.

Accountable
When a person or organisation is required or expected to justify their actions.

The legislative framework

The **legislative framework** that exists to promote and support health and well-being in Wales is a set of laws that have given people rights and also impose duties and responsibilities on NHS Wales and local authorities (councils) in Wales to provide certain health, social care and childcare services.

NHS and Community Care Act 1990

The NHS and Community Care Act 1990 introduced community care for adults with social care and support needs. Under the Act all local authorities are required to assess the social care and support needs of adults who have a physical disability, disabling illness, terminal illness, **sensory impairment**, learning disability or mental health problem. The local authority must then purchase care services to meet the individual's needs. The Act safeguards the interests of vulnerable adults by ensuring that they are appropriately catered for in the community.

Social Services and Well-being (Wales) Act 2014

The aim of this Act is to improve the well-being of people who need care and support, and carers who need support, and to transform social services in Wales. The Act requires that local authorities, health boards and Welsh Ministers (politicians) work in partnership to ensure:

- people have the support they need and can make decisions about their care and support as an equal partner
- assessments are focused on the individual in a person-centred way and that service providers share information or coordinate assessment to avoid unnecessary repetition
- carers also have an equal right to have their needs assessed
- safeguarding of vulnerable children and adults is a priority in all local authorities
- care providers adopt a preventative approach to meeting care and support needs
- local authorities and health boards form statutory partnerships to integrate health and social care provision and improve innovation and change in care services.

Further details about this Act can be found at https://gov.wales/docs/dhss/publications/160127socialservicesacten.pdf.

Public Health Wales Act 2017

This law aims to address **public health** concerns affecting the population of Wales. It also aims to create social conditions that support good health and prevent avoidable harms. It focuses on obesity, tobacco and nicotine products, special procedures (acupuncture, body piercing, electrolysis, tattooing), intimate piercing, health impact assessments, pharmaceutical services, and toilets for public use. More specifically, this law now:

- requires the Welsh government to publish a national strategy on preventing obesity and reducing obesity levels in Wales
- restricts smoking in school and hospital grounds, public playgrounds and outdoor care settings for children
- requires retailers of tobacco to be on a national register
- establishes a new licensing system to protect people from the risks of infection resulting from body piercing, electrolysis, acupuncture and tattooing
- prohibits the intimate piercing of those under 18

Key terms

Legislative framework
A set of laws.

Sensory impairment
A defect in one or more of a person's senses (sight, hearing, touch, smell, taste).

Key term

Public health
The health of the population as a whole, and the strategies used to prevent disease and promote health in a society.

- requires all providers of pharmaceutical services to be approved by the local health board as meeting a local need
- requires local authorities to ensure there is adequate access to toilets for public use in their local area
- requires public bodies to carry out health impact assessments when making plans or decisions that will affect people locally or nationally across Wales.

The Children Act 1989 and 2004

The Children Act 1989 established that care workers should see the needs of the child as most important when making any decisions that affect a child's welfare. Under the 1989 Act, local authorities were required to provide services to meet the needs of children identified as being 'at risk'.

The goal of the Children Act 2004 was to improve the lives of all children who receive informal or professional care. It covers all services that children might use, such as schools, day care and children's homes as well as healthcare services. The Children Act 2004 requires care services to work collaboratively so that they form a protective team around the child. It also requires organisations providing services for children to have:

- clear whistleblowing procedures
- safe recruitment strategies
- staff supervision and support, including safeguarding training.

> **Did you know?**
>
> The Children Act affects all health and social care, and childcare workers who provide services for children. Every worker must safeguard and promote the welfare of children.

Well-being of Future Generations (Wales) Act 2015

The aim of this law is to improve the future well-being of people living in Wales. The Act requires public bodies to work together, and with local communities in Wales, to achieve seven long-term well-being and development goals in a sustainable way.

A 'Sustainable Development Principle' works alongside these goals, highlighting how the goals and actions arising from the Act will be delivered. The five aspects that make up the Sustainable Development Principle are:

- long-term thinking
- prevention
- integration
- collaboration
- involvement.

The Act is explained in more detail by Public Health Network (https://www.publichealthnetwork.cymru/en/topics/policy/well-being-of-future-generations-wales-act-2015/) and at https://futuregenerations.wales/about-us/future-generations-act/.

▲ The seven well-being goals for Wales. Source: Public Health Network Cymru, 2018

Care Standards Act 2000–2017

This law introduced regulation for all providers of care services. It is the foundation of the regulatory system in Wales, setting national minimum standards for social care provision. The aim is to ensure that care providers deliver at least a minimum uniform level of care to every service user across the country, protecting their rights, welfare and dignity.

Government initiatives, strategies and frameworks

The Welsh government is responsible for making decisions about and providing services for health and, social care and childcare provision in Wales. Government policy is expressed and implemented through a range of initiatives, strategies and frameworks that all aim to improve the health, development and well-being of people living in Wales.

▼ Examples of Welsh Government initiatives to improve health and well-being.

Example of initiative	Purpose
New Treatment Fund	A way of providing Local Health Boards in Wales with money to quickly obtain the latest medicines for life-threatening conditions.
Building a Brighter Future	A plan that sets out the Welsh government's vision for services to promote and protect the health, well-being and development of children across the early years and to support their families.
Healthy Child Wales	A programme outlining the planned contacts children and their families can expect from their health boards between birth and starting school. Focusing on screening, immunisation and monitoring and supporting child development, it will ensure every child in Wales up to the age of seven receives consistent and universal healthcare services.
Flying Start	A programme that focuses on children under four years of age living in disadvantaged areas of Wales. It provides part-time childcare, health visiting services, parental support and speech, language and communication services. The aim is to overcome some of the effects that living in poverty can have on health and development, particularly during early childhood.
Welsh Network of Healthy Schools Schemes	Launched in 1999, it encourages the development of local healthy school schemes. Each local scheme is responsible for supporting the development of health promoting schools within their area. Within the scheme, there are seven different health topics that schools need to address: Food and Fitness; Mental and Emotional Health and Well Being; Personal Development and Relationships; Substance Use and Misuse; Environment; Safety; and Hygiene.
A Healthier Wales	The Welsh government's long-term vision and plan for achieving a 'whole system approach to health and social care', which involves bringing health and social care services together as a seamless service. There will be a shift towards community care with people only going into hospital when this is essential. The goal is that 'everyone in Wales should have longer, healthier and happy lives, able to remain active and independent, in their own homes, for as long as possible'.
Free prescriptions	The Welsh government provides free prescriptions for: • patients registered with a Welsh GP who get their prescriptions from a pharmacist in Wales • patients who live in Wales but are registered with a GP in England due to their address being close to the border (issued with 'entitlement cards'). The initiative aims to ensure everyone who needs a prescription gets it and to prevent health problems from worsening due to lack of available treatment.
A framework for delivering integrated health and social care for older people with complex needs	An initiative aiming to give older people with complex care needs more power and control over their care and support. The aim is for local authorities, healthcare, housing and voluntary sector service providers to work together, to delivery high quality integrated services, care and support.

▲ Sophie has a variety of care and support needs.

Case study

Sophie, who is 16 years old, has Down's syndrome. This condition has affected her health and personal development throughout her life and will mean that she has lifelong care and support needs. Sophie currently receives care and support from a range of care workers. Dr Hill is Sophie's GP. He works at a local health centre that is funded and run by the NHS (Wales). Alys Evans is a specialist learning disability social worker, employed by the local authority, who organises and monitors the special education and social care services that Sophie uses. Sophie attends the Stepping Stones day centre three days each week, where she takes part in a range of education and leisure activities. The centre was established and is still managed by MENCAP (Wales), a voluntary group. Sophie's parents also pay for her to attend a riding school on Thursdays that provides specialist classes for people with learning disabilities.

1. Describe how one regulatory body in Wales influences the care and support that Sophie receives.

2. How does the Children Act 1989, 2004 protect Sophie's interests as a user of care services?

3. Explain how three Welsh government initiatives, frameworks or strategies aim to help and support people such as Sophie.

Check your understanding

1. List the three regulatory bodies that set and monitor standards of care in Wales.

2. Which regulatory body carries out inspections of education providers in Wales?

3. Describe the main aims of two different pieces of **legislation** affecting care provision in Wales.

4. Explain how the Welsh government tries to improve the health, development and well-being of people living in Wales. You should refer to at least one initiative, strategy or framework in your answer.

Key term

Legislation
Written laws, such as Acts of Parliament.

2 Care sectors and healthcare provision in Wales

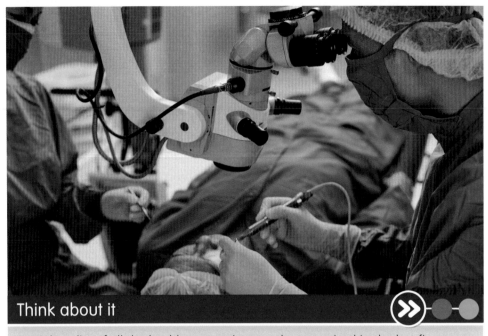

◄ Adam was able to have cataract surgery on his eye at his local hospital, which improved his vision.

Think about it »

1. Make a list of all the healthcare services you have received in the last five years.

2. Describe three examples of healthcare services that you believe should be provided for older people.

3. Give three reasons why you think some people choose to be volunteers in healthcare settings.

Care service provision in Wales

You probably know about a range of health, social care and early years services in your local area. For example, there may be a hospital, health centre, family doctor service, nursery or residential home near to where you live. Local care services like those mentioned are provided by a range of different organisations and by self-employed care workers. One way of understanding how care services are provided is to identify the sector they are part of. The three main sectors providing care services are the statutory, private and **voluntary sectors**.

The statutory care sector

The government is responsible for controlling and running the part of the care system known as the **statutory sector**. This sector includes organisations such as the National Health Service (NHS Wales) and Local Authorities (local councils). These organisations provide a lot of health and social care throughout Wales. By law (or 'statute'), the government must provide some healthcare services, such as NHS GP and hospital treatment, as well as some social services interventions. These services are 'free at the point of delivery' but are funded by general taxation.

Key terms

Voluntary sector
Registered charities and not-for-profit organisations.

Statutory sector
Care services that are provided on behalf of the state (government) because of a legal duty.

▲ NHS Wales is responsible for providing local accident and emergency services.

▼ People often refer themselves to an osteopath for treatment that relieves back pain.

Many NHS Wales healthcare services are free but some do have to be paid for, including include eye tests, glasses and contact lenses, dental treatment and cosmetic surgery (except for a medical reason), unless an individual is exempt (excused) from payment. In Wales, people who are exempt from payment include:

Who?	Exempt from paying for
Children and young people	NHS dental examinations carried out in Wales before their 25th birthday
Under 16s and those aged 16, 17, 18 in full-time education	NHS sight tests
Over 60s	NHS sight tests and NHS dental examinations
Those receiving benefits such as Income Support and Universal Credit	NHS dental treatment and eye tests; may be eligible to receive vouchers towards glasses or contact lenses and refunds for travel expenses for visiting health services

The private care sector

The **private sector** in Wales is made up of care businesses (such as private hospitals, high street pharmacists and nurseries) and self-employed care practitioners (such as childminders and counsellors). Many of the services that are provided by the private sector cannot easily be obtained in the statutory system and are specialist, non-emergency services. Day care nurseries and osteopathy services are examples.

Private sector organisations and self-employed practitioners usually charge people a fee for the health, social care or early years services they provide. Their aim is to make a financial profit whilst meeting service users care needs.

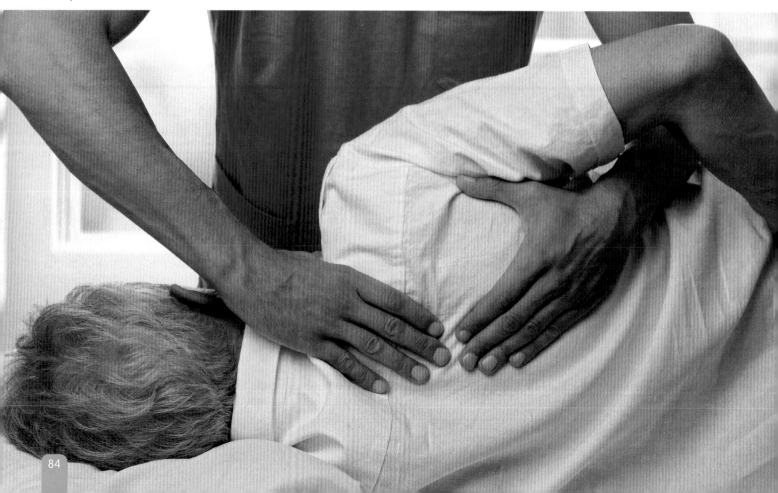

The voluntary care sector

The care system of Wales includes charities, local support groups and not-for-profit organisations. These are known as the voluntary sector or sometimes as the independent sector because they are independent of government.

The voluntary sector is made up from non-profit making organisations that provide care services because they see a need for them. Voluntary sector organisations are often registered charities and don't have a legal (or 'statutory') duty to provide care services. The sector is also called voluntary because many of the organisations have workers who are unpaid volunteers. Save the Children, Action for Children, Mind, Marie Curie, Scope and the Stroke Association are all examples of national voluntary sector organisations that recruit volunteers and operate throughout Wales. The voluntary sector also includes local support groups such as playgroups, counselling and bereavement groups who use volunteers and not-for-profit organisations with paid employees. These include Barnardo's, National Society for the Prevention of Cruelty to Children (NSPCC), Childline, Macmillan and Hospice of the Valleys.

Informal care

Many people who need care and support are unable to access or obtain assistance from statutory, private or voluntary sector providers. Instead, they are helped and supported by unpaid (and usually untrained) relatives, friends, neighbours and local faith groups. This is known as **informal care**. Examples of informal care provision include:

- babysitting
- shopping
- cleaning
- picking up **prescriptions**
- providing transport for appointments.

Children, older people and those with long-term care needs receive most informal care and support in Wales.

Healthcare services

Healthcare services in Wales are classified as either primary care services (GP services, opticians, pharmacies, dentists) or secondary care services (hospitals, occupational therapy, physiotherapy).

Primary health care involves assessment, **diagnosis** and non-emergency treatment services. Primary health care is provided for all **client groups** in community settings, such as health centres, clinics and service users' homes. Some people need to use primary healthcare services regularly because they have a chronic health problem or a disability that requires continuing treatment or monitoring. However, most people use primary healthcare services on an occasional basis for minor illnesses.

Secondary health care refers to the specialist types of care and treatment that are provided in a hospital or a specialist clinic. These focus on very specific, and often complex, health problems rather than on general illness. For example, large general hospitals usually have an accident and emergency (A&E) department that deals with life-threatening as well as minor injuries, a theatre or surgical department that deals with operations and a maternity unit that deals with childbirth.

How are healthcare services provided?

Most primary and secondary healthcare services in Wales are provided by NHS Wales, which is part of the statutory sector. Private sector organisations and private practitioners also provide a significant but smaller proportion of healthcare services. There are very few voluntary sector healthcare services.

The NHS in Wales was reorganised in 2009 to create single local health organisations that are responsible for delivering all healthcare services within a geographical area. NHS Wales now delivers services through seven Local Health Boards (LHBs) and three NHS Trusts.

▶ The seven Local Health Boards in Wales. Source: NHS Wales, 2019, http://www.wales.nhs.uk/nhswalesaboutus/structure

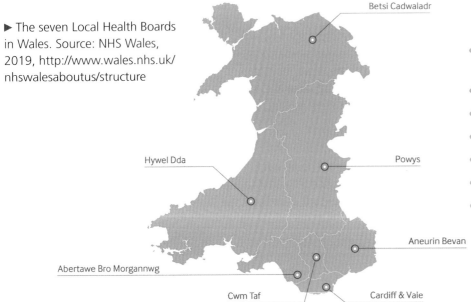

- Abertawe Bro Morgannwg University Health Board
- Aneurin Bevan University Health Board
- Betsi Cadwaladr University Health Board
- Cardiff & Vale University Health Board
- Cwm Taf University Health Board
- Hywel Dda University Health Board
- Powys Teaching Health Board

The seven LHBs in Wales now plan, secure and deliver healthcare services in their areas.

There are also currently three NHS Trusts in Wales that have an all-Wales focus. These are:

- Welsh Ambulance Services Trust for emergency services
- Velindre NHS Trust offering specialist services in cancer care and a range of national support services
- Public Health Wales.

Government money (also called 'funding') is used to employ about 78 000 people in a wide variety of NHS Wales care jobs, buy equipment and keep the statutory healthcare system running. NHS Wales provides most hospital services, funds GP practices and provides community health services across Wales.

▶ Some secondary healthcare services for client groups.

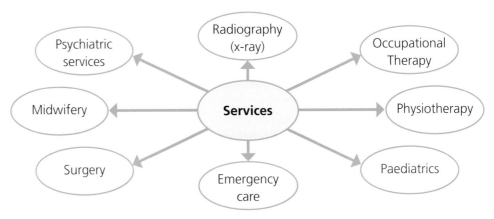

Private sector healthcare services

Private sector healthcare organisations include large care businesses, such as *BUPA*, *Spire* and *Nuffield Hospitals*. These organisations provide complex healthcare services, including surgery, in their own private hospitals in Wales. It is also possible to pay for care as a private patient in a ward or unit of some NHS Wales hospitals. The private sector in Wales also includes a wide range of self-employed private practitioners, including many dentists, **physiotherapists** and counsellors for example. Sometimes a private practitioner offers clients an alternative service from those freely available from local statutory or voluntary sector organisations. They can also offer specialist services that are not available in the statutory or voluntary sectors. An example might be osteopathy or acupuncture. Private sector healthcare clients pay for their care through health insurance or directly from their own finances.

Key term

Physiotherapist
A care professional who treats physical injury or movement problems with exercises and other physical treatments (such as massage).

Case study

Mrs Johnson is 81 years old and lives alone. She has some memory impairment, forgetting what time of the day it is, whether she has eaten, and people's names. She does remember the name her daughter Helen and granddaughter Sara who both live nearby, and also her neighbour, Mrs Scott. Mrs Johnson is unable to walk far due to her arthritis, very rarely goes out alone, and feels frightened of using her bath as she has difficulty getting in and out of it.

1. What forms of informal care would Mrs Johnson benefit from?

2. Who might be able to provide each form of informal care for Mrs Johnson?

3. If you were a relative or neighbour of Mrs Johnson, how would you feel about giving up some of your time to offer her informal care and support?

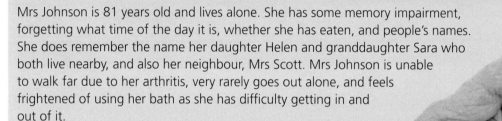

▲ Memory can start to fail in later adulthood.

Check your understanding

1. What is the name of the Local Health Board that provides NHS healthcare services where you live?

2. List three examples of healthcare services provided in secondary care settings.

3. Give two reasons why the voluntary sector is called 'voluntary'.

4. Describe two examples of private sector health and social care, or childcare services.

3 Social care and childcare provision in Wales

▶ Local playgroups are an example of voluntary sector childcare services.

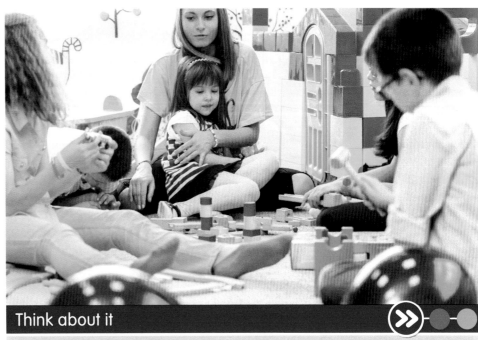

Think about it

1. Make a list of any social care and childcare services you know about in your local area.

2. Describe three examples of social care services that you think should be provided for older people.

3. Give three reasons why you think people use local or national childcare services.

Key terms

Social care
Social work, personal care, protection or social support services to children or adults in need or at risk.

Childcare
Services that safeguard or promote the development of children.

Foster care
Full-time substitute care of children, not in their own home, by people who are not their biological or adoptive parents.

Did you know?

Social care and support services are provided by large, national organisations across Wales as well as by small groups and local organisations set up to meet specific needs in a local area.

Social care and childcare services

Social care and **childcare** services help people with a range of non-medical support and personal development needs. Social care services respond to the needs of people in all life stages. Childcare services focus on meeting the needs of younger children (usually under 8) and their parents or carers.

Social care services

Social care is a general term used to describe non-medical support and social care services for people who have personal, emotional or financial problems, either temporarily or over a long period of time. Examples of social care services available in Wales include:

- **foster care**, residential care, child and family support services
- youth offending services, youth work
- homeless shelters, day centres, sheltered/supported housing
- lunch clubs, service user organisations
- support groups, counselling services, advice bureau
- care and support at home (domiciliary care and personal assistants).

How are social care services provided?

Local authorities (local councils) have a long history of providing statutory social care services in counties across Wales. More specifically, the **social services departments** of local authorities have responsibility for statutory social care services for adults in Wales. The Children Act 1989 also makes social services departments legally responsible for the welfare of children in need.

◄ Some statutory social care services for client groups.

Voluntary social care services

The voluntary sector began as a way of tackling major social problems such as poverty, unemployment and poor housing in 19th century Britain. A variety of voluntary social care services are now available for all client groups in Wales. However, unlike **statutory services**, they are not always available in every part of the country. This is because voluntary organisations differ considerably in the size and scope of their work. Some organisations, such as the NSPCC or MIND, offer social care services to children and people with mental health problems throughout Wales. Other organisations are smaller, focus on specific local issues and have very small budgets. Overall, though, the voluntary social care sector is a major provider of social care services in Wales.

Did you know?

Voluntary social care organisations often provide services to fill the gaps left by the statutory sector and play a vital part in supporting vulnerable people of all ages.

Key terms

Social services departments
The departments of a local authority that deal with non-medical social work, social care and safeguarding needs of children and adults.

Statutory services
Services that are funded and run by the government (state).

◄ Housing and residential social care services are often provided by voluntary sector organisations.

Private social care services

Compared to the statutory and voluntary sectors, the private social care sector in Wales is small. The private providers that do exist tend to specialise in residential care services for older people or people with disabilities and **domiciliary services**. People who use private sector social care services either pay for the cost of the services themselves or, if they meet the **eligibility criteria**, they may have their fees paid by their local authority social services department.

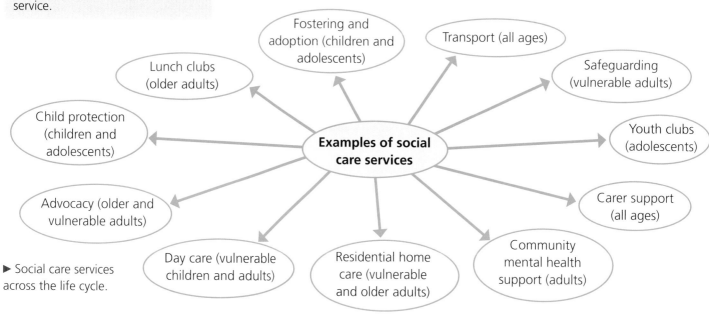

▶ Social care services across the life cycle.

Childcare services

Childcare organisations and self-employed practitioners such as childminders provide early education and childcare services for children under the age of eight. The aim of childcare services is to help young children to meet their physical, intellectual, emotional and social needs, often through play, and to safeguard children who are 'at risk'.

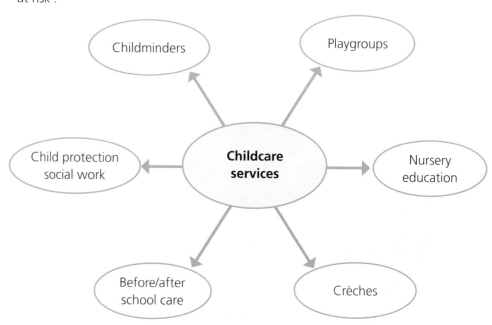

▶ Some examples of childcare services.

There are very few statutory childcare services in Wales. This is because childcare is generally seen as the responsibility of parents and other relatives. However, the Welsh government and local authority organisations are involved in providing some childcare services and there is a lot of voluntary and private sector provision for young children throughout Wales. The Welsh government currently funds 30 hours a week of free early years education and childcare for working parents of three- and four-year-olds in Wales through the 'Talk Childcare' scheme.

Statutory childcare services

Local authorities are responsible for purchasing (buying) care for children in need in their area. These services are typically provided for families where a child is 'at risk' or where family pressures and problems can be reduced by childcare support. Children with disabilities and children who have health or developmental problems are also eligible for these statutory services, such as playgroups, nurseries, childminders and family centres. Children and families who use these services must have unmet care and development needs that have been identified by a social worker or other early years professional.

Voluntary childcare services

The voluntary childcare sector consists of some large national organisations, such as Barnardo's, NSPCC and Childline, and a larger number of small, local voluntary groups that provide playgroups, nurseries and other support groups for children under the age of eight and their parents. The voluntary sector is a major provider of childcare services in Wales and is made of many support groups developed and run by parents with children who are not eligible for statutory services and cannot afford or don't wish to pay for private childcare services.

Private childcare services

Childcare services available from the private sector include nursery schools, playgroups, crèches and childminding services. These organisations provide services to young children who have needs that are not met by the limited range of statutory sector services. A child's parents must be able to afford to pay the fees charged, so private sector childcare services are not available to everyone who might need or benefit from them.

Some childcare workers also work in their own homes on a self-employed basis. Registered childminders are the largest group working in this way. Like all self-employed carers, they charge the people who use their services a fee for their time and expertise.

▲ Carla needed temporary alternative care.

Case study

Carla was six years old when her mum, a lone parent, was admitted to hospital for a major heart operation. Carla's mum, a local authority social worker called Jeff and Carla herself decided that the best option was for Carla to live with foster carers for two months. Jeff arranged for Carla to live with the Wilson family for most of the summer until her mum recovered from the operation and was able to return home. Carla said that she missed her mum a lot at first and felt like she didn't fit in. She did grow to like the Wilson family, particularly Sara, aged 14, who remains a friend.

1. Give three reasons why Carla needed care at this point in her life.

2. What kinds of care and support do you think a foster family would provide for children such as Carla?

3. Which care sector provided the foster care support for Carla when her mum was in hospital?

Check your understanding

1. What is the name of the local authority that provides statutory social services where you live?

2. List three examples of social care services provided by the voluntary sector.

3. What kinds of childcare services are available from private sector providers?

4. Describe two ways in which statutory and private sector childcare services differ.

4 Working in health, social care and childcare

Think about it

1. List the work roles (or job titles) of people employed in your local health centre or GP practice.

2. With a partner, identify as many different kinds of healthcare role as you can think of (for example, doctor, district nurse, practice nurse) and say something about what each role involves.

3. What health, social care or childcare roles interest you? Explain why and share what you know about the qualifications and experience needed for your preferred work roles.

▶ It's not all doctors and nurses – there are many different specialist work roles within a health and social care organisation!

Work roles in health, social care and childcare

Working in healthcare, social care or childcare roles in Wales can be rewarding and also challenging. Services that provide a high standard of effective care to a diverse population need to employ skilled, knowledgeable and experienced care workers. There are a wide variety of work roles across the health, social care and childcare sectors in Wales.

Healthcare work roles

People employed in healthcare roles deal with individuals of all ages who have medically-based physical problems such as a disease, injury or acute illness, or mental health problems such as anxiety or depression. NHS Wales is the largest employer in Wales with approximately 78 000 members of staff. The main healthcare job areas are as follows:

Healthcare work areas	Number of NHS employees
Medical and dental staff	6 321
Nursing, midwifery and health visiting staff	29 523
Healthcare assistants and other support staff	9 704
Ambulance staff	2 084
Scientific, **therapeutic** and technical staff	12 799
Administration and estates staff	17 384
Other non-medical staff	101

◀ Healthcare workers employed by NHS Wales (2017).

Key term

Therapeutic
Another word for healing.

Working in medicine

A qualified doctor has a degree in medicine. This involves attending a university medical school for five years to gain the basic academic knowledge and practical experience to pass this first stage of medical training. To gain entry to medical school, an applicant usually needs at least five GCSEs and three A Levels, or their equivalent, with very high grades. Most students enter medical school at the age of 18.

When a person qualifies at university, they must then work for at least a year as a junior doctor in a hospital setting, rapidly gaining experience of a range of diseases, illnesses and medical problems. Doctors spend most of their time examining patients, diagnosing their health problems and prescribing treatments. Doctors often work long hours and many work at weekends, in the evenings and at night to deal with the very large caseloads of patients they must see and treat. They also have to keep studying and take professional examinations to become specialists (consultants) in areas of medicine such as surgery, general practice or psychiatry.

Working in nursing

Nurses make up the largest group of care staff in Wales.

There are important differences in the type of training and work that the different groups of professionally qualified nurses do. Additionally, nurses also perform a different role from healthcare support workers (also known as nursing assistants).

Professionally qualified or **registered nurses** take an approved nurse training programme that lasts for three years and results in a registered nurse qualification. The minimum entry qualifications are passes in three A Levels or an equivalent Level 3 qualification. When qualified, a registered nurse generally works as a staff nurse to gain experience and improve their practical skills. The day-to-day work that nurses do depends on the specialist area of care in which they work. For example, mental health nurses talk with service users and provide emotional support, whereas nurses working in accident and emergency treat people's wounds and injuries.

Generally, nurses spend a lot of time in very close contact with patients, providing a wide range of direct care and support. Nursing is often a physically and emotionally tiring job. Caring for people who are sick and dependent can involve carrying out tasks that are unpleasant and physically demanding, such as changing and remaking soiled beds. As well as carrying out their care role, nurses have to complete administrative work relating to patients and often have a role in training student nurses.

Healthcare support work

People who are interested in direct care work can gain some vocational training and experience as a healthcare support worker. Many healthcare support workers take a vocational course and gain their training and experience under the supervision of registered nurses. Healthcare support workers are employed in all areas of health care. They often have a lot of direct patient contact, assisting registered nurses and other care staff in providing care.

Did you know?

There are four main branches of nursing: adult (also called general) nursing, children's nursing, learning disability nursing and mental health nursing.

Key term

Registered nurse
A nurse who has met the standards of practice and achieved a qualification that allows them to register with the Nursing and Midwifery Council.

The role of a healthcare support worker is different from that of a registered nurse in a number of important ways:

- Healthcare support workers carry out most of the domestic tasks in a care setting, such as making beds.

- The physical care that healthcare support workers provide relates to routine procedures such as lifting, bathing and dressing patients.

- Healthcare support workers carry out care planned by registered nurses.

Like nurses, healthcare support workers work day and night shifts and may also work at weekends. Personal maturity is one of the key factors that employers take into account when recruiting people to posts of support worker.

Social care work roles

People employed in social care roles usually deal with people who are vulnerable and who have care needs that are mainly social, emotional or financial rather than physical. Social care roles can include forms of direct care such as counselling, or indirect help such as arranging housing or access to other support services. Social care services are provided by workers who have a variety of different job titles, such as project workers, community workers and social workers.

Social work roles

A social worker is a person who has gained a professional social work qualification (normally a degree or diploma in social work), and who has experience of working with clients who have social, financial and emotional problems. Social work courses are available in further and higher education colleges. Applicants usually need a minimum of A Level or other Level 3 qualifications, and some social care experience.

Most professionally qualified social workers have a caseload of people they work with in community and institutional settings. Some social workers specialise in working with particular types of clients, such as those in child protection, safeguarding or psychiatric social work. Others operate as non-specialised social workers and see people referred to them with various problems. Some social workers work as care coordinators or care managers and specialise in assessing clients' needs and purchasing care packages for them.

Social care roles

Social care support workers tend to have vocational training gained through experience. They work under the supervision of qualified social workers, often providing practical help and support for clients that requires a lot of direct client contact. Social care workers are employed in a range of different settings, including domiciliary (home) care, residential care and day care settings, for example.

Social care workers may work a variety of different shift patterns. Day care workers tend to work from 9am to 5pm, Monday to Friday; domiciliary care workers may work at any time of the day from early morning to late evening; residential social care workers may work day and night shifts and weekends. There is no official minimum age for entry into this type of care work. Like healthcare support worker posts, employers look for people with personal maturity and some life experience that gives them the ability to help and support others.

Did you know?

As social work can be a difficult and stressful job that requires maturity and life experience, most courses have a minimum entry age of between 18 and 21 years old.

Childcare work roles

People working in childcare roles are usually employed in providing direct childcare and early education services for children under the age of eight. There is a wide range of care roles and career opportunities in childcare and early years education. Childcare and early years workers may have qualifications or may gain work because of their own experience in bringing up children. Many nursery, playgroup and classroom assistants now also undertake vocational training, for example, to add new knowledge and skills to their childcare work experience.

Childcare and early years work involves lots of busy, hands-on activities with children. Care workers in this area are responsible for the safety and development of the children they care for and work with. Some early years workers specialise in working with children who have physical or **sensory impairments**, whereas others specialise in working with children who have **learning difficulties**.

Within each area of work there are many specialist roles. Care workers tend to become more specialist as their careers progress. For example, within childcare a person could begin their career as a nursery assistant, then qualify and work as a nursery nurse and, with further experience and training, go on to become a classroom teacher in primary education, a nursery manager or an early years practitioner for a local authority.

Key terms

Sensory impairment
A defect in one or more of a person's senses (sight, hearing, touch, smell, taste).

Learning difficulty
An impaired or reduced ability to learn.

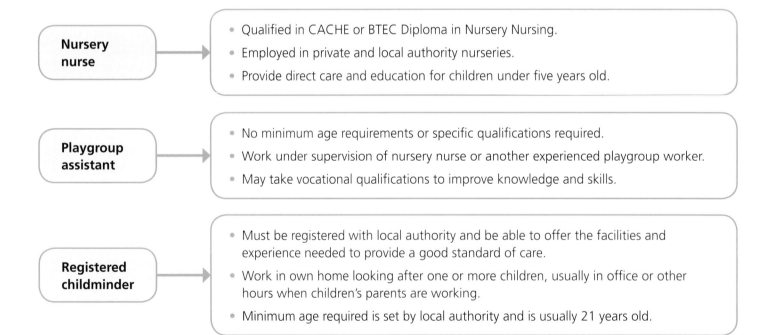

Nursery nurse
- Qualified in CACHE or BTEC Diploma in Nursery Nursing.
- Employed in private and local authority nurseries.
- Provide direct care and education for children under five years old.

Playgroup assistant
- No minimum age requirements or specific qualifications required.
- Work under supervision of nursery nurse or another experienced playgroup worker.
- May take vocational qualifications to improve knowledge and skills.

Registered childminder
- Must be registered with local authority and be able to offer the facilities and experience needed to provide a good standard of care.
- Work in own home looking after one or more children, usually in office or other hours when children's parents are working.
- Minimum age required is set by local authority and is usually 21 years old.

▲ Examples of childcare roles.

Partnership and multi-agency working

Healthcare, social care and childcare workers and statutory, private and voluntary care agencies often work together to provide services for people in Wales. This is because care workers and organisations now rarely work on their own or provide services in isolation. Partnerships and **multi-agency working** are common and healthcare, social care and childcare service provision for client groups, like children or older people, is increasingly **integrated**. At the same time, collaboration and **co-production** are also resulting in new forms of partnership between care agencies, care workers and the people who use care services.

Ways of working together

Partnership and multi-agency working can be organised in different ways.

Multi-agency panels
- Practitioners employed by a variety of different care organisations meet regularly as a panel to discuss service users with complex needs.
- Child protection panels are an example of a multi-agency service.

Multi-agency and multi-disciplinary teams
- A group of care practitioners with different backgrounds form a team that provides assessment, intervention and monitoring for groups of service users with specific needs.
- Multi-agency disability teams and virtual wards are an example of this type of multi-agency service.

Integrated services
- A range of separate services merge and work in a collaborative way to meet the broad but closely-related needs of a specific client group.
- *Flying Start* teams have a group of care workers who are members of different professions, including social workers, speech and language therapists, health visitors and childcare workers, each providing specific care for the individual child and their parents or carers.

The aims of partnership and multi-agency working are to:
- improve access to services not previously available to service users
- make access to services and care worker expertise easier and quicker
- encourage early identification of and intervention in health, social care and developmental problems
- reduce replication of services
- provide better links between service providers
- provide better quality, seamless services
- reduce the costs of providing care
- improve the efficiency and effectiveness of local care services
- organise locally-based services around the needs of the individual, their family and an informal support network to provide person- / child-centred care.

▲ The three main ways of effective partnership and multi-agency working.

Legislation has been passed to ensure that partnership and multi-agency working happens throughout Wales. This includes:

- *Social Services and Well-being (Wales) Act 2014*, which ensures that local authority, social services and other care and support services work together in partnership with individuals, taking into account their needs, preferences and strengths, to provide person- / child-centred care.

- *Well-being of Future Generations (Wales) Act 2015*, which makes public bodies work better with people, communities and each other (to take a more joined-up approach).

▲ Peter benefits from multi-agency support.

Case study

Peter is 64 years of age. He has mental health problems, diabetes and had a serious heart attack a year ago. Peter tries to be as active as he can. He sees a social support worker at a MIND day centre on three days each week, goes to an exercise group run by a physiotherapist at his GP practice for people recovering from heart problems and enjoys socialising with other residents in the small private sector care home where he lives. Peter also has a social worker who coordinates the care he receives. The people who work with Peter meet a couple of times each year to discuss his needs and what they can do as a team to help him.

1. Identify the work roles of the people who provide care and support for Peter.

2. Describe the qualifications and training that Peter's social worker and GP have undertaken to obtain their work roles.

3. How does Peter benefit from a partnership approach to his care?

Check your understanding

1. Identify an example of a healthcare, social care and childcare role that involves direct contact with service users.

2. Describe the work role of a healthcare support worker.

3. Explain what multi-agency working involves in health, social care and childcare.

4. Outline three benefits or advantages of multi-agency working.

2.2 PUBLIC HEALTH AND HEALTH PROMOTION ACROSS THE LIFE CYCLE
5 Public health in Wales

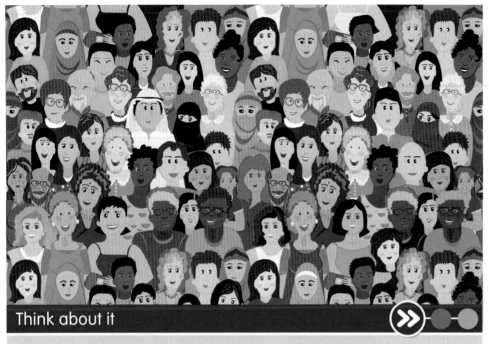

Think about it

1. List three lifestyle choices that affect public health in Wales.

2. What public **health promotion** campaigns can you recall seeing or reading about?

3. Why do you think reducing pollution is now seen as a major public health issue?

◀ Public health focuses on the health, development and well-being of large groups of people.

Understanding public health in Wales

Public health services focus on health issues affecting large groups of people (populations and communities) in Wales rather than on the personal health of individuals. For example, they focus on:

- lifestyle choices (smoking, alcohol consumption, healthy eating) and their impact on health and well-being
- the effects that the natural environment can have on people (sunburn and skin cancer, for example)
- the links between human activities (such as industrial production and pollution), environmental change and health.

Understanding public health issues in Wales will help you to see how individual health problems are really part of a 'bigger picture'. Health and illness experiences are often socially patterned, collective issues that impact on society as well as being individual experiences.

Key terms

Health promotion
The process of enabling people to increase control over, and to improve, their health.

Public health
The health of the population as a whole, and the strategies used to prevent disease and promote health in a society.

Key terms

Interventions
Actions or activities designed to improve health and well-being.

Health inequalities
Differences in the health status or the influences on health between groups in the population.

Life expectancy
The average period a person may expect to live.

What is the purpose of public health?

The purpose of public health activity in Wales is to improve the health and well-being of individuals, communities and the whole population. Public Health Wales, along with a range of other healthcare providers, do this through a variety of ways:

- They provide people with information, education and advice that will make them aware of risks to health. They also enable them to make healthy lifestyle choices and increase control over their own health.

- They design social and environmental **interventions** aimed at benefitting and protecting individuals' health and well-being.

- They address and prevent the root causes of ill health, not just focusing on treatment and cure.

Public health is about helping individuals to stay healthy and protecting them from threats to their health. The Welsh government wants everyone to be able to make healthier choices, regardless of their circumstances, and to minimise the risk and impact of illness.

What are the public health challenges facing Wales?

The population of Wales is healthy in some ways but has poorer health compared with many other Western nations. There are also significant **health inequalities** within the Welsh population, with those in poverty experiencing poorer health than others who are less poor. For example, there is a difference in healthy **life expectancy** of over 18 years between the most and least deprived sections of the population of Wales.

Health life expectancy at birth, Wales 2005–2009 and 2008–2012

▶ Health life expectancy at birth, Wales 2005–2009 and 2008–2012. Source: Public Health Wales Observatory, cited in Riordan, P. (2014).

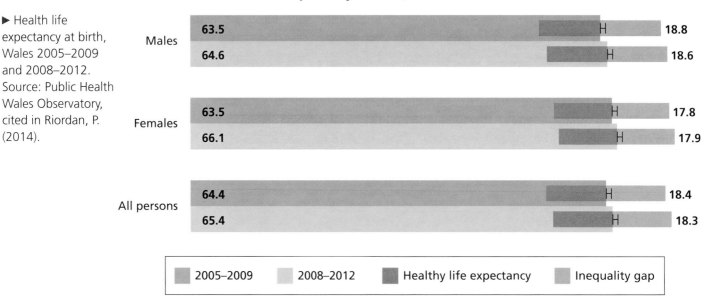

| | 2005–2009 | 2008–2012 | Healthy life expectancy | Inequality gap |

Males: 63.5 | H | 18.8
Males: 64.6 | H | 18.6

Females: 63.5 | H | 17.8
Females: 66.1 | H | 17.9

All persons: 64.4 | H | 18.4
All persons: 65.4 | H | 18.3

The causes of ill health in the Welsh population are linked to income, housing, opportunities for work and education. They are also strongly connected to lifestyle factors such as smoking, alcohol misuse, obesity, diet and exercise. The Welsh Health Survey (2012) found evidence of high levels of drinking, smoking and obesity combined with poor diets and a lack of exercise. For example:

- Just a third (33 per cent) of adults in Wales reported eating five or more portions of fruit and vegetables the previous day, while even fewer (29 per cent) reported being physically active on five or more days in the past week.

- The number of adults in Wales classed as overweight or obese had increased to 59 per cent, with 23 per cent in the 'obese' category, while 34 per cent of children were classified as overweight or obese.

- 23 per cent of adults still smoked (a figure that had only fallen by 1 per cent since the 2007 smoking ban), while 42 per cent reported drinking above the guidelines and 26 per cent admitted binge drinking on at least one day within the past week.

Who is responsible for public health in Wales?

Public Health Wales (www.publichealthwales. wales.nhs.uk) is the national public health agency in Wales. Its purpose is to protect and improve health and well-being and reduce health inequalities for people in Wales. Public Health Wales is part of the NHS and reports to the Cabinet Secretary for Health, Well-being and Sport in the Welsh Government. Public Health Wales, health boards and local authorities across Wales work closely together to promote public health in their areas. They also work in partnership with communities, housing and education departments, police, fire and rescue, and the voluntary sector to identify and set local health promotion and improvement targets.

> **Did you know?**
>
> Some lifestyle choices affect an individual's chances of developing cancer and circulatory and respiratory diseases, which then influence differences in life expectancy. Public health strategies and interventions are needed to combat these factors and address health inequalities.

▼ Agencies involved in health promotion in Wales.

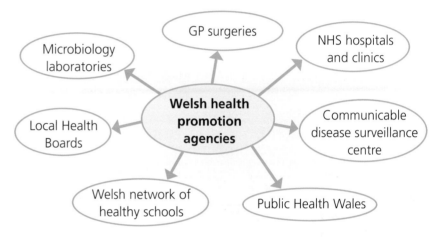

Who benefits from public health activity?

The public health work of government agencies and healthcare workers aims to improve the health and well-being of:

- individuals with specific health problems or needs
- communities or social groups with specific health improvement needs
- the nation as a whole.

Individual benefits
Effective public health activity can:

- increase an individual's understanding of health issues
- motivate people to take greater personal responsibility for their health and well-being
- reduce the individual's risk of experiencing disease or injury by changing their lifestyle choices or behaviour practices
- improve the quality of a person's life by boosting their health and well-being
- increase the individual's life expectancy by promoting a healthier and safer lifestyle.

National benefits

Governments and local agencies view public health activity as an effective way of improving the health and well-being of communities and the nation. For example, large-scale health promotion campaigns and interventions can:

- reduce levels of illness and disease in the population as a whole
- help to tackle inequalities in health and illness experienced in different sections of the population
- reduce crime and accident levels (related to road safety, drug use and alcohol-related violence, for example) locally and nationally
- increase participation in vaccination and screening programmes within targeted sections of the population
- raise awareness of and help to tackle current and emerging health and well-being concerns within the Welsh population (obesity levels, heart health, drug use and sexually transmitted infections, for example)
- reduce the financial cost to NHS Wales and government of having to treat preventable health problems (diet, smoking and alcohol-related, for example)
- reduce the cost to the police, courts and prison service of dealing with alcohol, drug and road safety-related crime and disorder incidents.

▲ Jamie wants to quit smoking.

Case study

Jamie is 34 years of age, works as a plasterer for a building company and smokes 20 cigarettes a day. He knows that smoking is a risk to his health and wants to quit as soon as possible. Jamie started smoking at school because many of his friends also smoked. He has carried on smoking because many of his workmates, as well as his parents, also smoke. His wife Emma has encouraged him to give up, telling Jamie that he is setting a bad example to their son. Jamie has seen a few posters about quitting smoking and recently picked up a leaflet about it when he was at the local gym.

1. Give two reasons why cigarette smoking is considered a public health issue in Wales.

2. What role does Public Health Wales have in helping people like Jamie to quit smoking?

3. Who would benefit, directly and indirectly, if people such as Jamie could be persuaded and helped to quit smoking?

Check your understanding

1. Give three examples of public health issues affecting Wales.

2. Using your own words, describe the purpose of public health activity.

3. Summarise the potential benefits of public health activity to individuals.

4. Explain how effective public health activity can benefit Wales as a nation.

6 Health promotion in Wales

▲ Fitness classes are an example of a positive health promotion activity.

Think about it

1. Name three health promotion campaigns that you are aware of.
2. Describe three health and well-being benefits of taking part in a fitness class like the one pictured.
3. What single lifestyle change would most improve the health and well-being of people in your local area?

Health promotion and health promotion methods

Have you ever set yourself a goal of 'being healthier' or 'getting fit'? A common time to do this is just after Christmas, when people often feel they've had too much to eat or drink. Other people change their diet and do their best to get fit when the summer is approaching or when they have a big occasion, such as a wedding, to attend. We've probably all wanted to improve our health and well-being at one time or another, although it is best to have a healthy lifestyle all year round.

Health promotion involves providing information and education containing **health messages** to individuals, to various social groups, to a whole community or, on a larger scale, to the wider nation.

Health promotion issues

Health promotion activity often focuses on lifestyle issues and health behaviour that present a risk to health. For example, smoking, poor diet, lack of exercise, alcohol and drug misuse, and unprotected sex are all important health promotion issues. Health promotion activity isn't just about health dangers and giving warnings though. Increasingly it is about promoting positive health.

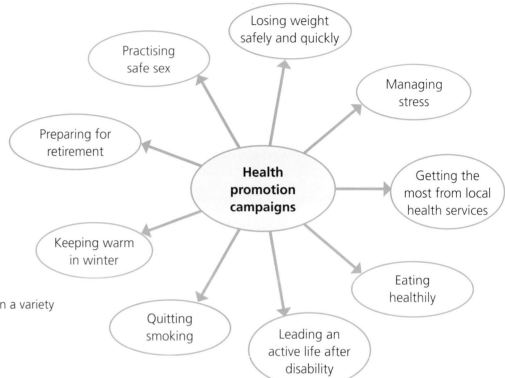

▶ Health promotion activities focus on a variety of campaigns.

Types of health promotion activity

Health promotion activity can occur in different ways. This includes giving individuals information, advice and guidance about ways to improve their health, well-being or safety and much larger-scale health promotion campaigns that are directed at the whole population or at groups within it.

Promoting healthy lifestyles

Health workers encourage people to make lifestyle changes as a way of improving their health and well-being. 'Do more exercise', 'lose some weight' or 'stop smoking' might form part of a health promotion message during a **consultation** with a health professional, for example. As well as raising awareness of health risks by giving information and advice, healthcare workers also:

- identify lifestyle issues that may lead to health problems and encourage people to adopt healthier lifestyles
- develop health improvement plans that focus on improving personal health, physical fitness and general well-being
- monitor health and well-being through **screening** and other health assessments, and provide services such as **immunisation** to prevent ill health from occurring.

Health workers such as GPs, community nurses, occupational therapists and physiotherapists also work with individual service users to set personal health improvement targets. They do this after undertaking a thorough assessment of the person's current health status. Part of the health worker's role is to provide support

Key terms

Consultation
A meeting with a doctor or another health professional to diagnose and discuss health problems or treatments.

Screening
A strategy used with a population to identify the possible presence of as yet unidentified disease in those without signs or symptoms.

Immunisation
Making people immune to infection.

and encouragement when the person struggles to make the necessary lifestyle changes or finds that their motivation to achieve their targets is slipping. Many people are very motivated to adopt a healthier lifestyle if they believe that it will reduce their risk of health problems, such as heart disease, obesity or cancer, in the future.

Health promotion campaigns

Public Health Wales often uses large-scale health promotion campaigns to raise national awareness of health risks and lifestyle issues such as healthy eating, drug misuse and HIV infection. They also work in partnership with Local Health Boards, voluntary groups and other agencies to develop and run health promotion and intervention projects targeted at specific groups or communities or the national population of Wales.

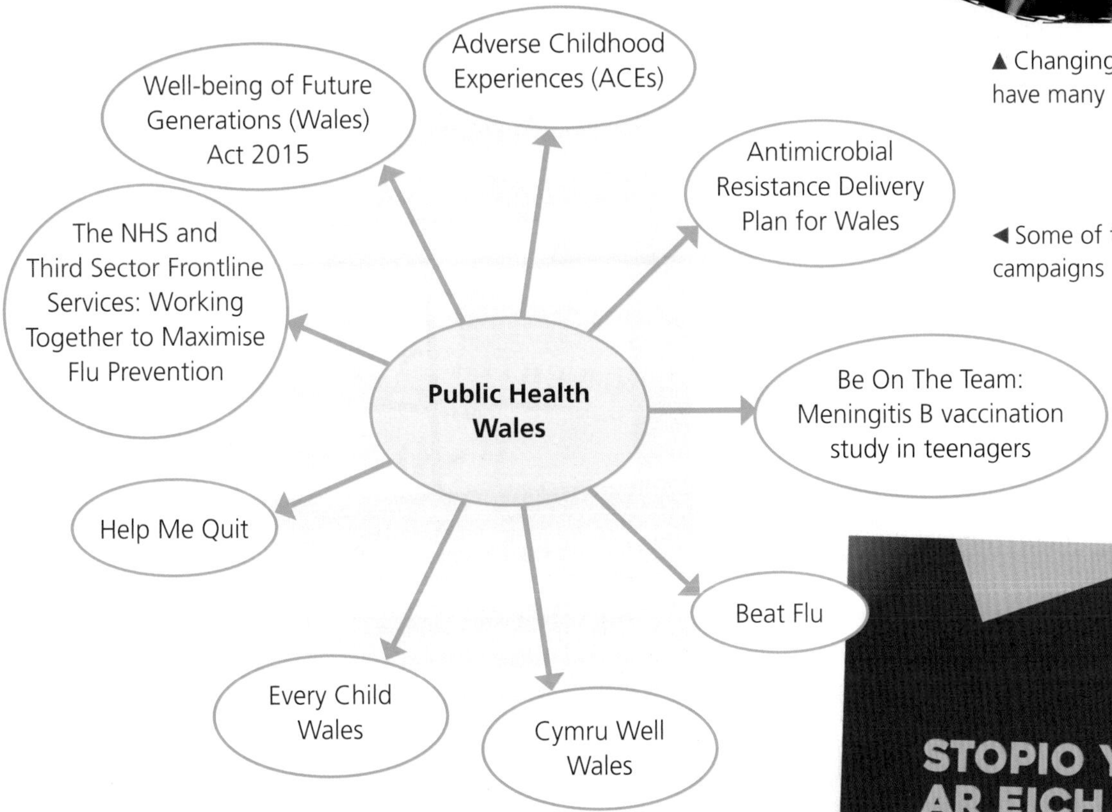

▲ Changing to a healthier lifestyle can have many benefits.

Well-being of Future Generations (Wales) Act 2015

Adverse Childhood Experiences (ACEs)

The NHS and Third Sector Frontline Services: Working Together to Maximise Flu Prevention

Antimicrobial Resistance Delivery Plan for Wales

Public Health Wales

Help Me Quit

Be On The Team: Meningitis B vaccination study in teenagers

Every Child Wales

Cymru Well Wales

Beat Flu

◄ Some of the health promotion campaigns run by Public Health Wales.

Further information on these campaigns and their health promotion aims can be found on the Public Health Wales website (www.publichealthwales.wales.nhs.uk).

STOPIO YSMYGU AR EICH PEN EICH HUN NEU GYDA HELP AM DDIM GAN Y GIG?
QUIT SMOKING ON YOUR OWN OR WITH FREE NHS HELP?

0800 085 2219

Ewch i helpafiistopio.cymru
Tecstiwch HMQ i 80818
Visit helpmequit.wales
Text HMQ to 80818

HELPA FI I STOPIO · HELP ME QUIT

► An NHS (Wales) leaflet from the Help Me Quit campaign.

Health promotion materials

Health promotion campaigns can make use of a variety of communication methods and materials to deliver health messages or information. These include:

- posters and leaflets
- websites and apps
- games and role plays
- presentations (talks and lectures)
- seminars and workshops
- information films and videos
- television and radio campaigns.

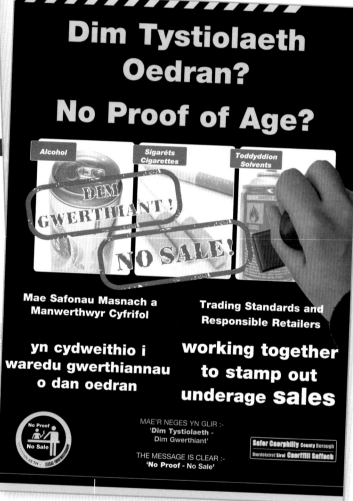

▲ Two of the health promotion campaigns in Wales.

The materials or delivery methods used must appeal to and be effective in reaching the **target groups** they are intended for. The types of materials or methods used must also be:

- capable of achieving the overall aims of the health promotion activity
- an appropriate way of explaining the health risk and providing health advice
- cost effective (TV adverts are very expensive, posters are not, for example)
- relatively easy to understand and use.

Health promotion aims or purpose	Appropriate methods/materials
Raising awareness of health issues	Talks/presentations Group work Mass media Displays Poster campaigns Leaflets
Improving knowledge/providing information	Websites and apps Presentations Games Posters Leaflets Mass media
Empowering people by improving self-awareness, self-esteem and decision-making	Group work Social skills training Role play Assertiveness training Counselling
Changing attitudes, behaviour and lifestyles	Websites and apps Games/group work Skills training Self-help groups Presentations Group or individual work

◄ Health promotion aims and the methods of promoting them.

The mass media (newspapers, magazines and television adverts) as well as booklets, leaflets, posters, websites, emails and text messages can be used to communicate information about a variety of health risks to the whole population, or large sections of it, during these campaigns. The purpose is to give people information about health risks and encourage everybody to take responsibility for making healthier or safer lifestyle choices. Some large-scale health promotion campaigns, such as the Christmas anti drink-driving campaign and the summer skin cancer awareness campaigns, are carried out every year. Other local initiatives related to safe drinking, road safety or personal safety, for example, may be targeted at a local population by the NHS Wales Local Health Board, police or fire service because there is a specific need for information in that area.

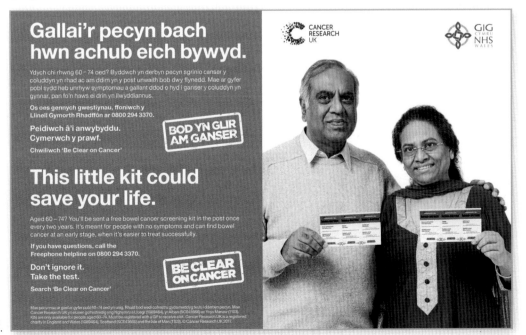

▶ A Welsh health promotion campaign for bowel cancer screening from Cancer Research UK.

▲ Why is Aled already overweight?

Case study

Aled is 12 years old. He lives on a small estate on the edge of town with his parents. Aled plays a lot of computer games on his console. He's also a keen keyboard player, practising for a couple of hours each day. Aled is popular at school, partly because he is very funny. He uses his humour to defend himself when people laugh at his size. Aled is 6.5kg overweight. His parents are concerned about this, though his mum insists he does not overeat. She believes that lack of exercise and 'genetics' has led to his weight problem.

1. What factors might be contributing to Aled being overweight?

2. Why is Aled's weight likely to lead to health problems if he doesn't do something about it?

3. How might Aled and others benefit from health promotion activities that focus on the value of exercise and participation in sport?

Check your understanding

1. Using your own words, explain what 'health promotion' activity is.

2. List five different health promotion issues that are relevant to adolescents.

3. Explain how healthcare workers promote healthy lifestyles and promote health improvement in their day-to-day work.

4. Describe three methods of health promotion, giving a reason for using each in a health improvement campaign.

2.3 FACTORS AFFECTING HEALTH AND WELL-BEING ACROSS THE LIFE CYCLE

7 Indicators of health

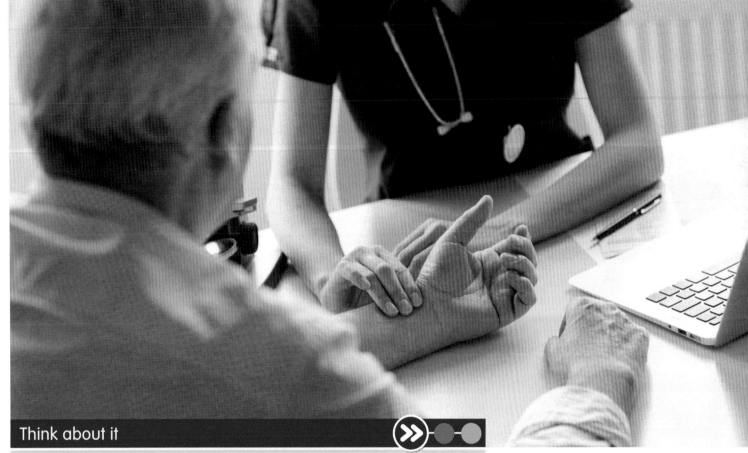

Think about it

1. Identify two places on the human body where it is possible to feel a person's pulse.

2. What effect do you think a diet high in fat and salt has on a person's blood pressure?

3. Describe three health problems that are associated with having a higher body mass index (being overweight) than recommended.

▲ Routine measurements, like the pulse rate, are taken to assess a person's general health.

How can we know a person is healthy?

One way of knowing if a person is healthy is to measure specific indicators of their physical health. This topic will focus on what these indicators are, how they can be measured and how the results of health assessments can be used to develop realistic health improvement plans.

The different indicators of physical health are all based on the same basic process: the healthcare worker measures and records something and then compares the individual's 'score' against a standard scale. To make sense of the results, the healthcare worker must take the person's age, sex and lifestyle into account. This is important because a pulse rate of 100 beats per minute would be fast for an adult but normal for a baby, for example. You are probably familiar with the way that blood pressure and pulse are measured. However, there are a range of other techniques that provide useful information about physical health too.

Key term

Obese

Having excess body fat that may have a negative effect on health.

Body mass index (BMI)

The relationship between height and weight can be an indicator of good or ill health in adults. Health professionals recommend that a person's weight should be in proportion to their height. A person is considered **obese** when their weight is more than 20 per cent above the average weight for people of the same height.

▶ People who are obese or whose weight is much greater than recommended run the risk of developing a range of health problems.

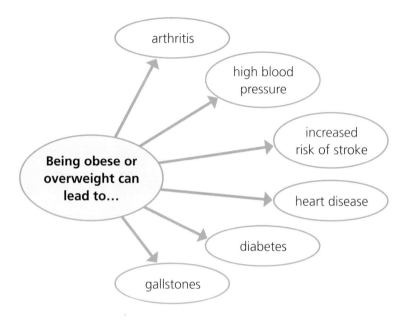

Health professionals calculate body mass index (BMI) to assess whether a person is overweight. A person's BMI score is calculated by dividing their weight in kilograms by their height in metres squared. This produces a number which is then checked against the categories in the table below.

▶ BMI scores and implications for health.

Female BMI score	Indicates	Male BMI score	Indicates
Under 18	Underweight	Under 18	Underweight
18–20	Lean	18–20	Lean
21–22	Normal	21–23	Normal
23–28	Overweight	24–32	Overweight
29–36	Obese	32–40	Obese

The NHS website (https://www.nhs.uk) has a useful BMI calculator that will do all the maths for you. You just need to know your height and current weight to obtain your score.

In most cases a person's BMI result will provide some useful information about their physical health. Being over- or underweight can have significant negative effects on physical health, for example. However, one of the limitations of BMI scores is that they don't take a person's body shape and composition into account. For example, a very fit and muscular person, such as a rugby player or weightlifter, may also have a high BMI score because their body contains lots of heavy muscle but little fat.

Blood pressure

Healthcare professionals routinely measure their patients' blood pressure as well as their pulse rate. This is a direct way of checking heart functioning and, indirectly, physical fitness.

> **Systolic blood pressure** → The force (or pressure) of blood on the artery walls when the heart beats

Then

> **Diastolic blood pressure** → The pressure that blood puts on the arteries between heart beats

SYSTOLIC In the systolic phase the heart contracts, blood pressure rises and blood moves out along the vessels.

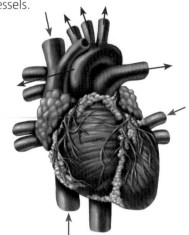

DIASTOLIC In the diastolic phase the heart relaxes, blood pressure falls and blood fills the heart.

Key terms

Systolic blood pressure
The blood pressure on the artery walls when the heart is contracting or pushing blood out.

Diastolic blood pressure
The minimum pressure on the arteries when the chambers of the heart fill with blood.

A person's blood pressure reading is recorded and written as two numbers. The systolic measure comes first, followed by the diastolic measure. On average, a healthy young adult will have a blood pressure reading of 120/80 mm Hg (millimetres of mercury).

A person's blood pressure fluctuates throughout the day and night. It increases when the person is active and decreases when they are inactive, resting or sleeping. A person's blood pressure will usually be taken when they are resting. A younger adult should have lower blood pressure than an older adult. If a person's blood pressure is higher or lower than average for a person of their age, it will need to be checked on several more occasions to establish whether this is due to a health problem.

Did you know?

Consistently high blood pressure (hypertension) is linked to a higher risk of heart attacks and strokes. Low blood pressure (hypotension) may be an indicator of heart failure, dehydration or other underlying health problems.

Peak flow

A person's respiratory health (breathing) can be assessed by a peak flow meter. You may have seen or used a peak flow meter, especially if you have asthma or have had other respiratory health checks. The person is asked to take a deep breath and then breathe out as hard as they can into the peak flow meter.

A peak flow meter measures the maximum rate at which air is expelled (pushed out) from the lungs when a person breathes out as hard as they can. A healthy adult should produce a peak flow result of 400–600 litres of air per minute. Peak flow tests can be used to diagnose whether a person has a problem with the use of their lungs, because there is a standard scale of expected scores against which the results can be compared. People with chronic (long-term) asthma usually record a measurement that is lower than 350 on the peak flow scale when they breathe out as hard as they can.

▼ A peak flow meter being used.

Key terms

Radial artery
An artery that begins at the elbow and extends down the forearm.

Carotid artery
Either of the two large arteries, one on each side of the head, that carry blood to the head and which can be felt in the neck.

Resting pulse and recovery after exercise

The pulse rate, both before and after exercise, is often used to determine a person's general health or physical fitness. The pulse rate indicates how fast the heart is beating. For adults, the average (or normal) resting rate is usually between 70 and 80 beats per minute. Babies and young children normally have a faster pulse rate than adults.

The pulse can be felt at any artery. In conscious people, it is usual to use the **radial artery**, which can be felt at the wrist. In unconscious people, the **carotid artery**, which can be felt at the neck, may be used (most conscious people would find it uncomfortable if you pressed on their carotid artery). A person's pulse rate increases when they exercise, when they are emotionally upset, or if they develop a form of heart or respiratory disease. People who are unfit, who smoke or who are overweight have a faster resting pulse rate than normal.

Case study

Emlyn recently turned 49 years of age. He was concerned about this birthday because he's always believed that people over the age of 50 suffer from ill health. His parents died of heart and lung diseases when they were in their late 50s. Emlyn tries to live a healthy life. However, he smokes a few cigarettes occasionally, drinks in moderation and rarely exercises. He was worried enough about his health to go to a private clinic to have a range of health checks carried out. These revealed:
- his blood pressure is 190/110 mm Hg
- his breathing rate is 28 respirations per minute
- his pulse is 92 beats per minute.

1. Should Emlyn be pleased or worried about the results of his health checks?
2. Describe how Emlyn's pulse rate would have been measured.
3. What kind of blood pressure problem(s) would be cause for concern in someone like Emlyn?

▲ Emlyn decided to have a series of health checks.

Check your understanding

1. List three different indicators of physical health that can be measured.
2. What is a normal body mass index (BMI) score for a) a man and b) a woman?
3. Explain how a person's blood pressure is recorded and what this says about their physical health.
4. Why is a person's resting pulse always lower than their pulse after exercise? Give the biological reason(s) for this.

8 Influences on health and well-being

Think about it ⟫ ● ○ ●

1. Make a list of five factors that you think are part of a 'healthy' lifestyle for an adult.

2. How 'healthy' are your current lifestyle choices?

3. Explain how the elements of a 'healthy' lifestyle might change over the course of a person's life?

▲ Dafydd has been wondering if it's time to start making healthier lifestyle choices.

Influences on good health and well-being

Would you like to be healthy? Most people would answer 'Yes' to this question. Research has shown that people say being healthy is just as likely to make them feel happy as winning lots of money. Winning lots of money relies on luck. However, being healthy is a bit easier to achieve if you understand how different factors affect health and well-being. These include:

- *physical factors* such as a balanced diet, adequate rest, enough sleep and regular exercise

- *social factors* such as stimulating work, education and leisure activity

- *economic factors* such as enough **income**.

Key term

Income
The money a person receives usually from work.

113

Key terms

Nutrients
Substances found in food that are essential for growth and the maintenance of life. The five main nutrients are protein, carbohydrates, vitamins, minerals and fats.

Carbohydrates
A nutrient found in bread, pasta and potatoes, for example, that provides the body with energy.

Fats
An essential nutrient that stores energy, absorbs vitamins and maintains core body temperature.

Proteins
Nutrients found in meat, eggs and milk that are needed for human growth.

Minerals
Micronutrients such as calcium and iron that are needed in small amounts to allow the human body to function.

Vitamins
Micronutrients such as vitamin C that are needed in small amounts to keep the body healthy and functioning well.

Hydration
The process of making your body absorb water or other liquid.

Nutrition, hydration and diet

Nutrition

Food plays a very important role in health. The food we eat should be nutritious if it is going to be beneficial to our physical health. This means it should contain a variety of **nutrients**.

Nutrients are naturally-occurring chemical substances found in the food we eat.

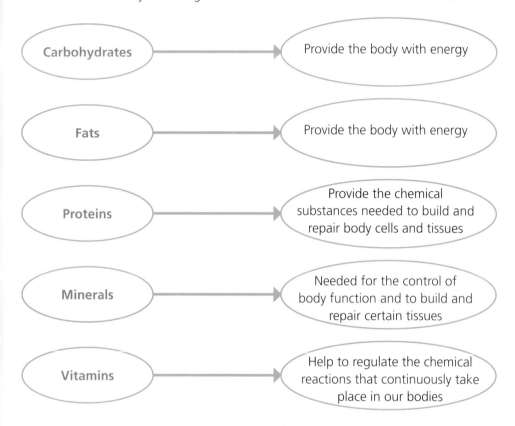

Carbohydrates	→	Provide the body with energy
Fats	→	Provide the body with energy
Proteins	→	Provide the chemical substances needed to build and repair body cells and tissues
Minerals	→	Needed for the control of body function and to build and repair certain tissues
Vitamins	→	Help to regulate the chemical reactions that continuously take place in our bodies

▲ The five basic nutrients help the body in different ways.

As well as eating food that contains a balance of these five nutrients, we also need to consume fibre and water. Fibre is not a nutrient but is important as it improves digestion, prevents constipation and is associated with a lower risk of heart disease, stroke, type 2 diabetes and bowel cancer.

Staying hydrated

The human body needs adequate **hydration** to function properly. This is because water in the body regulates temperature, transports nutrients and blood compounds, removes waste products in urine, and acts as a lubricant and shock absorber in our joints. Water is lost through sweat and urine and through breathing. This needs to be replaced by consuming food and drinks to avoid dehydration. Mild dehydration causes a dry mouth, headaches and poor concentration. Feeling thirsty and producing urine that is darker than the normal straw or pale-yellow colour is an indication that you are a little dehydrated.

Did you know?

Consuming six to eight glasses of fluid a day is usually enough to stay hydrated. More is needed if the weather is hot or you have been physically active or exercising.

Eating a balanced diet

A healthy intake of food, also known as a **balanced diet**, contains suitable amounts of each basic nutrient. The amount and types of foods that are healthy for a person to eat varies for each individual. The following factors will affect how much and what types of food we need to consume:

- age
- gender
- body size
- height
- weight
- the environment (for example, whether you live in a cold or a warm country)
- the amount of physical activity you do in your daily life.

Nutrition is very important in the early years of life. Babies and infants need the right types of food to help them grow and develop normally, and to prevent them from developing certain illnesses. Children and adolescents also need the right types of food to promote their physical growth and to provide 'fuel' or energy for their high level of physical activity.

People who have special diets, for example vegetarians and vegans, leave out or include specific food groups to meet their personal values or special physical needs. Vegetarians don't eat meat or fish but they can still get all the nutrients they need. They can get proteins from cereals, beans, eggs and cheese. Vegans, who eat no animal products at all, can still get all their essential nutrients provided their food intake is varied. For example, they can get protein from nuts and pulses.

Adequate rest and sleep

Do you get enough rest and sleep? How much sleep do you need to be healthy? If you want to be healthy you've got to take rest and sleep seriously. Not everyone does. Some people work too much and spend their life feeling tired. This isn't healthy.

People should rest every day to maintain their health and well-being. The amount of sleep a person needs varies according to their age. Babies, young children, older people and pregnant women tend to need a period of rest during the day.

Most healthy adults and older children need to rest only at the end of their active day. Even so, people need varying amounts of sleep depending on their life stage and physical needs. For example, a four- year-old child sleeps an average of 10 to 14 hours a day, whilst a ten-year-old needs about 9 to 12 hours. Most adults sleep from seven to eight and a half hours every night. Others require as few as four or five hours or as many as ten hours each night.

▲ A balanced diet provides a range of nutrients that are essential for good health.

Key term

Balanced diet
A diet consisting of a variety of different types of food and providing adequate amounts of the nutrients necessary for good health.

Did you know?

Most people find that they need slightly less sleep as they grow older. A person who slept eight hours a night when they were 30 years old may need only six or seven hours when they are 60 years old.

Regular exercise

Do you like doing exercise? Some people really enjoy playing sports, going to the gym or taking exercise classes. You might be one of them. Or you might be one of the large number of people who don't do enough exercise. Unfortunately, exercise isn't as popular as eating food and is one of the things in lists of top health tips that many people struggle with. But it's still important and is very good for your physical health.

► Some benefits of exercise.

Exercise...
- helps the body to stay supple and mobile
- keeps the heart healthy
- improves circulation
- helps muscles, joints and bones to remain strong
- improves stamina
- reduces blood pressure
- increases self-esteem and self-confidence
- helps to control and maintain weight
- is a good way of socialising
- makes you feel more energetic

Regular exercise has a positive effect on both physical and mental health. But it's important not to do too much exercise. People are advised to find a balance between physical activity and rest to maintain good physical health and a sense of well-being. Too much exercise can lead to excessive weight loss and may result in physical damage or chronic injuries, to joints or ligaments for example.

So, what kinds of exercise should you do? The type and level of exercise that an individual can do safely will depend on their age, gender and health status. For example, moderate exercise can be safely undertaken by older and less physically mobile people, including women in the later stages of pregnancy and people with physical disabilities. Younger people who are physically fit can safely undertake more vigorous exercise.

▼ Exercise that is also fun to take part in has emotional as well as physical benefits.

Adequate financial resources

People need enough money (adequate finance) to afford the basic necessities of life, such as food, housing and clothing. People with more money generally have better housing and may eat better quality food. In this way money does affect basic physical health. People who have enough income are also less likely to worry about being able to cope with everyday life. They don't experience the same stresses as people who are worried about paying their rent or feeding their children, for example. Having a good income allows people to buy luxuries such as holidays, cars, electrical goods and other desirable things. It also has a positive effect on self-esteem as money is highly valued in Western societies. The reverse is true for people who lack sufficient income – they can be seen, and view themselves, in a negative way because they are poor.

Stimulating work, education and leisure activity

Work

For many people, work has a positive effect on their health and well-being. Work is good for mental health and social well-being when it provides an individual with:

- a sense of purpose and identity ('what do you do?')
- self-reliance
- self-esteem and a sense of self-worth
- positive social relationships.

Employment obviously provides the income people need for their financial well-being but it also provides people with social contacts and support and a sense of achievement.

Education

A person's educational achievements affect their outlook on life, their sense of emotional well-being and their self-esteem. People feel proud of passing exams and gaining qualifications and upset about failing them.

Personal, social and health education programmes are now also a part of every school's curriculum. Children and young people learn about physical, mental, emotional and sexual health as well as how the use of alcohol, tobacco and illegal drugs can affect their health and well-being. Increasingly, schools and colleges are also focusing on healthy eating and educating pupils and students about the need to eat a balanced diet.

More informal educational approaches are also used to target adults and older people with forms of health education (through leaflets, booklets, articles and programmes in the media, for example) in order to provide information and shape attitudes towards living a healthier lifestyle.

▼ Education improves knowledge about and attitudes towards healthy lifestyle choices.

Leisure activity

Leisure time, including having hobbies, enjoying a social life and simply relaxing, is part of a healthy life. The leisure activities that people take part in during their non-work time contribute to health and well-being because they:

- help people to form social relationships with each other
- provide opportunities to communicate with and feel valued by others
- enable people to develop social skills
- provide opportunities to develop and use physical and intellectual abilities and skills, depending on the leisure activity
- provide people with an important sense of belonging to a group or team.

Influence of others

Having a partner, supportive family and a network of friends has a positive effect on a person's physical and mental health and well-being. Feeling loved and cared about, having a sense of belonging and benefitting from the practical and emotional support that other people provide boosts a person's emotional and social well-being, for example. By contrast, people who are isolated and lonely are likely to experience poor mental health and lack the everyday connections and contact with others that contribute to well-being.

▲ What does Emma need to do to have a healthier lifestyle?

Case study

Emma is a 21-year-old student teacher. She is reluctant to talk about her size but knows that she is 'too heavy'. Emma rarely cooks for herself, eats a lot of take-away food and consumes several cans of fizzy drink each day. She also drinks twice the recommended number of units of alcohol for a woman in a week. Emma's knowledge of nutrition is poor. She says she just chooses food that she knows she will enjoy. As a result, Emma is now 30kg overweight and is developing health problems. Her feet are always cold and often 'blue' in colour. She becomes breathless if she walks any distance, tires quickly if she lifts things and says she often has aches and pains in her ankles, knees and shoulders.

1. What is wrong with Emma's dietary intake at the moment?
2. What does Emma need to do in order to eat a balanced diet?
3. How will eating a balanced diet help Emma's to improve her health?

Check your understanding

1. List three physical factors that influence a person's health and well-being.
2. Explain what a balanced diet is and describe what it should consist of.
3. How can stimulating work have a positive effect on a person's health and well-being?
4. Outline three ways in which leisure activity can have a positive effect on personal health and well-being.

9 Risks to health and well-being

Think about it

1. What precautions do you take to stay safe when out at night?
2. List five illegal drugs or substances that can have a damaging effect on a person's health and well-being.
3. Describe the negative effects of smoking on a person's physical health.

Understanding health risks

A range of factors can put an individual's health and well-being at **risk**. The lifestyle choices a person makes about drugs, alcohol and smoking, for example, will have definite consequences for their physical and mental health and well-being.

Staying safe

Bad things can and do happen in everyday life. By the time a person becomes an adult, and then a parent, they generally know there is a range of **hazards** and dangers that can be a risk to personal health, well-being and safety.

Hazard	What are the risks?
Stranger danger	'Stranger danger' highlights the risk that strangers shouldn't be trusted and can be a source of danger and harm. It is associated with the threat of child abduction, child abuse by paedophiles and unprovoked sexual and physical assault on adults. Rare and isolated incidents tend to be exaggerated by the media, although the small risk from strangers in online and everyday environments is taken seriously by parents, educators and the police.
Road safety	Roads are a part of most people's everyday life. It is the vehicles using them that present a risk of harm. Road safety campaigns that focus on safe crossing of roads, safe driving and accident prevention (such as using seatbelts and child car seats) make people aware of risks to health and well-being and provide information and education on how to minimise risk and stay safe.
Playground injury	Playgrounds are fun places to play, learn and develop with friends. The equipment in playgrounds needs to be used in a safe way to avoid injuries though. Swings, climbing equipment and water features (pools and ponds) can be hazardous and lead to fractures, brain injuries and drowning if a child is unable to use the equipment safely and is unsupervised. To minimise risks, safety notices should be displayed and followed in playgrounds. Equipment should be designed with safety in mind and appropriate supervision should be provided, particularly for younger children.
Sun safety	Exposure to too much hot sunshine can lead to burns to the skin and increases the risk of skin cancer later in life. Using sunscreen that is factor 15+, avoiding spending time in direct, hot sunshine and covering up with loose clothing are ways of minimising the risk.

▲ Megan always feels nervous on her way home late at night.

◄ Examples of risks to personal safety.

Key terms

Risk
Exposure to danger, harm or loss.

Hazard
Anything that can cause harm.

Key terms

Substance misuse
A term to describe illegal or unauthorised drug abuse or excessive use of alcohol that is damaging to health.

Psychoactive
A substance that has a major effect on mental (brain) processes.

Prescription
A doctor's written instructions to dispense medication.

Substance misuse

Substance misuse is widespread in many countries, including the United Kingdom. The substances that people are most likely to misuse and which have significant consequences for health and well-being are:

- illegal and **prescription** drugs
- **psychoactive** substances
- tobacco
- alcohol.

Misuse of any of these substances can have a range of adverse effects on a person's physical and mental health and may even prove fatal.

Misuse of illegal drugs

Drug misuse is very high up the list of ways to harm your health. Damage to health from drug misuse can be sudden and catastrophic (people die) or it can occur over a longer period of time. Either way, drug misuse is something to avoid if you wish to live a healthy life.

Drugs are chemical substances that affect the body's chemistry and functioning. They can be obtained through:

- a doctor's prescription if they are for medical treatment
- over the counter, by purchasing them in a chemist, supermarket or other shop (these drugs include medicines and legal substances such as alcohol and tobacco)
- buying 'street' or illicit and medicinal drugs illegally.

There were 6518 admissions related to illicit drugs in 2016–2017 in Wales, involving 5138 distinct individuals. In Wales, 192 people died as a result of drug misuse in 2016 (Smith and Turner, 2017).

For many years, newspapers and television have featured stories and programmes about drug misuse. Drug misuse is now a major cause of health problems and premature death in the United Kingdom. All sections of the population are affected by it, but young people are the most likely to risk their health through drug misuse. There are many complex reasons for this.

▶ Examples of illegal drugs.

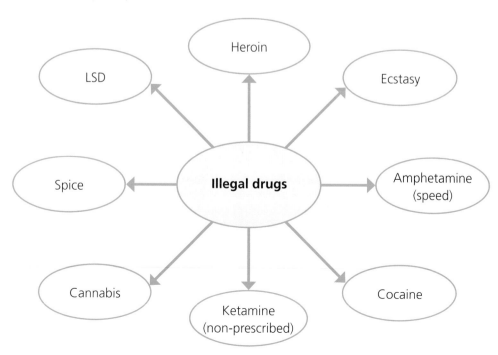

Misuse of prescription drugs

Any drug, whether it is legal or illegal, can cause harm if it is misused. For example, whilst medicines are used to treat disease and illness, they can also have physical and psychological side-effects. The doctor who prescribes them will know about these possible effects and will take care to monitor the patient. To limit side effects, the doctor will prescribe only the dose required. People may misuse prescription drugs by taking more than their doctor prescribes, or they may take medicine not prescribed for them. They then run the risk of experiencing harmful and even fatal side-effects.

Some drugs cause people to become psychologically dependent on them if taken over long periods. This applies to medicinal drugs as well as to illegal 'street' drugs. Long-term users often suffer very unpleasant side-effects and withdrawal symptoms when they try to stop taking these drugs.

Non-prescription drugs are usually illegal. Alcohol, cigarettes and medicines bought from chemists or supermarkets are the exceptions. People who use 'street' drugs such as heroin, cocaine, marijuana and ecstasy are usually trying to get the short-term feelings of mental pleasure, stimulation and physical energy that the drugs often give. However, in the longer-term, all 'street' drugs present major risks to the user's health. They usually have damaging effects on physical health, as well as on social, psychological and financial well-being.

New psychoactive substances

New **psychoactive** substances (NPSs) are substances that have been created to replicate the effects of illegal drugs, such as cannabis, cocaine and ecstasy, whilst remaining legal. This has led to them also to being called 'legal highs'. NPS products can no longer be bought in shops but are frequently purchased online. They often have brand names and packaging that are designed to be attractive and exciting. It is impossible for users to be certain about what chemicals the products contain. As a result, the effects of the drugs vary and can be very unsafe and harmful. These include:

- overdose and unpredictable behaviours
- sudden increase in body temperature, heart rate, coma and risk to internal organs
- hallucination and vomiting
- confusion leading to aggression and violence
- sudden low mood and suicidal feelings
- increased risk of developing long-term mental health problems
- physical and psychological dependency after short intense periods of use.

The Psychoactive Substances Act (2016) makes it an offence (punishable by up to 14 years imprisonment) to produce, possess or supply these substances for human use. DrugWise, an organisation providing information on drug use in the United Kingdom, identified the main users of NPSs as young men aged 16 to 24, with one in 40 (2.6 per cent) of young adults taking an NPS in

▲ Jodie realised she had a drinking problem.

Case study

Jodie started drinking in her local park with some older teenagers and a couple of her friends when she was 16 years old. She drank a couple of bottles of cider and any vodka that was available a few times a week. Jodie thought that drinking was fun and that it made her happy. She realised when she was 19 years of age that the opposite was true. Jodie found herself thinking about alcohol at work and would drink at lunch time. Three months ago she was sacked from her job for coming to work smelling of alcohol. Jodie hasn't drunk any alcohol since. Her GP (family doctor) also told her about the physical effects that long-term alcohol abuse and binge drinking could have on her health.

1. Why do some young teenagers like Jodie start drinking alcohol?

2. Identify four effects of long-term alcohol abuse or binge drinking on physical health.

3. What are the benefits, to Jodie and wider society, of sticking to the recommended safe limits for alcohol consumption if she does start drinking alcohol again?

Check your understanding

1. List three types of drug that present a risk to health if they are misused.

2. Describe three behaviours that put an individual's personal safety and health at risk.

3. What are 'new psychoactive substances' and why do they present risks to health?

4. Explain why the use of illegal/street drugs is likely to damage a person's physical and mental health.

10 Lifestyle risks to health and well-being

10 Lifestyle risks to health and well-being

Think about it

1. Identify three reasons why drinking alcohol to excess is a risk to health.

2. List five illegal drugs or substances that are addictive.

3. Describe the negative effects of smoking on a person's physical health.

Understanding lifestyle risks to health

A range of factors can put a person's health and well-being at risk. Lifestyle factors refer to behaviours and choices that have a direct impact on a person's health and well-being. These include the choice to smoke cigarettes or other forms of tobacco, to drink alcohol, as well as the impact of not exercising and the risks associated with unprotected sex.

▲ Drinking alcohol can be both beneficial and damaging to a person's health and well-being.

Smoking

Do you smoke cigarettes? If not, you probably know people who do. Smoking cigarettes is a prominent part of some people's social life. The *National Survey for Wales 2017–18* revealed that 21 per cent of men and 19 per cent of women in Wales were current smokers. People between 25 and 34 were most likely to smoke. In addition, adults living in the most deprived areas of Wales were more likely to smoke (28 per cent) than adults living in the least deprived areas (13 per cent). Despite it being legal for people age 18 or over to buy and smoke tobacco, cigarettes have a very bad reputation with healthcare workers.

► An X-ray revealing that this person has cancer in both lungs.

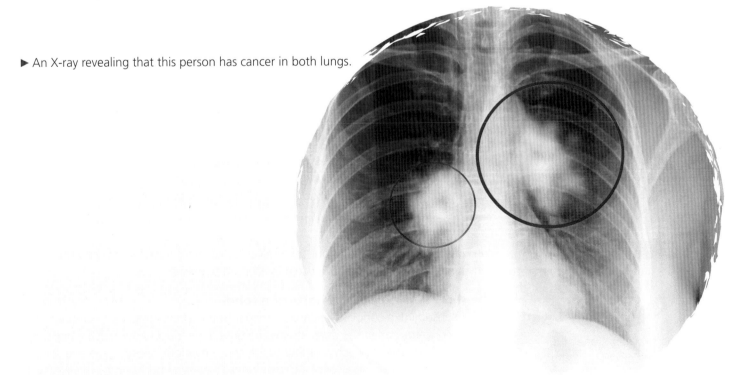

Key terms

Coronary heart disease
A disease in which a waxy substance called plaque gradually builds up inside the arteries that supply oxygen-rich blood to your heart muscle.

Stroke
The sudden death of brain cells due to a lack of blood flow (and oxygen) to the brain when an artery is blocked or ruptured. Loss of speech, weakness and loss of use of limbs on one side of the body may result.

Bronchitis
An infection of the main airways of the lungs (bronchi) resulting in them being irritated and inflamed and producing mucus.

Haemoglobin
The substance in blood that carries oxygen.

Cilia
The small hairs lining the lungs.

▲ Stopping smoking is one of the most important pieces of health advice.

Cigarettes and tobacco smoking have no health benefits at all. Instead, smoking directly damages your physical health. This is one of the most important pieces of information that health workers regularly give out to people. Their advice is always to stop smoking. You should be told this if you smoke cigarettes. People who fail to take note of this warning run a considerable risk of causing themselves long-term health damage and dying as a direct result of their smoking habit. The health problems associated with smoking tobacco include:

- **coronary heart disease**
- **stroke**
- high blood pressure
- **bronchitis**
- lung cancer
- other cancers, such as cancer of the larynx, kidney and bladder.

Why is smoking addictive and damaging?

The nicotine in cigarettes is a powerful, fast-acting and addictive drug. Smokers absorb it into their bloodstream and feel an effect in their brains seven to eight minutes later. Some smokers say this is 'calming'. However, the physical effects of smoking also include an increase in heart rate and blood pressure and changes in appetite. Cigarette smoke contains a high concentration of carbon monoxide – a poisonous gas. Because carbon monoxide combines more easily with **haemoglobin** than oxygen, the amount of oxygen carried to a smoker's lungs and tissues is reduced. This reduction in oxygen supply to the body then affects the growth and repair of tissues, and the exchange of essential nutrients.

The carbon monoxide inhaled by a smoker can also affect their heart. The changes in the blood associated with smoking can cause fat deposits to form on the walls of the arteries. This leads to hardening of the arteries and to circulatory problems, causing smokers to develop coronary heart disease.

Cigarette tar contains many substances known to cause cancer. It damages the **cilia** in the lungs that help to protect them from dirt and infection. Because these lung protectors get damaged, smokers are more likely than non-smokers to get throat and chest infections. About 70 per cent of the tar in a cigarette is deposited in the lungs when cigarette smoke is inhaled.

Misuse of alcohol

Alcohol is a very popular, widely available and accepted part of social life in Wales. Many people enjoy a drink and there is usually nothing wrong with that. In small, controlled quantities, alcoholic drinks can be part of a pleasurable social occasion. In moderation, some types of alcoholic drink, such as red wine, have been shown to be good for health. The weekly guideline amount for safe drinking is 14 units of alcohol. One unit of alcohol is the same as one small glass of wine, half a pint of ordinary strength beer, lager or cider or a 25 ml pub measure of spirits.

You should be aware that these recommended limits are based on 'pub measures'. People who drink at home or buy alcohol from an off-licence or supermarket to consume elsewhere, usually pour themselves larger measures of wines and spirits or consume stronger beer than that sold in licensed premises.

The short and long-term effects of alcohol

When consumed, alcohol is rapidly absorbed into the bloodstream. The amount of alcohol concentrated in the body at any one time depends on how much a person drinks, whether the stomach is empty or full and the height, weight, age and sex of the drinker. Nearly all the alcohol a person drinks has to be burnt up by the liver.

The rest is disposed of either in sweat or urine. The human body can get rid of one unit of alcohol in one hour. Smaller than average people, younger or older people and people who are not used to drinking are more easily affected by alcohol and take longer to get it out of their bodies.

The health risks associated with alcohol result from consuming it in large quantities, either regularly or in binges. The *National Survey for Wales 2017–18* revealed that 25 per cent of men and 12 per cent of women in Wales drink more than the weekly guideline of 14 units. People living in the most deprived areas of Wales are least likely to drink more than the guideline limits (15 per cent) whilst those who live in the least deprived areas are most likely to do so (21 per cent).

People who frequently drink excess amounts of alcohol have an increased risk of:

- high blood pressure
- coronary heart disease
- liver damage
- cancer of the mouth and throat
- psychological and emotional problems, including depression
- obesity.

Alcohol is also a depressant. This means that it reduces certain brain functions and affects judgement, self-control and coordination. This is why alcohol may be the cause of fights, domestic violence and accident-related injuries.

Lack of exercise and obesity

Lack of regular physical exercise can lead to ill health and disease. For example, lack of exercise is linked to an increased risk of diseases such as coronary heart disease, stroke, obesity and **osteoporosis**. Obesity is now a major health problem in Wales with 60 per cent of adults (three out of every five) in Wales classified as either overweight or obese (*National Survey for Wales 2017–18*).

The *National Survey for Wales 2017–18* found that over half (53 per cent) of all adults reported they had been active for at least 150 minutes in the previous week. Men were more likely to have been active than women and younger people aged 16 to 24 were the most physically active. Thirty-four per cent of adults were inactive (active for less than 30 minutes) the previous week. Inactivity was highest among older adults and adults in more deprived areas. There are many reasons why people don't take more exercise. These include not having enough time, not liking sport and being frightened of injuries.

Low risk alcohol guidelines for men & women*

To keep health risks from alcohol to a low level it is safest **not to regularly drink more than**

14 units a week

This means you **should not drink more than this amount of wine …**

175ml glasses of 13% wine

… **OR** this amount of **lager** or **ale**

568ml pints of 4% lager or ale

… **OR** this amount of **cider**

568ml pints of 4.5% cider

… **OR** this amount of **spirits**

25ml glasses of 40% spirits

*UK Chief Medical Officers' Low risk drinking guidelines, August 2016

▲ Recommended maximum units of alcohol for men and women.

Key term

Osteoporosis
A medical condition in which the bones become brittle.

Sexually transmitted infection
An infection transmitted through the exchange of semen, blood or other bodily fluids during sex.

Chlamydia
A curable bacterial infection spread through unprotected sex that can damage a woman's reproductive system.

▶ Sexually transmitted infections.

Unsafe sexual behaviour

The main health risk of unprotected sexual activity is from **sexually transmitted infections**. There are at least 30 different types of sexually transmitted infection. Sexually transmitted infections are caught by having unprotected sex with an infected person. A person can become infected after a single act of unprotected sex with an infected person.

Young, sexually active people are most at risk of catching a sexually transmitted infection. The most common sexually transmitted infection is **chlamydia**. This can cause serious problems such as pelvic inflammatory disease (PID) and inflammation of the fallopian tubes (oviducts) if it is not treated. However, it isn't fatal. People recover after treatment.

Girls	Boys
• A vaginal discharge that is thick or smelly, has a different colour, is more copious than usual or causes itching may indicate you have thrush or trichomoniasis.	• If blood or a discharge comes out of your penis, or passing urine (water) is painful, it may mean you have gonorrhoea, non-specific urethritis or chlamydia.
• If it hurts when you pass urine (water), you may have cystitis (inflammation of the bladder) or thrush.	• If you get warty lumps on or near your penis or anus (back passage), you may have genital warts.
• If your vagina itches or gets sore, you may have thrush.	• If you get painful sores or blisters on or near your penis or anus (back passage), you may have herpes.
• If you have an itchy vagina and pubic hair, you may have crabs (pubic lice – small wingless insects that live in pubic hair and feed on blood).	• If the tip of your penis or area around your anus (back passage) is red and itchy, you may have thrush.
• If you develop warty lumps around your vagina or anus (back passage), you may have genital warts.	• If you have an itchy scrotum and pubic hair, you may have crabs (pubic lice – small wingless insects that live in pubic hair and feed on blood).

Public Health Wales reported that in 2017 there were 6920 diagnoses of chlamydia, 3020 diagnoses of first episode genital warts, 1422 diagnoses of first episode herpes, 1190 diagnoses of gonorrhoea, 214 of syphilis and 86 of HIV in sexual health clinics (SHCs) in Wales (www.wales.nhs.uk).

▶ A sexual health clinic.

Case study

Miriam recently turned 21 years old. She went to a nightclub with friends and then had a party at her flat to celebrate. Overall, Miriam drank six glasses of wine and five vodka shots at the nightclub. She isn't sure whether she carried on drinking at home but she does remember being sick before she fell asleep. When she woke up, Miriam was lying on her bed next to Martin, a friend from college. Martin was only wearing boxer shorts, although she was fully clothed. Miriam doesn't remember speaking to Martin at the party or know why he is asleep and only partly clothed on her bed. She is now worried that they may have had unprotected sex.

▲ What risks has Miriam posed to her health?

1. How many units of alcohol did Miriam consume at the nightclub?

2. Explain why binge drinking like this presents a risk to Miriam's health and well-being.

3. Explain the risks associated with unprotected sex, referring to the names and symptoms of two sexually transmitted infections.

Check your understanding

1. Name three diseases associated with cigarette smoking.

2. Describe three long-term effects that drinking alcohol to excess can have on a person's health and well-being.

3. Identify two effects on health and well-being of not taking enough regular exercise or being physically inactive.

4. Explain why unprotected sex is a high-risk activity that can lead to health problems.

2.1 Health and social care, and childcare provision in Wales to promote and support health and well-being

Health, social care and childcare service provision in Wales is affected by a range of laws.

The Social Services and Well-being (Wales) Act 2014

The NHS and Community Care Act 1990, 2012

The Public Health Wales Act 2017

The Children Act 1989 and 2004

The Well-being of Future Generations (Wales) Act 2015

The Care Standards Act 2000–2017

Legislation aims to promote and support health and well-being in Wales.

Government regulation and policy

Standards of care are set and monitored by three regulatory bodies:

- Estyn
- Healthcare Inspectorate Wales
- Care Inspectorate Wales

Welsh government policy initiatives, strategies and frameworks on health, social care and childcare aim to improve the health, development and well-being of people living in Wales. Examples include:

- Flying Start
- Building a Brighter Future
- Healthy Child Wales
- Free Prescriptions

Care providers

Care is provided through the statutory, private, voluntary and informal care sectors in Wales by people working in healthcare, social care and childcare roles.

Care agencies and workers join together to provide care services through partnerships and multi-agency working.

2.2 Public health and health promotion across the life cycle

Public health provision

Public health services aim to improve the health and well-being of individuals, communities and the whole population of Wales.

Public Health Wales is responsible for providing health education and advice and health improvement campaigns that prevent and tackle the root causes of ill health.

Government regulation and policy

The causes of ill health in Wales are linked to low income, poor housing and lack of opportunities for work and education.

Public health methods include screening, immunisation and health education campaigns.

2.3 Factors affecting health and well-being across the life cycle

Personal health indicators and influences

Healthcare workers use body mass index (BMI), blood pressure, peak flow and pulse rate measures as indicators of physical health.

Positive influences on health and well-being include:

- Nutrition, hydration and diet
- Rest and sleep
- Regular exercise
- Adequate financial resources
- Stimulating work, education and leisure activity.

Risks to health

Stranger danger, road safety risks and sunburn

Substance misuse, including cigarette smoking, illegal drugs and psychoactive substances

Alcohol misuse

Lack of exercise

Unprotected sex

3 Health and Social Care, and Childcare in the 21st Century

This unit provides you with opportunities to gain knowledge and understanding of the ethical issues affecting service provision in Wales to provide and support a sustainable health and social care, and childcare system in the 21st century.

This unit consists of four main parts:

3.1 Equality, diversity and inclusion to include Welsh language and culture

3.2 Safeguarding

3.3 Contemporary issues in health and social care, and childcare

3.4 Supporting a sustainable health and social care, and childcare system in the 21st century

◄ Society must ensure that everyone has equal access and opportunities.

Each part of the unit has been broken down into shorter topics. These topics will help you understand a range of ethical and safeguarding issues that influence the provision of health, social care and childcare services in Wales. You will also consider a range of contemporary issues affecting the health and well-being of children and adults living in Wales. Finally, the unit will help you to understand how innovation and change are transforming health, social care and childcare services in Wales to make them more sustainable in the 21st century.

The unit will help you to understand how and why health, social care and childcare services are changing in Wales. It will also prepare you for the external test that you need to pass to complete this unit.

Assessment: 1.5 hour written examination

Part 3.1 Equality, diversity and inclusion to include Welsh language and culture

Topic 1: What are equality, diversity and inclusion?

Topic 2: Promoting equality, diversity and inclusion

Topic 3: Equality laws and protection

Part 3.2 Safeguarding

Topic 4: Understanding safeguarding

Part 3.3 Contemporary issues in health and social care, and childcare

Topic 5: Contemporary issues affecting adults and older people in Wales

Topic 6: Contemporary issues affecting children and younger people in Wales

Part 3.4 Supporting a sustainable health and social care, and childcare system in the 21st century

Topic 7: Holistic health, development and well-being

Topic 8: What is happening in Wales?

3.1 EQUALITY, DIVERSITY AND INCLUSION TO INCLUDE WELSH LANGUAGE AND CULTURE
1 What are equality, diversity and inclusion?

Think about it

1. In what ways is there diversity in your local community?

2. What factors or characteristics influence your sense of personal identity (who you are) and belonging to a community?

3. How is the right to be treated equally and fairly protected in your school or college?

Being treated fairly

▲ Diversity and difference are accepted by Seren's friends.

Do you expect to be treated fairly? How would you feel if you were treated differently and unfairly from others at school, at home or when you used care services? What if you were refused access to a service or were excluded from a place because of your gender, your appearance or your (dis)ability? How would you react if some people were hostile, abusive or avoided you because of your skin colour or the way that you dressed?

A teenager growing up in Wales today would probably object to being treated unfairly. Girls and women shouldn't be treated less favourably than boys and men in Welsh schools or in the workplace, should they? The same applies to people from black and minority ethnic groups, people with **disabilities** and people who identify themselves as lesbian, gay, bisexual or transgender. In 21st century Wales it is unlawful, and always wrong, to treat some people less favourably than others because of their personal characteristics. This hasn't always been the case and there are reasons why people **discriminate** unfairly against others.

A lesson in prejudice

In 1968 Jane Elliott, a white teacher from a mostly white town in Iowa (USA), carried out an experiment to demonstrate to the eight-year-old children in her class how **prejudice** (racism) worked and how it felt to be discriminated against. After break, the all-white class of children was divided into two groups based on eye colour.

The blue-eyed children were told they were superior to their brown-eyed classmates. The brown-eyed children, who had to wear identifying collars, were also told they were less intelligent and poorly behaved. Elliott found that the blue-eyed children soon began to behave in an arrogant way and the brown-eyed children soon began to accept their lower position.

The next day Jane Elliott reversed the experiment, and the results reversed. However, the brown-eyed children, having already experienced discrimination, were more sensitive to the suffering of their blue-eyed peers. When they were filmed years later, the classmates who had taken part remembered vividly how the experiment had made them feel and how it had changed their attitude towards race and discrimination.

Key terms

Disabilities
Impairments of physical, mental or sensory functions that affect a person's abilities or activities.

Discriminate
Act in an unfair and unequal way because of prejudice.

Prejudice
A strongly-held negative belief or attitude relating to a particular individual or group of people.

Understanding prejudice

Prejudice is usually the reason for unfair discrimination occurring. A person is prejudiced if they hold negative feelings and attitudes towards another person or group of people. Prejudiced attitudes are usually based on untrue, ill-informed or exaggerated ideas or beliefs about those they are hostile to.

Did you know?

In many cases, prejudice is a fear of the unknown or a fear of something or somebody who is simply different.

▶ Examples of prejudice.

Social group	Form of prejudice
Minority ethnic groups	Racism/racial hatred
Minority religious groups	Islamophobia; anti-semitism; sectarianism
Women	Sexism
Lesbians, gay men, bisexual and transgender groups	Homophobia
Older people	Ageism
People with disabilities or mental health problems	Disablism

Unfair discrimination

Unfair discrimination occurs when a person treats an individual or a group of people less favourably or unfairly because of their prejudice. The Equality Act 2010 makes it unlawful to unfairly discriminate against a person in Wales on the grounds of their:

- age
- disability
- gender reassignment
- marriage or civil partnership
- pregnancy and maternity leave
- race
- religion or belief
- sex
- sexual orientation.

The Equality Act 2010 calls these **protected characteristics**.

Key term

Protected characteristics
A characteristic or feature of a person that may not be used as a basis for decision-making as, if used, this might result in unlawful discrimination.

▶ Asmahan complained that Tom's 'jokes' about her clothing and appearance were an example of unfair discrimination.

Challenging prejudice and unfair discrimination

Care workers should never unfairly discriminate against service users, whatever their social characteristics or background. All care service users are entitled to non-discriminatory treatment and care workers should adopt an anti-discriminatory approach to practice. This means being:

- aware of the different forms of prejudice and unfair discrimination that can occur in care settings
- sensitive to the ethnicity, social background and cultural needs of each individual
- prepared to actively challenge any instances of prejudice or unfair discrimination they witness.

Promoting equality, diversity and inclusion

Wales is a diverse, multicultural society with a socially and ethnically mixed population. It is therefore important for care workers to recognise that each person they work with, as a service user or a co-worker, has the right to fair and equal treatment.

Knowing about and understanding how to put the principles of equality, diversity and inclusion into practice ensures that care workers treat all service users fairly. The following table explains how this should work in practice.

▼ Principles of equality, diversity and inclusion.

Principle	What does it mean?	What to do in practice
Equality	This refers to individuals being equal in terms of status, rights or opportunities.	Make sure individuals or groups of people are not treated differently or less favourably because of a specific protected characteristic, including their race, gender, disability, religion or belief, sexual orientation or age.
Diversity	This involves acceptance and respect for differences and an understanding that every individual is unique and valued.	Find ways of recognising individual differences (in 'race'/ethnicity, sexual orientation, gender, disability, age, for example) and embrace and celebrate the diversity of individuals within a community.
Inclusion	This refers to the universal human right to participate equally, confidently and independently in everyday activities.	Enable all people irrespective of race, gender, disability, medical or other need to have equal access and opportunities and to get rid of discrimination and intolerance (removal of barriers) in all aspects of public life.

The importance of addressing equality, diversity and inclusion issues in care settings in Wales is recognised by equality laws, the policies and procedures of care organisations and the codes of professional practice of care workers. This doesn't mean that there is no prejudice or that healthcare, social care and childcare services are free of unfair discrimination. However, knowing about and understanding the importance of equality, diversity and inclusion does help care workers to prevent and tackle unfair treatment when it does arise.

Case study

A reporter from the BBC programme *Inside Out West* carried out an investigation into employment agencies. The researcher telephoned 30 agencies to ask whether they could advertise a receptionist post to 'white only' workers. This is a selection of the replies:

▲ How easy is it to discriminate?

Agency 1: 'That's fine. You are not allowed to say it but, no, we certainly hear what you say. That's not a problem.'

Agency 2: 'We'll ignore it and pretend you didn't say it but listen to what you said, if you see what I mean.'

Agency 3: 'It's difficult with the accent over the phone isn't it? I understand that, yeah, shouldn't really say that but taken on board.'

Agency 4: 'OK. You are not supposed to tell me that but I will forget you did (laughter) but bear it in mind.'

Researcher: 'Just send through white.'

Agency 4: 'Yep. Normal people.'

Of the agencies contacted, 25 out of 30 agreed to provide 'white only' candidates.

1. What kind of prejudice is being expressed by the researcher?

2. How should the agency staff who are talking with the researcher respond to his request for 'white only' job candidates?

3. Why is it wrong to favour one ethnic group over another when trying to fill a job vacancy?

Check your understanding

1. List three forms of prejudice and identify the social groups on which each focuses.

2. Explain the link between prejudice and unfair discrimination.

3. Describe what 'protected characteristics' are and explain why all care workers need to be aware of them.

4. What does anti-discriminatory practice in care settings involve?

2 Promoting equality, diversity and inclusion

Think about it

1. List as many different ethnic groups as you can.

2. Apart from ethnicity, which other social or cultural characteristics are the basis of differences between people in Wales?

3. How do you know whether a person is being respectful towards you?

▼ Inclusive childcare services provide equality of opportunity for all children.

Wales: A picture of diversity

Diversity is about difference. Health, social care and childcare workers in Wales need to recognise and respect individual differences. The first step is to raise your awareness of the diversity that exists within the population of Wales.

According to the 2011 Census:

- Just over 3 million people (3 063 456) were resident in Wales in 2011.

- This included slightly more females (1 559 228) than males (1 504 228).

- The largest ethnic group in Wales is white British (93.2%).

- The population of Wales also included 70 128 (2.3%) Asian or Asian British and 18 276 (0.6%) black or black British people as well as 31 521 (1.0%) of people whose ethnicity is described as British mixed.

According to StatsWales (2016):

- In the year ending December 2017, there were an estimated 391 500 (20.8%) people aged 16–64 in Wales with a disability. In addition, as many as a third of people of retirement age (65+) could have a disability.

- Most people in Wales identify themselves as heterosexual/straight (94%) with a minority identifying themselves as gay, lesbian or bisexual (2%). The remaining people (4%) didn't know or refused to identify their sexual orientation.

These data snapshots provide examples of similarities and differences between people living in Wales. There are many more examples, all of which can be important to individuals with care needs.

Key term

Diversity
A range of different and varied things.

Promoting equality, diversity and inclusion

Health, social care and childcare workers must value and treat each person who needs care or support fairly and equally.

▶ How to ensure service users are treated and valued fairly and equally.

Principle	What this means in practice
Value diversity and promote equality of opportunity	• Produce and put into practice equal opportunities policies • Celebrate a range of religious and cultural festivals (Eid, Hanukkah, Christmas, Diwali)
Recognise the needs of people from diverse backgrounds, including those who come from minority religious and cultural backgrounds	• Provide dietary choices (vegan, halal, kosher) that are acceptable to all • Ensure female staff are available to meet individuals' religious and cultural needs
Adapt service provision to meet the diverse needs of different individuals	• Provide a range of activities and outings to meet different interests, abilities and preferences • Ensure buildings and facilities are fully accessible to all users
Create an inclusive culture for all staff and individuals	• Ensure each individual's identity and beliefs are recognised and respected • Use non-discriminatory language and have an easy-to-use complaints procedure to report instances of discriminatory behaviour

Responsibilities of care organisations and agencies

Care organisations and agencies must have equal opportunities policies and training for staff as well as work procedures that protect an individual's rights and prevent discrimination. Other examples of organisational strategies used to promote **equality**, diversity and **inclusion** are:

• ensuring the access needs of individuals are met and any barriers that create separation are removed

▶ Books, toys and images used in nurseries must represent and reflect diversity.

- providing training to raise staff awareness of equality, diversity and inclusion issues and equip them with the skills to challenge inequality and discrimination when it occurs

- providing continuous professional development opportunities that enable all staff to develop to their full potential

- using varied materials to portray positive images of diversity – visual displays should avoid stereotypes and celebrate diversity and difference, for example

- organising diverse activities that celebrate different religious festivals and promote understanding of different religious beliefs and cultures

- using books and toys that avoid stereotypical images of men and women, ethnic groups and other social differences, so they do not discriminate against any individuals or groups

- adapting and providing appropriate care to meet the diverse needs of different individuals

- providing equality of access to health, social care and childcare services and opportunities to enable individuals to fully participate in their care and/or learning process.

Responsibilities of care workers

An organisation's induction training and policies usually tell care workers what their equal opportunities responsibilities are.

Strategies for providing care and support in positive, non-discriminatory ways include:

- finding out about the preferences, needs and wishes of service users when providing care or support

- encouraging people who use care services to make choices and respecting their decisions, wishes and preferences

- facilitating religious worship and the expression of personal identity and beliefs

- ensuring that the food offered to an individual meets their religious and dietary needs

- protecting the privacy and dignity of individuals when personal care is being provided (for example, a person should not be exposed to the view of others when they are being dressed, undressed, taken to the toilet or being helped to wash)

- respecting individuals' rights to privacy in their room (for example, knocking before entering and checking that it is all right to come in is much more respectful than simply throwing the door open; not carrying out tasks without asking or not sitting on a person's bed or chair without asking permission).

Working with colleagues

Working with colleagues in a health, social care or childcare setting should be a supportive and enjoyable experience. However, this is not always the case as tensions can arise over the best or most appropriate ways of doing things. Direct and indirect discrimination can also occur and should always be challenged. A care worker who witnesses discrimination by a colleague must report this to their employer or manager.

Did you know?

Care workers need to respect and meet the individual needs of each service user and treat their colleagues fairly and with professional respect.

Case study

Jenny, aged 17, has started working at the Little Feet Nursery three days a week. She has settled in quickly and enjoys the work she does. Mari, the nursery manager, has noticed that Jenny spends a lot of her time with Eli and Erin, both aged four. She also chooses them first when organising games, holds their hands when on outings to the park and gives them more praise than the other children. When asked about this, Jenny told Mari that Eli and Erin are her favourite children at the nursery as they remind her of her nephew and niece. None of the parents have complained about Jenny, although some of the children say she doesn't like them as much as she likes Eli and Erin.

1. Explain whether, and if so why, you think Mari should be concerned about the way Jenny relates to the children at the nursery.

2. Identify three ways in which Jenny could be more inclusive in the way that she works with the children at Little Feet Nursery.

3. What would you say to Jenny about equality, diversity and inclusion if you were Mari?

► Is Jenny discriminating?

Check your understanding

1. Describe three ways a care organisation can show that it values diversity.

2. What is wrong with care workers 'treating everybody the same'?

3. Describe three ways in which a health, social care or childcare worker could work in a non-discriminatory way.

4. What should a health, social care or childcare worker do if they experience or witness discriminatory behaviour?

3 Equality laws and protection

Think about it

1. What does the idea of 'equality' mean to you?

2. In what ways is the town, village or area in which you live 'diverse'? Identify at least three forms of difference between people.

3. How does your school or college promote and support inclusion?

▲ Equality and inclusion are human rights issues that affect everyone.

Equality laws and protection from discrimination

All work in healthcare, social care and childcare settings in Wales is underpinned by **legislation**. Equality laws are a key part of the legal framework of care. They make clear what individuals can expect when they use different services.

The laws that apply in Wales have been established by the Welsh government, the United Kingdom Parliament in Westminster, or by the European Parliament. The laws that are summarised below relate to equality, diversity and inclusion and promote individuals' rights.

Equality laws

The rights that people living in Wales have to fair and equal treatment are contained in equality laws. The Equality Act 2010 and the Human Rights Act 1998 express the basic rights and legal protections that make individuals equal before the law.

The Equality Act 2010

This law provides protection against discrimination for people who possess one or more of the nine protected characteristics. Overall, it aims to ensure that people can't be treated unfairly because of their differences.

Key term

Legislation
Written laws, such as Acts of Parliament.

▶ Examples of unlawful responses to protected characteristics.

Protected	Example of unfair and unlawful treatment
Age	Advertising for a 'young nurse' when a qualified nurse's age is irrelevant to their ability to do the job.
Disability	Locating health promotion information on the first floor of a building accessible only via stairs.
Marriage and civil partnership	Only consulting with married people about the effectiveness of a 'couples' counselling' service.
Pregnancy and maternity	Making a woman redundant shortly after she notifies her employer that she is pregnant.
Race	Never shortlisting black male applicants for nursery worker roles because 'parents don't trust them'.
Religion and belief	Not supporting a Muslim woman's request to see an Imam (a Muslim leader) at the nursing home where she lives.
Sex	Making sexual jokes and comments 'to relax' women who attend a fitness class at the local community centre.
Gender reassignment	Refusing to accept a booking for a dance class from a transgender couple because of their 'unusual' appearance.
Sexual orientation	Using derogatory language and nicknames to refer to a colleague who has a same-sex partner.

The Equality Act 2010 also refers to four main types of unfair discrimination:

▶ Four main types of unfair discrimination.

Direct discrimination

A person is treated less favourably as a direct result of a protected characteristic they have (for example, they are lesbian or Muslim) or are thought to have.

Indirect discrimination

An individual or group of people are treated unfairly and unequally because a practice, system or condition is applied (for example, must wear a hat as part of their uniform) that does not take into account a protected characteristic (for example, Sikh faith which requires a turban to be worn by men, which might make hat-wearing more difficult).

Harassment

A person is subjected to 'unwanted conduct' linked to one of their protected characteristics that intimidates them or violates their dignity. Bullying, making belittling comments and sexual harassment are examples.

Victimisation

Treating a person less favourably and unfairly because they have made, or are supporting somebody who has made, a complaint or allegation against another individual or the service.

The Human Rights Act 1998

Every individual in Wales has basic human rights. These are set out and protected by the Human Rights Act 1998. It requires that all public organisations (government, NHS Wales, care homes, local authorities, the police) treat people fairly and with dignity and respect. Every individual has the right:

- **to liberty and security**, for example, the right not to be locked in a care home bedroom

- **to life**, for example, the right to life-saving treatment

- **to respect for private and family life**, for example, the right to privacy in a residential care home

- **not to be tortured or treated in an inhumane or degrading way**, for example, the right to be clean and fed when unable to meet own needs in hospital or a care home

- **to freedom from discrimination**, for example, the right to treated fairly and equally.

Laws that protect and promote individuals' rights

In addition to general equality legislation, laws also exist to protect the rights of people who have specific health, support or social care needs. These focus on protecting the interests of people who are vulnerable to abuse or exploitation or who have additional needs for support.

The Mental Capacity Act 2005

A person with **mental capacity** is capable of making their own decisions. People can lack or lose mental capacity, either temporarily or permanently, because of conditions such as brain injury, dementia or learning disability. The Mental Capacity Act 2005 is a law that aims to protect an individual's rights to independence, dignity and freedom when this happens.

> **Did you know?**
>
> The FREDA acronym is a reminder of what is covered by the Human Rights Act 1998: people expect to be treated with **F**airness, **R**espect, **E**quality, **D**ignity and **A**utonomy.

> **Key term**
>
> **Mental capacity**
> The awareness and ability to make informed decisions or choices.

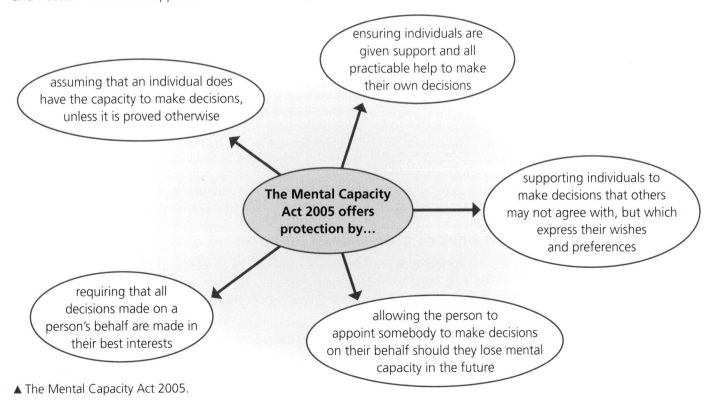

▲ The Mental Capacity Act 2005.

The Mental Capacity Act 2005 includes the Deprivation of Liberty Safeguards (DoLS). These aim to help people who cannot consent to their care arrangements in a care home or hospital in order to maintain their independence, dignity and the right to freedom.

If a person is continuously supervised and is not free to leave the care home or hospital because of their lack of mental capacity, the local authority must authorise care practices that deprive the person of their liberty (freedom). The DoLS procedures ensure that a person can have any restrictions on their freedom reviewed, can challenge this in court and will have a personal representative appointed to protect their best interests.

The Mental Capacity Act 2005 and the DoLS procedures ensure that the rights of vulnerable people in care homes and hospitals in Wales are monitored and legally protected.

The Social Services and Well-being (Wales) Act 2014

This Act aims to improve the well-being of people who need social care and support, and carers who need support, in Wales. The Act changes the way people's needs are assessed and the way services are delivered. In particular,

- it requires local authorities in Wales to treat people who need care as equal partners

- assessments must focus on what matters to the individual, their strengths and the support available to them from family, friends and others in their local community

- assessment is simplified and can be carried out by one person on behalf of a number of organisations

- services will aim to prevent a person's problems from getting worse.

The aim of the Act is to boost the well-being of people who have support needs by ensuring that each individual has more of a say in the care and support they receive. This should lead to a reduction in the person's need for formal, planned support.

Additional Learning Needs and Education Tribunal (Wales) Act 2017

Until recently, children with special educational needs (SEN) and those with **learning difficulties** and/or disabilities received support from separate services in Wales. This Act provides a legal framework for improving the planning and delivery of support for all learners from 0 to 25 years of age who have additional learning needs (ALN).

The Act is part of a transformation plan that will ensure ALN support in Wales is based on a person-centred approach, identifies individual support needs early, puts effective support and monitoring into place for each individual and ensures that different agencies collaborate and adapt interventions to deliver desired outcomes. The new ALN system in Wales is due to come into operation in 2020 with an individual learning plan being developed for each person with ALN by 2023.

Codes of professional practice

The standards of practice that care workers must meet are set by their **regulatory bodies**. These are independent organisations, such as the Nursing and Midwifery Council and Social Care Wales, who set out the standards in a code of professional practice.

Codes of professional practice provide guidance and rules on ways of behaving and standards of practice. They identify what a care worker should do in specific situations and establish what 'good practice' involves in care settings. They cover issues such as equality, diversity and inclusion and explain how care workers should protect the interests of the people they care for and support.

Key terms

Learning difficulty
An impaired or reduced ability to learn.

Regulatory body
An independent organisation, such as the Nursing and Midwifery Council, that makes rules and sets standards for a profession such as registered nurses.

The Nursing and Midwifery Council produces a code of practice for nurses and midwives, whilst Social Care Wales produces a code of practice for social care workers. Health and social care workers who breach the code or practice of their regulatory body are liable to be disciplined and may even be barred from working in their profession if they have demonstrated dangerous or sub-standard care practice.

Welsh language and culture

The Welsh government policy *Cymraeg 2050: A Million Welsh Speakers* (http://www.assembly.wales/Laid%20Documents/GEN-LD11108/GEN-LD11108-e.pdf) describes the Welsh language as a key feature of the culture and identity of Wales as a nation. Opportunities to use the Welsh language in care settings are closely linked to equality, diversity and inclusion issues in Wales.

Cymraeg 2050 outlines a vision of Welsh being used in every aspect of daily life, including in workplaces, in services and in everyday social settings. The three main aims of this policy are to:

* increase the number of Welsh speakers

* increase the use of Welsh

* create favourable conditions for the increased use of the Welsh language.

Welsh speakers now have the legal right to receive Welsh-language services, and a Welsh Language Commissioner monitors the implementation of these rights.

More than just words

The Welsh government's strategy *More Than Just Words* launched in 2012 aims to ensure Welsh speakers receive healthcare, childcare and social care services in their first language. Receiving services, and being able to talk to staff, in Welsh is seen as especially important for vulnerable people and their families who need to access services in their first language. This includes older people suffering from dementia or stroke who may lose their second language, and very young children who may only speak Welsh. Regardless of their age or health condition, people whose first language is Welsh may feel more comfortable and be more able to express their needs to care workers in their chosen language. This is also likely to empower people and enable them to participate more actively in their care.

> **Did you know?**
>
> Speaking to people in their first language ensures they are treated with respect and dignity and can support their sense of identity.

The active offer

More Than Just Words requires healthcare, social care and childcare services to provide Welsh-language training to staff and bilingual services to cater for Welsh- and English-language speakers. However, it is also important that Welsh-language services should be offered to Welsh speakers without them having to ask for them. This is known as the 'active offer'. As a result, care organisations need to make the Welsh language visible and services in Welsh readily available to everyone. They shouldn't be seen as something 'extra' or unusual. This 'active offer' principle reflects the core values of the NHS to treat people as individuals and ensure that their needs are central to care delivery.

Case study

Frances Hoggan (née Morgan) (1843–1927) was born in Brecon, mid Wales, and became the first British woman to gain a medical degree. She completed a six-year medical degree in just three years in Zurich, Switzerland, because no British medical schools would admit women in the 19th century.

▲ Dr Frances Hoggan.

Frances was a medical doctor, researcher and campaigner for the education of girls and women at a time when women's opportunities were very limited. She was finally able to enter the Medical Register in 1877, following a change in the law. However, she still faced hostility and opposition to her campaigns to improve the education of girls and women in Wales at this time. She spoke about the need for gender equality at the National Eisteddfod in Denbigh in 1878 and Cardiff in 1883, proposing that both genders would benefit from being educated together and having the same opportunities. Frances also campaigned to raise awareness of women's health issues and the need for a preventative approach to public health. She did this at a time when many men in authority argued that the mental effort of education would damage the development and functioning of the female reproductive system and so should be avoided.

1. Identify the type of unfair discrimination that Frances Hoggan experienced in trying to become a doctor.

2. Describe the benefits of there being both male and female doctors within healthcare services.

3. Explain how current equality laws would have helped Frances to achieve her goal of becoming a doctor.

Check your understanding

1. Identify three examples of legislation that promote equality and protect individuals from unfair discrimination.

2. Identify one 'protected characteristic' referred to by the Equality Act 2010 and describe three examples of unfair discrimination that would be unlawful as a result of this law.

3. What is 'mental capacity' and how does the law in Wales protect people who lack this?

4. Give three reasons to explain why the availability of Welsh-language provision is an equality issue in healthcare, social care and childcare settings in Wales.

3.2 SAFEGUARDING
4 Understanding safeguarding

Think about it

1. List as many forms of abuse or mistreatment of vulnerable people as you can.

2. Give three reasons why parents or care workers sometimes abuse or mistreat their children or the people they should be caring for.

3. What are the procedures in your school or college for reporting mistreatment or abuse?

What is safeguarding?

All health, social care and childcare workers have a duty to safeguard the children and adults they have contact with. **Safeguarding** involves:

• promoting healthy physical, intellectual (educational), emotional and social development appropriate to a child's or adult's age and expected level of development

• ensuring a child or adult is provided with a safe environment and nurturing care and support

• protecting all individuals from maltreatment.

It is important to note that safeguarding involves promotion of health, development and well-being as well as protection from harm. Children and adults in need of protection are usually vulnerable in some way. Children lack the maturity as well as the ability to meet their own needs and act in their own best interests. Most adults can protect themselves from threats of harm and meet their own daily living and care needs. However, some adults require safeguarding because they lack the mental capacity, physical ability or social skills to meet their own needs independently.

Forms of abuse and neglect

Some individuals in society may experience abuse, neglect and maltreatment that damages their personal development. These include children and young people, vulnerable adults, older people and people with disabilities who do not receive protection and safeguarding from parents or care workers. Abuse and neglect are most commonly perpetrated by parents on children, by one partner or another and by carers of people who are unwell, frail or who have developmental problems. The different forms of abuse that members of vulnerable groups experience include:

• physical

• sexual

• emotional and psychological

• financial exploitation

• neglect.

▲ Alex was often bullied by other children because his **autism** made him vulnerable.

Key terms

Safeguarding
Protecting children and vulnerable adults from abuse or neglect and educating those around them to recognise the signs and dangers.

Autism
A lifelong condition that affects how an individual communicates with, and relates to, other people and the world around them.

Did you know?

Abuse and neglect can affect personal development in various ways but is particularly damaging to an individual's social and emotional development.

▶ Forms of abuse and neglect.

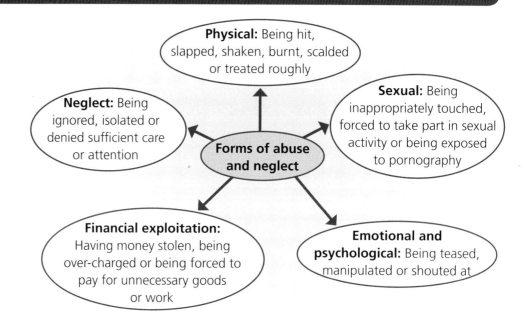

Reasons for abuse and ill treatment

The perpetrator, or person who carries out abuse, neglect or ill treatment, is ultimately responsible for their actions. Their employer, the police or the courts won't allow them to make excuses for harming a child, a vulnerable relative or a service user. However, there are a number of factors that increase the risk of abuse or neglect.

▶ Reasons for abuse and ill treatment.

Care workers should be aware of factors that contribute to the ill treatment of vulnerable people. They may be able to alert others to situations that could lead to the ill treatment of service users. For example, when care workers are poorly trained, unsupervised or have insufficient support, managers should be alerted because this can lead to neglect and abuse of service users. Similarly, where a care worker is working on their own with service users, or if there are too few staff to provide services, standards of care can fall to unacceptable levels. In these situations, it is often complaints from service users or their relatives that bring abuse and neglect to light.

Safeguarding strategies

Many people who use care services are at a vulnerable point in their life. They put a lot of trust in health, social care or childcare workers to provide them with the protection, help and support that they need. Some groups of service users, including children, people with disabilities, older people and people with mental health problems, are more at risk of abuse, maltreatment or neglect. Older, frail people, those with learning disabilities or people with dementia may also find it difficult to follow basic health and safety precautions that protect them from the dangers of everyday life. Consequently, a number of safeguarding strategies are used in care settings to minimise risks and protect people from harm.

Safeguarding laws and policies

A number of different laws have been passed to protect and safeguard the interests of vulnerable children and adults. Healthcare, social care and childcare workers should be aware of these laws and should know how they apply to the work they do with service users. At a general level, the purpose of safeguarding legislation and policies includes:

- promoting and maintaining the safety of individuals (and care workers)
- developing and maintaining effective lines of communication whilst also maintaining **confidentiality** of information
- ensuring appropriate vetting procedures when recruiting new employees.

Current legislation and policies that affect safeguarding provision include:

- United Nations Convention of the Rights of the Child 1989
- Human Rights Act 1998
- The Children Act 1989
- The Children Act 2004
- All Wales Protection Procedures 2008
- Safeguarding of Vulnerable Groups Act 2006
- Social Services and Well-being (Wales) Act 2014
- Violence against Women, Domestic Abuse and Sexual Violence (Wales) Act 2015

United Nations Convention of the Rights of the Child 1989

This convention outlines the rights that all children have, as well as the obligation of adults and governments to work together in ways that promote and uphold these rights. The convention says that children's rights must be prioritised to enable them to survive and develop in dignity. Children's human rights apply to all children at all times, without exception. Children's rights under the convention include:

- protection (for example, from abuse, exploitation and harmful substances)
- provision (for example, for education, health care and an adequate standard of living)
- participation (for example, listening to children's views and respecting their evolving capacities)
- specific protections and provisions for vulnerable populations such as Aboriginal children and children with disabilities.

> **Key term**
>
> **Confidentiality**
> Keeping information private, or restricting access only to those authorised to know.

Human Rights Act 1998

This Act applies to all 'public authorities', including care homes, hospitals and social services departments.

What human rights are covered?	What does this mean in practice?
Right to life	Decisions to **resuscitate** or turn off life support machines cannot be made by care workers alone.
Right to respect, privacy and family life	Service users are entitled to confidentiality of personal information. People with learning and physical disabilities are entitled to live independently and form personal relationships.
Right to liberty and security	A person cannot be detained in hospital or a care home unless they have been sentenced by a court or have been admitted under the Mental Health Act as a danger to themselves or others.
Right to freedom from discrimination	A person cannot be treated less favourably than others because of their physical, social or cultural characteristics.
Right to freedom of expression	Individuals have the right to express their views and to make their own choices about treatment.
Right to freedom of thought, conscience and religion	Individuals can choose and express their own faith and beliefs. They should be supported and given opportunities to do this in care settings.

▲ The Human Rights Act 1998 outlines the rights and freedoms that every person in the United Kingdom is entitled to.

The Children Act 1989

This Act established that care workers should see the needs of the child as most important when making any decisions that affect a child's welfare. Under this Act local authorities are required to provide services that meet the needs of children identified as being 'at risk'.

The Children Act 2004

The Children Act 2004 aims to improve the lives of all children who receive informal or professional care. It covers all services that children might use, such as schools, day care and children's homes as well as healthcare services. The Children Act 2004 now requires care services to work collaboratively so that they form a protective team around the child.

All Wales Child Protection Procedures 2008

These procedures determine how child protection referrals, actions and plans are carried out by Local and Regional Safeguarding Children Boards across Wales. They are based on the idea that protecting children from harm is everybody's responsibility. The procedures require a multi-agency partnership in order to identify vulnerable children.

Safeguarding of Vulnerable Groups Act 2006

Staff recruited to work with children or vulnerable adults must pass a safety vetting check carried out by the Disclosure and Barring Service (DBS). There are three levels, or types, of DBS check:

- Standard – checks for criminal convictions, cautions, reprimands and final warnings
- Enhanced – an additional check for any information held by police that is relevant to the role applied for
- Enhanced with list checks – additional checks are made of List 99, the **PoCA** (children and young people) and **PoVA** (adults) lists of individuals barred from working with vulnerable people.

Key terms

Resuscitate
Bring back to life.

PoCA
Protection of Children Act 1999.

PoVA
Protection of Vulnerable Adults.

Social Services and Well-being (Wales) Act 2014

This Act provides the legal framework for social service provision in Wales. Locally, Regional Safeguarding Children's Boards coordinate and ensure the effectiveness of work to protect and promote the welfare of children. They are responsible for local child protection policy, procedure and guidance. Each board includes any:

- local authority
- chief officer of police
- local health board
- NHS trust
- provider of probation services

that falls within the Safeguarding Board area.

Violence against Women, Domestic Abuse and Sexual Violence (Wales) Act 2015

This legislation aims to improve the public sector response in Wales to violence against women, domestic abuse and sexual violence. The Act will:

- improve ways that awareness, prevention, protection and support for victims of gender-based violence, domestic abuse and sexual violence are organised
- ensure that agencies and organisations responsible for violence prevention and protection develop shared strategies that focus on real needs and for which they will be accountable
- ensure a ministerial adviser works with Welsh ministers and improves multi-agency working on these issues across Wales
- improve consistency, quality and coordination of service provision in Wales.

Mental Health Act 1983 and 2007

These Acts are the main laws affecting the treatment of adults experiencing serious mental disorders in England and Wales. The Mental Health Act 2007 seeks to safeguard adults who are mentally unwell by ensuring that they can be monitored in the community by care workers and admitted to hospital if they don't stick to their treatment. The Mental Health Act 1983 and 2007 also protects the rights of mental health service users in a number of ways. Both Acts give individuals the right to appeal against their detention in hospital and gives them some rights to refuse treatment. The 2007 Act now gives individuals detained in hospital the right to refuse certain treatments, such as electroconvulsive therapy, and ensures that a person can only be detained in hospital if appropriate treatment is available for them.

Safeguarding policies and procedures

Care organisations always have a safeguarding policy and a set of procedures for staff to follow in order to prevent, or respond to, safeguarding incidents. Care workers are expected to know and understand this policy and procedure. It will usually be explained during a person's induction training when they first join the care organisation.

▶ What should an organisation's safeguarding policy and procedures ensure?

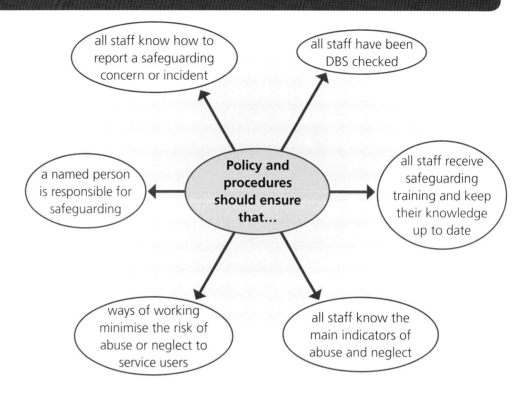

Care organisations also have a range of procedures about care practices that can become safeguarding concerns if they are not properly dealt with.

▶ Safeguarding concerns for care practices.

Care practice	How can this be a safeguarding concern?
Administration of medicine	Giving medication late or at an incorrect dose can put the person at risk physically.
Moving and handling people	Unsafe moving and handling can put individuals at risk of physical injury or falls and may be seen as physical abuse.
Checking pressure sores	Neglecting to check the condition of a person's skin can lead to infected pressure (bed) sores.
Responding to call bells	Failure to respond to call bells could be very distressing for an individual and may put them at risk of a fall or other physical injury.
Eating and drinking	Poor nutritional support may lead to malnutrition or may put those with chewing and swallowing problems at risk.
Lack of social time or activity	Failure to provide or support stimulating social or physical activity could lead to psychological abuse and social isolation.
Rough and rushed treatment	This can lead to fear and physical injury and could be seen as physical abuse.
Managing money and valuables	Inappropriate storage or theft of money or other valuables or staff acceptance of inappropriate gifts may be seen as financial exploitation.

Case study

Gavin's parents argue a lot. They shout and swear at each other and at him if they think he has misbehaved in any way. Gavin's father has a very short temper and sometimes threatens to hit Gavin with a belt. He has never done so but Gavin is still frightened of his dad when he starts shouting and jabbing his finger at him. This happens so often that Gavin says it is 'normal' for parents to behave in this way and he can't remember the last time that his dad was affectionate or said something positive to him. Gavin has learnt that protesting his innocence or arguing back only leads to harsher punishment. One recent Saturday morning, he was sent to his room and had to stay there without food until the following day. This really upset Gavin and made him think that he is a bad person.

1. What kinds of ill treatment does Gavin experience from his parents?

2. Which aspects of Gavin's development and well-being may be affected by his ill treatment?

3. Explain whether, and if so why, you think Gavin may benefit from a safeguarding intervention.

◄ Gavin is badly treated by his parents.

Check your understanding

1. Using your own words, explain what safeguarding involves in a health, social care or childcare context.

2. List five different forms of maltreatment that would lead to a safeguarding concern.

3. How does the Disclosure and Barring Service (DBS) help to safeguard vulnerable children and adults?

4. Identify three pieces of safeguarding legislation or policy that protects the rights of children and young people.

▶ Wales has an ageing population. Being active promotes health and well-being in later life.

Think about it

1. What health and welfare needs do you associate with older people?
2. List three health problems that are associated with obesity.
3. What are mental health problems and why do some people experience them?

▼ Ysbyty Cwm Cynon is an innovative hospital looking to the future.

Health and well-being challenges in Wales

What are the main health and well-being challenges facing the adult population of Wales? This is an important question for the Welsh government and for those planning personal and public health services in Wales. Identifying and targeting the right issues matters for both the current and future population of Wales. The right kind of services in the right areas of Wales are needed to meet people's current health needs. At the same time, **public health** strategies to prevent disease and illness are also needed to ensure that services are effective, affordable and sustainable in the future.

Identifying population health needs

The starting point for addressing public and personal health issues is to obtain data about the Welsh population and the patterns of health and illness that people living in Wales experience. Government and service planners need to know about:

- the age structure of the population
- the trends in birth rate
- the trends in **life expectancy**
- levels of unemployment
- variations in the size and structure of the population in different parts of Wales
- levels of **migration** into and emigration out of Wales
- patterns of **disease** and illness within the population.

Demographic data is used by governments, planners and social scientists to identify and monitor the size, structure and changing features of the population of Wales. This, together with other health-related data, is also used by government and politicians to plan and develop appropriate health and care services to meet people's predicted needs for care and support.

Data about the structure and health experiences of the population of Wales is obtained from various sources.

▼ Some of the sources of population and health data for Wales.

Data source	What is it?
The Census www.ons.gov.uk/census	The Census is a detailed count of the population carried out every ten years. Next due in 2021, it covers all nations of the United Kingdom.
The Office for National Statistics www.ons.gov.uk/	The United Kingdom's independent producer of population, social and health statistics.
StatsWales https://statswales.gov.wales/Catalogue	A free Welsh government service that provides data and statistics on Welsh population, health and social issues.
Public Health Wales http://www.wales.nhs.uk/sitesplus/888/home	The national public health agency in Wales that provides information and publications on public health issues and campaigns.
Public Health Wales Observatory www.publichealthwalesobservatory.wales.nhs.uk/home	A part of Public Health Wales that provides data and reports on a range of public health concerns affecting Wales.
The National Survey for Wales https://gov.wales/statistics-and-research/national-survey/	An annual survey of people in Wales on a range of health and social issues carried out on behalf of the Welsh government.

Key terms

Life expectancy
The average period a person may expect to live.

Migration
Movement of people from one place to another with the intention of settling.

Disease
An abnormal condition that negatively affects part of a person's body.

Demographic data
Information about the size and structure of the population.

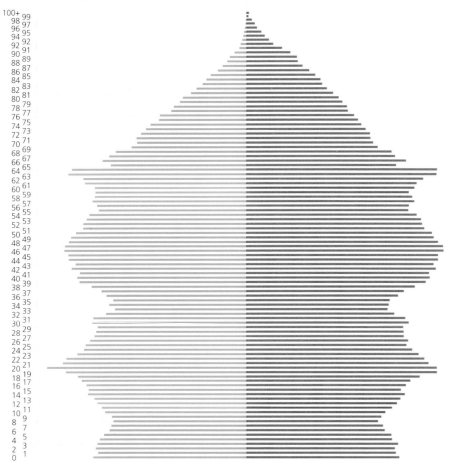

Female
Male

▲ The population structure of Wales.

An ageing population

The population of Wales is ageing. In 2008, 18 per cent of the Welsh population was over 65; by 2033 this is expected to rise to almost 26 per cent. Currently, one in every four adults in Wales is over 65 years old. By 2031, this will rise to one in every three adults. As in much of the developed world, increased wealth, health and standards of living mean that as people in Wales grow older they can look forward to a far longer and healthier retirement than their own parents. The Office for National Statistics has predicted that:

- The number of people in Wales aged 16–64 is projected to **decrea**se by 81,000 (4.2%) between 2016 and 2041.

- The number of people in Wales aged 65 and over is projected to **increase** by 232,000 (36.6%) between 2016 and 2041.

An ageing population presents a range of challenges for Welsh society. For example, there are likely to be fewer people in paid work generating taxes to pay for services or to train and become care workers but more older people in need of care and support services. Older people are more likely to experience chronic conditions, multi-morbidities (two or more chronic conditions) and **cognitive** impairments than younger people. The gap between the need for care and the resources available to meet those needs will mean that services will have to adapt and people will need to take more personal responsibility for being healthy as they age. In order to tackle this challenge, the Welsh government is considering different strategies which include:

- supporting people to 'age in place' by staying at home rather than moving into residential or nursing home care

- making effective use of assistive technologies (for example, a stairlift) to maximise independence

- adapting services to prevent as well as meet the needs of older people.

Obesity

Obesity is a major public health concern in Wales. It is the result of a range of other health issues, such as poor diet, lack of exercise and an inactive lifestyle. It raises a person's risk of experiencing a range of other health problems, including type 2 diabetes, **cardiovascular disease** and some forms of cancer. As a result, obesity places a huge strain on NHS Wales.

The *Welsh Health Survey 2015* showed that 24 per cent of adults are classified as obese and 59 per cent of adults are classified as overweight or obese. Being overweight and obese as an adult in Wales is linked to deprivation. Of the people living in the least deprived areas of Wales, 54 per cent were overweight or obese compared with 63 per cent living in the most deprived areas.

Key terms

Cognitive
Relating to mental processes involved in knowing, learning and understanding.

Cardiovascular disease
A disease that involves the heart or blood vessels.

Mental health issues

Mental health problems are increasingly being recognised as a serious public health concern in many countries. There is no single cause of mental health problems. They can be triggered by biological, psychological, social or environmental factors. People have an increased risk of developing a mental health problem if, for example, they:

- are living in poverty or on a low income

- are unemployed, lonely or socially isolated

- misuse drugs or alcohol

- have an existing medical illness

- experience trauma, injustice or discrimination

- have poor access to support and services.

Conditions such as anxiety, depression, eating disorders and self-harming behaviour are all being diagnosed more frequently in Wales. Data from the *Welsh Health Survey 2015* showed that:

- 13 per cent of adults in Wales reported being treated for any mental illness.

- 10 per cent of adults reported being treated for depression, 8 per cent for anxiety, and 2 per cent for another mental illness.

- The percentage of adults who reported being treated for any mental illness in Wales increased towards middle age before decreasing in retirement age.

- A higher percentage of women (16 per cent) than men (10 per cent) in Wales reported being treated for a mental illness.

- Self-harm is a growing problem in Wales, with approximately 5500 emergency admissions to hospital each year.

Percentage who report being treated for any mental illness, by age and sex

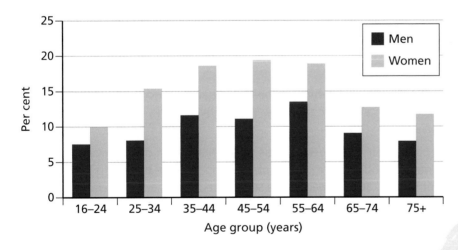

◄ Adults in Wales reporting treatment for any mental illness in 2015.
Source: Welsh Health Survey (2015).

Substance misuse

Substance misuse covers the misuse of both drugs (illicit or prescribed) and alcohol. Both are major public health concerns in Wales.

A Public Health Wales report, *Alcohol and Health in Wales 2014*, revealed that:

- Around 1500 deaths in Wales are due to alcohol each year (one in 20 of all deaths).

- one in six boys and one in seven girls aged 11–16 drink alcohol at least once a week. Around 400 young people under 18 are admitted for alcohol-specific conditions per year in Wales, although the rate has been decreasing for several years.

- Generally, consumption of alcohol has slightly decreased and adults under 45 in Wales now drink less.

- Deaths and hospital admission due to alcohol are strongly related to deprivation, with rates in the most deprived areas much higher than in the least deprived. There is no sign of improvement in the inequality gap in mortality over time.

On the issue of drug misuse, a Public Health Wales report, *Piecing the Puzzle 2016*, revealed that:

- Hospital admissions in Wales related to use of illicit drugs rose by 9% compared with 2014–2015.

- Admissions data also suggested that use of multiple drugs may be increasing.

- Deaths from drug misuse rose 48.7% to 168 in 2015. This increase reversed the declining trend seen over the previous five years.

- Hospital admissions involving illicit drug use by people over the age of 50 rose 4.8% in 2015–2016 compared with the previous year.

Public Health Wales' *Annual Profile for Substance Misuse 2016–17*, reported that fewer people in Wales are being assessed or admitted to hospital for drug misuse than in previous years, but that deaths from drug misuse have been increasing.

Sustainability of health and social care, and childcare in Wales

Achieving long-term **sustainability** of health, social care and childcare services in Wales is a fundamental challenge for the Welsh government, care workers and the people of Wales.

An ageing population, rising levels of obesity, mental health difficulties and substance misuse problems are putting pressure on the government to find enough **funding** for services and to adapt these services to meet changing needs.

The Welsh government is trying to achieve sustainable health, social care and childcare services in Wales by:

- investing in public health initiatives that focus on prevention and population health

- motivating people to take greater personal responsibility for their health and well-being so that preventable health problems are actually prevented

- adapting services so they are fit to meet the needs of the future population

- providing care in less costly settings such as primary and community services

- maintaining spending on effective health, social care and childcare services to keep up with demographic change

- developing and motivating a high quality health, social care and childcare workforce with the right skills to deliver services in the future.

The sustainability of care services in Wales is an ongoing challenge. It is achievable in the long term if government, care workers and the population of Wales each do what they can to tackle current population health issues and accept that prevention is better than 'cure' in the long run.

Case study

Bianca Edwards is a student living in Cardiff. She has attended the accident and emergency department of her local hospital six times so far this year. She has been taken there by friends twice and by ambulance on the other occasions. On each occasion, she had collapsed in a bar or on the street after drinking heavily and taking ecstasy tablets. Bianca accepts that she has a binge drinking problem but says she drinks to make herself feel better. She has felt depressed and lonely since moving away from home to live in Cardiff a year ago. Bianca saw a mental health nurse the last time she was assessed in accident and emergency. The nurse gave Bianca information about a support group for young people and referred her to a university counselling service. Bianca knows that she is risking her health but doesn't know what else to do to get help for her problems.

1. Which of Bianca's health problems could be seen as preventable?

2. What could Bianca do to avoid future admissions to the accident and emergency department for the same reasons in future?

3. How does referring Bianca to a support group and counselling help to make accident and emergency services more sustainable in future?

◄ Bianca is often seen at her local Accident and Emergency department.

Check your understanding

1. What is demographic data and how do governments use it to plan care services?

2. What evidence is there that Wales has an obesity problem?

3. Give an example of two chronic health problems within the Welsh population.

4. Describe three ways in which the Welsh government and population can help to make the provision of care services more sustainable.

6 Contemporary issues affecting children and young people in Wales

▶ Menai is currently a foster carer for both Emily and David, who are **looked after children**.

Think about it

1. List three issues or problems that affect Welsh children's health, development or well-being.

2. If you could improve one aspect of your own health or well-being, what would you change?

3. Explain how parents can promote the health and well-being of their children.

Challenges to children's health and well-being

The health, development and well-being of children and young people in Wales are also important issues for government, service providers, families and children themselves. This is because a child's experiences of health and well-being tend to follow them into adulthood and later life. Unhealthy children tend to become unhealthy adults.

Government and public health agencies have identified a range of contemporary challenges affecting children in Wales. Each challenge outlined below presents a risk or threat to the health and well-being of children and young people in Wales. These challenges need to be addressed to avoid ill health in the Welsh population in future.

Childhood obesity

The World Health Organisation (WHO) has identified childhood obesity as one of the most serious public health challenges of the 21st century. The WHO defines overweight and obesity as 'abnormal or excessive fat accumulation that presents a risk to health'. Childhood obesity is mainly the result of unhealthy eating and low levels of physical activity. The fundamental cause is an energy imbalance – more energy (calories) is consumed than the person uses.

Childhood obesity is a growing problem globally with an estimated 41 million children under five being overweight. Wales has the largest proportion of overweight or obese children in the United Kingdom. Public Health Wales published research in 2014 that showed:

- Nearly three-quarters (73 per cent) of the 29 238 children measured had a body mass index (BMI) classified as healthy.

- Of the 26 per cent of children with a BMI classified as unhealthy, 11.3 per cent were classified as obese.

- Children living in Merthyr Tydfil (34 per cent), Gwynedd and Bridgend (30 per cent) are most likely to be overweight and obese. Children living in Monmouthshire (21 per cent) and the Vale of Glamorgan (22 per cent) are least likely to be obese.

Childhood obesity is a major health problem in Wales because it increases the risk of high blood pressure, type 2 diabetes and sleep problems. Obesity can also affect mental health by reducing a child's confidence and self-esteem. More positively, being overweight or obese, and their related health problems, can be prevented. This is why healthy eating, exercise and weight management strategies are given a high priority by public health, NHS and education services in Wales.

Poverty and childhood

People who live in poverty live in a household with little or no money, few possessions and few resources to support themselves. The United Kingdom government says that people living in households that receive less than 60 per cent of median (average) income are living in poverty. The organisation Children in Wales defines poverty more broadly saying that 'poverty happens when a family's resources are below what they need, including taking part in their local community or society more generally'.

There are approximately 600 000 children living in Wales. The charity Save the Children reports that in 2018:

- Almost one-third of children (200 000) were living in poverty. This is a higher proportion than in any other nation in the United Kingdom.

- 90 000 children (14 per cent) are living in severe poverty (in households at or below 50 per cent of median income).

- More than half (53 per cent) of Welsh children in low-income families are worried their parents are finding it harder to pay for everyday necessities such as food, heating and clothes.

- A fifth (20 per cent) of Welsh parents on low incomes say stress about money affects their relationship with their children.

Experiencing poverty in childhood matters because it affects a person's health, development and well-being. For example:

- Children who experience poverty are more likely to suffer ill health because of cold, damp and overcrowded housing conditions, lack of indoor and outside space to play, and diet which is insufficient and of poor quality.

- Children living in poverty tend to do less well at school. There is a 28 per cent gap between children from wealthier families and those who receive free school meals in achievement of five GCSEs, grades A* to C.

Blaenau Gwent has the highest rate of child poverty in Wales. You can check rates of child poverty in your own area of Wales by visiting the website for end child poverty: www.endchildpoverty.org.uk.

> **Did you know?**
>
> Other sources of information about childhood obesity in Wales include:
>
> - NHS Wales: www.wales.nhs.uk/healthtopics/lifestyles/obesity
> - Public Health Network Cymru: www.publichealthnetwork.cymru
> - Public Health Wales Observatory: www.publichealthwalesobservatory.wales.nhs.uk

> **Did you know?**
>
> Further sources of online information on child poverty in Wales include:
>
> - Children in Wales – www.childreninwales.org.uk
> - Oxfam – www.oxfam.org.uk/cymru/poverty-in-wales
> - The Welsh government – https://gov.wales/topics (search for 'child poverty').

Food poverty

The term **food poverty** is used when a person, or members of a family, don't have the means to buy enough food for themselves. This means that the person or family members will go hungry and will not have access to a diet that is nutritionally, socially or culturally acceptable. A person or family that just about has enough money to afford food, may still experience food poverty if they can't obtain or get access to the kinds of foods they would like to eat. Lack of choice due to poor availability of fresh, unprocessed food means that some people in Wales only have access to low quality but affordable food. Places where there are very few opportunities to buy fresh foods, or even a variety of food types, are referred to as 'food deserts'. These places may only offer fast food outlets rather than places to buy ingredients to make your own food.

The use of food banks and 'community fridges' to support people in food poverty is rising throughout the United Kingdom, including Wales. Data and statistics on food poverty are difficult to obtain because it is a 'hidden' problem, unrecorded by government and unreported by people who experience it because of shame and embarrassment. However, the charity Oxfam has reported that over two million people in the United Kingdom are estimated to be malnourished and three million are at risk of becoming so.

Bullying

Bullying is behaviour that is deliberately hurtful, repeated over a period of time and difficult for victims to defend themselves against. A person can be bullied verbally (name-calling, teasing, threats), physically (hitting, pushing, attacking) or psychologically (spreading malicious rumours, social media posts and messages). Cyberbullying also occurs through the use of digital devices such as mobile phones, computers and tablets. It involves sending SMS, texts or emails or sharing images or information with the intention of embarrassing or humiliating a person, and is an increasing problem for children and young people.

Bullying can have a very negative effect on a person's mental health and well-being. This includes developing social anxiety, depression and even suicidal thoughts. The impact of cyberbullying tends to be worse and last longer than bullying that happens in person. The immediate upset and trauma of being bullied can also have longer-term effects, as people can struggle to regain their confidence and sense of self-worth.

A Welsh government survey of year 6, 7 and 10 pupils attending schools in Wales in 2009 found that:

- 32 per cent of pupils in year 6 reported being bullied within the last two months, rising to 47 per cent who reported being bullied in the last school year

- 30 per cent of pupils in year 7 reported being bullied within the last two months, rising to 44 per cent who reported being bullied in the last school year

- 15 per cent of pupils in year 10 reported being bullied within the last two months, rising to 25 per cent who reported being bullied in the last school year.

This also means that 53 per cent of pupils in year 6, 56 per cent of pupils in year 7, and 75 per cent of pupils in year 10 did not report being bullied in the last year. The survey also found that most pupils who are bullied are bullied infrequently and most are only bullied for a relatively short period (typically one or two weeks). The frequency and incidence of bullying also tends to decline as pupils get older.

Protecting children from harm

Bullying is an example of a risk to children's development and well-being. Exploitation, radicalisation, female genital mutilation and substance misuse are further examples of threats or risks to health, development and well-being during childhood and adolescence.

Radicalisation

Radicalisation occurs when someone begins to adopt extreme political, religious or social views, which might lead them to them acting (or intending to act) in a way that could harm themselves or others. Radicalisation is a gradual process, so a child or young person may not realise it is happening. Radicalisation is a form of harm and a safeguarding issue. It is associated with the attempts that some extreme political and terrorist groups, and their members, make to recruit vulnerable children and young people. Radicalisation may involve:

- being groomed online or in person
- exploitation, including sexual exploitation
- psychological manipulation
- exposure to violent material and other inappropriate information
- the risk of physical harm or death through extremist acts.

> ### Key term
>
> **Self-identity**
> An individual's view of themselves, which is usually influenced by personal perceptions of their own abilities, flaws and status and by feedback received from others.

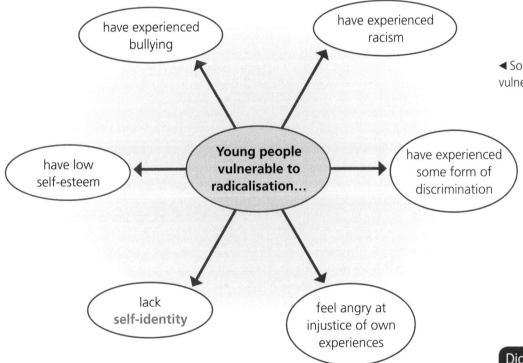

◄ Some young people may be more vulnerable to radicalisation.

The National Society for the Prevention of Cruelty to Children (NSPCC) lists the following as potential warning signs:

- isolating themselves from family and friends
- talking as if from a scripted speech
- unwillingness or inability to discuss their views
- a sudden disrespectful attitude towards others
- increased levels of anger
- increased secretiveness, especially around internet use.

> ### Did you know?
>
> Further sources of information on radicalisation include:
>
> - Dewis Cymru: https://www.dewis.wales/radicalisation-cyp
> - NSPCC: https://www.nspcc.org.uk/what-you-can-do/report-abuse/dedicated-helplines/protecting-children-from-radicalisation/.

Female genital mutilation

Female genital mutilation (FGM) involves deliberately cutting, injuring or changing the genitals of a girl or young woman where there's no medical reason to do so. FGM usually happens to girls whose mothers, grandmothers or extended female family members have had FGM themselves or if their father comes from a community where it's carried out. It is typically carried out for cultural, religious and social reasons, although there are no religious texts that say it should be done. The mistaken belief that FGM will benefit the girl in some way (for example, as a preparation for marriage or to preserve her virginity) is often used to justify it. There are, in fact, no medical benefits to having FGM.

FGM is a very painful procedure that can have serious short- and long-term health effects. These include:

- constant pain
- pain and/or difficulty having sex
- repeated infections, which can lead to infertility
- bleeding, cysts and abscesses
- problems passing urine or incontinence
- depression, flashbacks and self-harm
- problems during labour and childbirth, which can be life-threatening for mother and baby.

FGM is typically carried out against a girl's will by a non-medically qualified, traditional circumciser or 'cutter' without anaesthetic. It is illegal in Wales and the rest of the United Kingdom and is a safeguarding issue. A person who performs FGM can spend up to 14 years in prison. Anyone found guilty of failing to protect a girl from FGM can also be imprisoned for up to seven years.

Substance misuse

Young people often begin using alcohol and drugs as part of adolescent experimentation. The likelihood that a young person will use drugs increases with age. Though nearly half of young people between 16 and 24 have used illicit drugs, most don't go on to develop a drug problem. It is difficult to know how many children and young people misuse drugs and alcohol as it is a largely hidden activity. Often an individual's family is unaware of their substance misuse, for example. In addition, the data is compiled from school-based surveys, inevitably missing out children excluded from mainstream schools. Alcohol and cannabis are the substances that young people are most likely to misuse.

Public Health Wales report *Annual Profile for Substance Misuse 2018/2019* provides the following data on children's substance misuse:

- the number of children in need for whom own substance misuse was identified as a problem was 1020 (4.6% increase on the previous year).
- In 2014–2015, the most recent year for which statistics are available, the number of school exclusions related to drugs or alcohol rose overall from 370 to 380 (2.7% increase).
- There were 922 admissions involving young people aged 25 or under with an alcohol-specific condition in 2016–2017 (decrease of 11.6% compared with 2015–2016).
- There has been a decline in hospital admissions of young people for alcohol-related reasons between 2013–2014 (1251 admissions) and 2016–2017 (922 admissions).
- There were 1296 admissions of young people aged 25 or under for conditions related to illicit drugs in 2016–2017, a decrease of 1.4% on 2015–2016.

Did you know?

Sources of information on FGM include:

- Forward UK: https://forwarduk.org.uk/key-issues/fgm/
- Childline: www.childline.org.uk

Did you know?

Further sources of information on young people and substance misuse include:

- National Survey for Wales: https://gov.wales/statistics-and-research/national-survey/?lang=en
- Public Health Wales: http://www.wales.nhs.uk/.

Looked after children

There were 6407 looked after children in Wales at the end of March 2018. This was an 8 per cent increase on the previous year. Wales has a rate of 102 looked after children per 10 000 children aged 18 or under. This compares to a rate of 62 per 10 000 children in England.

Looked after children are typically living in one of the following settings:

- with foster parents
- in a residential children's home
- in residential settings such as schools or secure units.

A child may need to be looked after if there is no responsible adult to care for them (because of bereavement or they are an unaccompanied asylum seeker, for example), if their parents have requested or agreed to this (because of parent or child disability or illness, for example) or if the child is at significant risk of harm living within their family.

Looked after children and young people are a vulnerable group because of previous experiences of abuse or neglect, unstable relationships as they move in and out of care or between placements, or running away that puts them at greater risk of physical abuse, grooming and sexual exploitation. Compared with children in the general population, looked after children have poorer mental and physical health and lower educational attainment.

Did you know?

Sources of information on looked after children include:

- Children in Wales: http://www.childreninwales. org.uk/resources/looked-after- children/page/2/
- StatsWales: https://statswales.gov.wales/ Catalogue/Health-and-Social- Care/Social-Services/Childrens- Services/Children-Looked-After.

Children as carers

Young carers are children and young people under 18 years of age who look after a member of their family. This may be because their relative has a physical or mental illness, a substance misuse problem or is disabled in some way. A young carer may be responsible for cooking, cleaning, shopping, providing nursing or personal care or emotional support.

Young carers are a hidden group within the population of Wales. Welsh government figures from 2014–2015 show that there are only 741 young carers known to their local authorities. However, according to the 2011 Census, Wales has over 11 000 carers under the age of 18, caring, unpaid, for a friend or family member. This is the highest proportion of carers under the age of 18 in the United Kingdom.

Young carers can become isolated, with little relief from the pressures of being responsible for providing care at home and are less likely to experience a normal childhood. They are also likely to struggle educationally, worry about letting their family or the person they care for down, and are at risk of bullying for being 'different'.

Did you know?

Sources of information about children as carers/young carers include:

- Children in Wales: http://www.childreninwales.org. uk/resources/young-carers/
- Barnardo's: http://www.barnardos.org.uk/.

Case study

Daisy is 17 years of age and has been her mum's main carer for the last five years. Her mum has primary progressive multiple sclerosis. This causes her to feel tired and weak, gives her back, neck and joint pain, and prevents her from walking due to problems with balance and coordination. Daisy has learnt to be a very effective carer since her mum became unwell. She helps her mum to go to the toilet, use the shower and get dressed every morning. They take turns to cook and she always goes with her mum to the shops to buy food and other everyday items. Daisy does most of the cleaning and tidying at home, which takes up a lot of her time and energy. She doesn't get to see her own friends very often as she is either at home in case her mum needs her or is taking her out somewhere. Daisy managed to pass her GCSEs, despite missing a lot of school. She often feels that she has missed out on having a normal adolescence but still thinks it is important to do whatever she can for her mum.

▲ Daisy has a busy life caring for her mum.

1. Describe how being a carer might affect Daisy's social development during adolescence.

2. What kinds of emotional support would you expect Daisy to provide for her mum?

3. Explain why carers such as Daisy are described as a 'hidden' group in the Welsh population.

Check your understanding

1. List four health and well-being challenges facing children and young people in the Welsh population.

2. What is obesity and why is it a health challenge affecting children in Wales?

3. What is bullying and how can it affect a child or young person's health, development or well-being?

4. Explain why either looked after children or young carers in Wales face health, development and well-being challenges.

3.4 SUPPORTING A SUSTAINABLE HEALTH AND SOCIAL CARE, AND CHILDCARE SYSTEM IN THE 21ST CENTURY
7 Holistic health, development and well-being

Think about it

1. Make a list of activities or forms of exercise that have physical, emotional and social benefits.
2. How do you take personal responsibility for your health and well-being?
3. Explain how the everyday choices people make have an impact on their health and well-being in both the short and long term.

Key terms

Disease
An abnormal condition that negatively affects part of a person's body.

Illness
A form of sickness affecting the person's body or mind.

Holistic
Focusing on the whole person, physically, intellectually, emotionally and socially.

◄ Katrin takes responsibility for her personal health by focusing on activities that are good for her body, mind and spirit.

Approaches to health

'Health' can be understood in a number of ways. Unit 1 presented you with various definitions of health, both positive and negative. When health is defined in a positive way, healthy behaviours (eating a balanced diet, taking regular exercise and getting enough sleep) and characteristics associated with being healthy (feeling happy, physical fitness and being a healthy weight) are mentioned. When health is defined in a negative way, the focus is on the absence or lack of **disease** and **illness**. Both approaches can help us to understand what 'health' means and what 'being healthy' involves. However, using them hasn't prevented or been able to address the major health problems and challenges now faced by the population of Wales. To do this, the Welsh government believes that a more **holistic** approach to health is needed.

▲ Key aspects of living a healthy life.

The holistic approach to life

The holistic approach to health and well-being is a whole person approach that addresses the body, mind and spirit or the physical, emotional/mental and spiritual aspects of an individual and their interaction with the environment.

Traditionally, healthcare workers have specialised in particular areas of physical or mental health. This has resulted in them focusing on identifying problems (illness and disease) within a specific part of a person's body or mind. Physical health specialists have tended to ignore mental health issues and mental health workers have not paid too much attention to physical health issues. Increasingly, though, these two aspects of health are seen as closely linked. Health and social care workers are now trained and encouraged to consider the 'whole person' and to find out about all aspects of the individual's lifestyle and the environment in which they live to understand and respond to any health issues holistically.

Holistic health care

Holistic health care is an **integrated** approach to health care. It treats the 'whole' person, not simply symptoms and disease. Mind and body are seen as integrated and inseparable. Health and social care workers are now expected to do more than just identify and treat a specific ailment. They are trained to look at the various aspects of an individual's lifestyle and health issues, and to offer treatment and support that helps each person to reach their best possible level of wellness. The World Health Organisation (WHO) sums up this approach when it defines health holistically as:

> 'a state of complete physical, mental and social wellbeing, not merely the absence of disease or infirmity'. (WHO, 1946)

The holistic approach to health recognises that the human body can malfunction and become sick. However, instead of just focusing on treating the cells, organs or body systems that are affected, users of the holistic approach to health look for long-term, sustainable solutions that target the cause of the illness or disease rather than just the symptoms. It sees the mind and body as interlinked and the environment in which a person lives as a key influence on their health and well-being.

As well as changing the way practitioners in Wales think about and practise 'health' care, adopting the holistic approach should also affect the attitudes and health behaviour of people in Wales and the way healthcare services are organised and provided.

▲ The holistic approach to life recognises several interlinked aspects of human experience.

Key term

Integrated
Another term for linked or coordinated.

◄ Health services such as well women clinics adopt an holistic and preventative health approach to the 'whole person'.

Taking responsibility for personal health

Traditionally, people have taken 'health' for granted, assuming that they are 'healthy' and will be in future so long as they don't experience illness or disease. If this happened, going to see a GP or to hospital for **diagnosis** of the health problem and then receiving treatment were seen as the next steps. The limitations of this approach to personal health are:

- it is too passive – it falsely assumes that 'health' can be taken for granted and a person's lifestyle choices don't matter
- it assumes that illness and disease can be treated and 'health' will return
- it requires access to a range of good quality healthcare services
- it puts healthcare workers and services under pressure.

The rising costs and increasing demand for healthcare services in Wales means that services will not be sustainable unless people accept more responsibility for their personal health. The holistic approach to health provides a way of overcoming this, as it sees each person as an active participant in achieving and maintaining the best possible state of personal health and well-being. Everyday choices about diet, exercise, lifestyle and attitudes about what constitutes wellness are the responsibility of the individual. Healthcare workers take on the role of supporting people to make appropriate choices and to take responsibility for their well-being. When more people take personal responsibility for their health and well-being, fewer people need the help of care services.

The holistic approach to health also encourages a preventative approach that should reduce the risk of a person developing long-term health problems. Adopting a healthy lifestyle and making everyday choices (to eat well, to exercise, to maintain a healthy weight) that have a positive effect on health and well-being lowers the risk of chronic ill health. This reduces demand on healthcare services, makes waiting lists shorter and allows time and resources to be targeted at those most in need.

What is holistic health?

- Holistic health is not only concerned with the absence of disease, but also with a positive state of being.
- Real health involves the 'whole' person.
- Mind and body are integrated and inseparable.
- Holistic health treats the 'whole' person, not just symptoms and disease.
- Real health is not just the absence of disease, but is also a positive state of being.
- Real health is achieved with treatment of causes rather than symptoms, using natural and preventive approaches to health.
- Each person has a responsibility for their own health and must be an active participant in their own healing.

Key term

Diagnosis
The process of identifying an illness or disease.

The impact on services

The holistic approach to health will have an impact on the types of healthcare services that are provided in Wales. For example, services will focus on:

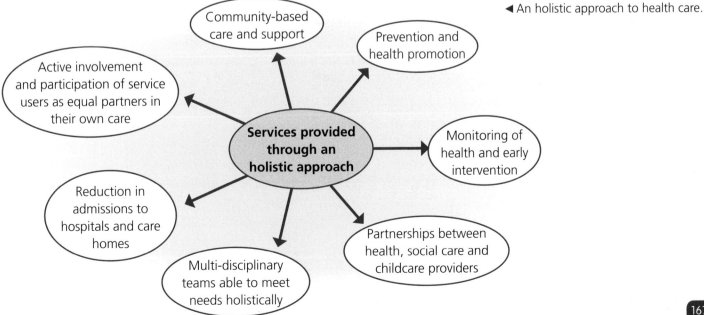

◄ An holistic approach to health care.

Health, social care and childcare services adopting an holistic approach to health will be based on partnerships between care organisations and agencies. They will need to involve individuals and communities in the co-production of services and find ways of activating people to take greater responsibility for their personal health. This will ensure that services across Wales are sustainable in the long term. This kind of innovation will also move them away from being a national 'illness' service dealing with high levels of sickness and chronic health problems to services that promote, support and help the population of Wales to experience a positive state of health.

▲ How could Dave change his lifestyle?

Case study

Dave Phillips is 32 years old. He works as a lorry driver for a livestock transport company. Dave spends long hours working, driving between farms and livestock markets around Wales. He describes his diet as 'terrible' and says that he does no exercise due to tiredness and lack of time. Instead, Dave's leisure time is spent drinking beer and eating crisps in front of the television. He has a few friends but rarely sees them. Dave hasn't been to see his GP for several years. He knows that he is overweight and unfit but says he is 'not ill, so there's no point' in having his health checked.

1. How would you describe Dave's approach to 'health'?

2. Give two reasons why Dave should adopt a more holistic approach to his health and well-being.

3. What everyday choices could Dave make that would improve his health and well-being?

Check your understanding

1. Using your own words, describe the 'holistic approach to life'.

2. Give two reasons why a person should not take their 'health' for granted.

3. Describe what a person could do to take personal responsibility for their health and well-being.

4. Explain, giving two examples, how the holistic approach to health affects the way services are provided.

8 What is happening in Wales?

◄ Wales faces health and social care challenges in the 21st century.

Think about it

1. How do you expect Wales (and the world) to change by the middle of the 21st century? Make a list of five ideas that come to mind.

2. What do you think needs to change in Wales to make it a healthier place to live?

3. What services or opportunities are there in your local area for people to improve their health and well-being?

Partnership working in Wales

We have seen that Wales faces a number of health, social care and childcare challenges. Whether this is due to the ageing population, rising obesity levels or to lifestyle issues associated with alcohol, exercise or illegal drug misuse, care systems in Wales are under pressure. The Welsh government has concluded that major change is needed to modernise health, social care and childcare services and make them sustainable in future.

Changing the way care services are provided in Wales is one of the key strategies for tackling the challenges faced. The use of **partnership working** and **multi-disciplinary teams** is at the heart of this. It involves closer working between NHS Wales, Local Health Boards, council social services departments and private and voluntary sector organisations. Legislation and Welsh government initiatives and programmes have been developed to make this happen.

Key terms

Partnership working
Collaboration and cooperation between different organisations to achieve a common aim.

Multi-disciplinary team
A group of care practitioners with different specialisms (doctors, nurses, social workers) working together to meet people's care needs.

Social Services and Well-being (Wales) Act 2014

This Act is designed to transform social care provision in Wales. It provides a legal framework for improving the well-being of all adults, children and young people who need social care and for carers who support them.

▼ The four values of the Social Services and Well-being (Wales) Act 2014 should influence all social care provision in Wales.

Values of the Act	Aims
Voice and control	The individual and their needs should be the main focus of their care with a voice in, and control over, any choices or decisions made to help them achieve well-being.
Prevention and early intervention	Preventative services within the community should be increased to minimise the escalation of people's needs.
Well-being	People should be supported to achieve their own well-being and the success of care and support should be measured.
Co-production	Individuals should become more involved in the design and delivery of services.

Assessment of needs

The 2014 Act changed the way an individual's social care and support needs are assessed. It introduced **proportionate assessment**, focusing on the individual. This is a simpler type of assessment focusing on what matters to the individual. The person's strengths and the resources they have to achieve their daily living goals are taken into account alongside problems that they have. Where a person has multiple or complex needs, one care worker can carry out an assessment on behalf of several agencies or organisations. This avoids the person having to go through repeated assessments. The 2014 Act also gave carers an equal right to assessment of their needs.

Integration of services

The Social Services and Well-being (Wales) Act 2014 says that local partnership boards consisting of representatives from the local authority (council), local health board and NHS Wales must be established to make integration of health and social care happen. Their role is to prioritise the integration of services in relation to:

- older people with complex needs and long-term conditions, including dementia
- people with learning disabilities
- carers, including young carers
- Integrated Family Support Services
- children with complex needs due to disability or illness.

The social care and support needs of a local population must be assessed by the local authority and health board for the area working together. Local authorities are also responsible for arranging preventative services that reduce the need for formal services. Bi-lingual information, advice and guidance on support and local services must also be made available in each local authority area.

▲ The Social Services and Well-being (Wales) Act 2014 sets the direction for providers of social care and support services in Wales.

Well-being of Future Generations (Wales) Act 2015

This Act also focuses on sustainability, well-being and modernising care services in Wales. The goal of this law is to improve the social, economic, environmental and cultural well-being of the people of Wales now and in the future. It requires public bodies (including Welsh Ministers, local authorities, Local Health Boards, Public Health Wales and NHS Trusts) to work together to improve the quality of life of people and communities in Wales over the long term.

To tackle the well-being challenges that the people of Wales face now and in the future, the Act requires public bodies to:

- apply sustainable development principles
- **implement** a well-being duty
- meet well-being goals.

Sustainable development principles

The Act refers to a 'sustainable development principle'. This means that the public body, such as a local authority or NHS Wales, must act in ways that meet people's needs now without damaging the ability of future generations to meet their own needs. To show that they have applied the sustainable development principle, a public body must:

- think long term, balancing what they want to do now with its future impact
- prioritise prevention, ensuring that problems don't occur or don't get worse
- identify integration opportunities, considering how their decisions will impact on their well-being goals or on other public bodies
- collaborate with others to meet their well-being goals
- involve and include others in a local area who have an interest in meeting the organisation's well-being goals.

Well-being duty
The 2015 Act places a well-being duty on public bodies in Wales. This states that each public body must set and publish 'well-being objectives' that help to achieve Wales's well-being goals (see below) and do its best to meet those objectives.

Well-being goals
Public bodies, such as local authorities, NHS Wales and Public Health Wales, must work to achieve each goal of the 2015 Act, not just one or two of them.

▼ The seven well-being goals of the Well-being of Future Generations (Wales) Act 2015.

Well-being goal	What does this involve?
A prosperous Wales	An innovative, productive and low carbon society which recognises the limits of the global environment and therefore uses resources efficiently and proportionately (including acting on climate change); and which develops a skilled and well-educated population in an economy which generates wealth and provides employment opportunities, allowing people to take advantage of the wealth generated through securing decent work.
A resilient Wales	A nation which maintains and enhances a biodiverse natural environment with healthy functioning ecosystems that support social, economic and ecological resilience and the capacity to adapt to change (for example, climate change).
A healthier Wales	A society in which people's physical and mental well-being is maximised and in which choices and behaviours that benefit future health are understood.
A more equal Wales	A society that enables people to fulfil their potential no matter what their background or circumstances (including socio-economic).
A Wales of cohesive communities	Attractive, viable, safe and well-connected communities.
A Wales of vibrant culture and thriving Welsh language	A society that promotes and protects culture, heritage and the Welsh language, and which encourages people to participate in the arts, and sports and recreation.
A globally responsible Wales	A nation which, when doing anything to improve the economic, social, environmental and cultural well-being of Wales, takes account of whether doing such a thing may make a positive contribution to global well-being.

The way that health, social care and childcare services are provided by public bodies such as local authorities and NHS Wales must contribute to achieving these well-being goals. The well-being duty requires each public body to say how they will do this.

Supporting the Well-being of Future Generations (Wales) Act 2015
The Act establishes a statutory *Future Generations Commissioner for Wales*, whose role is to act as a guardian for the interests of future generations in Wales, and to support the public bodies listed in the Act to work towards achieving the well-being goals.

Did you know?
The Auditor General for Wales and the Future Generations Commissioner both have a role in examining these goals.

Did you know?

Further information about this Act can be found in the Essentials Guide produced by the Welsh Government (https://gov.wales/docs/dsjlg/publications/150623-guide-to-the-fg-act-en.pdf).

▶ The Well-being of Future Generations (Wales) Act 2015 sets out well-being goals that aim to build a better future for people living in Wales.

Key term

Prudent healthcare
Doing less in a cautious way, to achieve better outcomes for patients in greatest need.

Did you know?

Making Prudent Healthcare Happen (http://www.prudenthealthcare.org.uk/) provides further information about the meaning of prudent healthcare and case studies that show how it affects people working in and using healthcare services in Wales.

The Act also establishes Public Services Boards (PSBs) for each local authority area in Wales. Each PSB must improve the economic, social, environmental and cultural well-being of its area by working to achieve the well-being goals.

Prudent healthcare in Wales

NHS Wales is the main provider of health services for the population of Wales. It has the difficult task of providing high quality services at a time when more people are using services and the costs of providing are increasing. NHS Wales has responded to this challenge by adopting the principles of **prudent healthcare**.

Principles of prudent healthcare

Prudent healthcare is based on the principle that health services and healthcare workers should:

* achieve health and well-being with the public, patients and professionals as equal partners through co-production

* care for those with the greatest health need first, making the most effective use of all skills and resources

* do only what is needed, no more, no less; and do no harm

* reduce inappropriate variation using evidence-based practices consistently and transparently.

The use of these principles to plan and deliver health care is an important way of modernising NHS Wales. Reducing waste, inefficiencies and unnecessary use of services is part of this process. Putting these principles into practice in hospitals, clinics and GP surgeries across Wales can then help to ensure that high quality and sustainable health services with improved outcomes can be provided for people living in Wales.

Government strategies, initiatives and programmes

Using legislation to introduce new ideas and change into the way care and support services are provided is an important part of the Welsh government's attempt to modernise health and social care provision. A range of other initiatives and programmes aimed at supporting sustainable health and social care, and childcare provision have also been developed in Wales.

Lifestyle advice and information

Information, advice and guidance on healthy living, as well as signposting to public health interventions and services is provided through initiatives such as:

Health Challenge Wales

Health Challenge Wales is a national initiative that focuses people on efforts to improve health and well-being. The key themes of this are:

- smoking
- obesity
- accidents and injuries
- alcohol and other substance misuse
- infections
- mental health and well-being.

The purpose of Health Challenge Wales is to help to improve people's health.

Beat Flu

Beat Flu is a campaign in Wales raising awareness of flu (influenza) and sharing information on the benefits of the annual flu vaccination. It provides information for children and adults as well as health and social care workers about flu, ways of minimising and managing it and immunisation campaigns.

Combined nutrition and physical activity programmes

A range of programmes that provide combined nutrition and physical activity interventions are delivered in key settings. These include:

Healthy Start Programme

The Healthy Start Programme is a voucher scheme for women who have young children or who are pregnant and receiving benefits. Healthy Start vouchers can be used to buy some basic foods, such as milk, fruit and vegetables and infant milk formula. Women who use the scheme are also given coupons to swap for free Healthy Start vitamins designed for pregnant and breastfeeding women and developing children.

Welsh Network of Healthy School Schemes

The Welsh Network of Healthy School Schemes (WNHSS) began in 1999 to encourage the development of local healthy school schemes across Wales. Local schemes are responsible for supporting the development of health-promoting schools within their area. Within the scheme, there are seven different health topics that healthy schools need to address. These include:

- food and fitness
- mental and emotional health and well-being
- personal development and relationships
- substance use and misuse
- environment
- safety
- hygiene.

Healthy schools can address these issues through teaching and learning, their policies and through staff development, for example.

Primary School Free Breakfast Initiative

This Welsh government initiative offers all children at a local authority maintained primary school a free breakfast. The aim is to increase healthy eating and reduce breakfast skipping among children from disadvantaged backgrounds.

Food and Nutrition for Childcare Settings

The Welsh government has produced food and nutrition guidelines for childcare settings across Wales. The purpose is to ensure that childcare services provide healthy food and drink so that children start school at a healthy weight. Young children who attend childcare settings may receive up to 90 per cent of their food and nutritional intake there if they attend.

Guidance on best practice

Information, advice and guidance on best practice approaches to getting fit, eating well and making lifestyle changes to improve health and well-being are provided through:

Dragon Multi-Skills and Sport

This Sport Wales initiative aims to improve the physical skills of seven- to eleven-year-olds, which are fundamental across a range of different sports. These are ability, balance and coordination (the ABCs). Every child develops at their own pace, so sessions are tailored to meet each child's individual needs. Children are introduced to and participate in a range of sports that support their physical development in a progressive way.

Community Food Co-operatives programme

The Community Food Co-operatives programme makes fresh fruit and vegetables available to local residents in Wales at very affordable prices and encourages local people to include them in their families' diets. There are around 300 community food co-ops across Wales. They operate in places such as schools, community centres, church halls, workplaces and many other different venues. They promote and provide access to healthy eating as well as a supportive network of people. Further information can be found at the Community Food Co-operatives website (http://www.foodcoopswales.org.uk/).

The Eatwell Guide

The Eatwell Guide is a United Kingdom-wide initiative that is designed to show how much of what we eat should come from each food group to achieve a healthy, balanced diet. Further information and can be found at the Eatwell website (https://www.nhs.uk/live-well/eat-well/the-eatwell-guide/).

Change4Life

Change4Life is also a United Kingdom-wide health promotion initiative that provides information, guidance and advice on healthy food, activity and weight. As well as providing nutritional information about food, it also includes healthy recipes and activity ideas for both children and adults. Further information and health improvement resources can be found at the Change4Life website (https://www.nhs.uk/change4life).

5x60

5x60 is a Sport Wales secondary school sport programme run by local authorities across Wales. The aim is to work with students, parents and local communities (including sports clubs and coaches) to create a range of sport and exercise opportunities for young people locally. A key principle of the programme is that the young people choose the activities themselves. Activities include:

- competitive sport
- informal activities, such as dance and aerobics
- coached activities
- outdoor activities.

Case study

Ieuan Evans is proud to be Welsh. He is 12 years old and supports the Wales football and rugby teams as well as his hero Geraint Thomas, the Welsh cyclist. Ieuan is a member of his local football team and has recently joined a cycling club. This keeps him busy and very active at weekends and when he goes to training session after school. Ieuan has learnt about the importance of a healthy lifestyle and being physically fit at school and at his sports clubs. He would really like to represent Wales at sport one day, but his current goals are to get into the school football team and to complete a long-distance cycle race.

1. List three Welsh government programmes that would help Ieuan to stay fit and healthy if he participated in them.

2. How is the sustainable development principle introduced by the Well-being of Future Generations (Wales) Act 2015 intended to benefit children in Wales like Ieuan?

3. Explain how Ieuan would benefit from going to a school that is part of the Welsh Network of Healthy Schools scheme.

▲ Ieuan leads a healthy, active life.

Check your understanding

1. Identify two laws that focus on improving the health and well-being of the Welsh population now and in the future.

2. Outline the four values that should influence social care provision in Wales.

3. Explain what is meant by 'prudent healthcare'.

4. Identify three government strategies, initiatives or programmes that have the goal of improving the health and well-being of people living in Wales.

3.1 Equality, diversity and inclusion to include Welsh language and culture

Respecting diversity and promoting equality and inclusion are important principles affecting the provision of healthcare, social care and childcare services in Wales.

Equality refers to individuals being equal in terms of status, rights or opportunities.

Diversity involves acceptance and respect for differences and an understanding that every individual is unique and valued.

Inclusion refers to the universal human right to participate equally, confidently and independently in everyday activities.

Equality laws, policies, procedures and codes of professional practice.

Some of the legislation that respects diversity and promotes equality and inclusion:

- The Equality Act 2010
- The Human Rights Act 1998
- The Mental Capacity Act 2005
- The Social Services and Well-being (Wales) Act 2014
- Additional Learning Needs and Education Tribunal (Wales) Act 2017

Providing and supporting opportunities to use the Welsh language in care settings is closely linked to equality, diversity and inclusion issues in Wales.

3.2 Safeguarding

Safeguarding

Safeguarding involves promoting healthy development, providing a safe environment, nurturing care and support and protecting all individuals from maltreatment.

Abuse, neglect and maltreatment can include physical, sexual, emotional and psychological abuse; financial exploitation; and neglect.

Abuse and neglect can affect a person's development, particularly their social and emotional development and mental well-being.

Safeguarding laws and policies

- The United Nations Convention of the Rights of the Child 1989
- The Human Rights Act 1998
- The Children Act 1989, 2004
- The All-Wales Child Protection Procedures 2008
- The Safeguarding of Vulnerable Groups Act 2006
- Social Services and Well-being Act (Wales) 2014
- Violence against Women, Domestic Abuse and Sexual Violence (Wales) Act 2015

Care organisations always have a safeguarding policy and a set of procedures for staff to follow to prevent, or respond to, safeguarding incidents.

3.3 Contemporary issues in health and social care, and childcare

Health challenges faced by adults and older people in Wales

An ageing population

Rising obesity levels

Mental health problems

Substance misuse problems

Achieving sustainable health, social care and childcare services

Health challenges faced by children and young people in Wales

Obesity Poverty Food poverty Bullying Radicalisation Substance misuse

3.4 Supporting a sustainable health and social care, and childcare system in the 21st century

Holistic health

Holistic approaches to health focus on the whole person (the body, mind and spirit) and their interaction with the environment.

The World Health Organisation (WHO) defines health holistically as 'a state of complete physical, mental and social wellbeing, not merely the absence of disease or infirmity' (WHO, 1946).

People who use an holistic approach take personal responsibility and a preventative approach to their health and well-being.

Partnerships and Prudent healthcare

The holistic approach to health requires prevention and health promotion services, partnerships between care agencies and the active involvement of service users in their own care.

Modernising care services in Wales through partnership working, prudent healthcare principles and the integration of health and social care services will make health, social care and childcare provision more sustainable in future.

4 Promoting and Supporting Health and Well-being to Achieve Positive Outcomes

This unit provides you with opportunities to gain knowledge and understanding of the way health and social care, and childcare services support individuals in Wales to achieve health and well-being.

This unit consists of four main parts:

4.1 How public health and social care, childcare and the National Health Service Wales (NHS Wales) have improved the health and well-being of the nation

4.2 How types of care can support individuals to achieve positive outcomes

4.3 Supporting self-identity, self-worth and sense of security and resilience across the life cycle

4.4 Meaningful activities to support and promote health, development and well-being

Each part of the unit has been broken down into shorter topics. These topics will help you understand how public health, social care and childcare services aim to meet the care, support and development needs of the whole population of Wales. You will also learn about the way different services are provided to meet the varying needs of individuals and client groups within the population. The unit will explore factors that contribute to positive self-identity and the role that meaningful activity plays in promoting and supporting health and well-being.

Assessment: A Non-Exam Assessment (NEA) that is composed of one task set by WJEC.

◀ Providing support is an important part of ensuring positive care outcomes.

Part 4.1 How public health, social care, childcare and NHS Wales have improved the health and well-being of the nation

Topic 1: Improving health in Wales

Part 4.3 Supporting self-identity, self-worth, sense of security and resilience across the life cycle

Topic 4: Understanding self-identity

Topic 5: Developing psychological security and resilience

Part 4.2 How types of care can support individuals to achieve positive outcomes

Topic 2: Care for all in Wales

Topic 3: Meeting individuals' needs

Part 4.4 Meaningful activities to support and promote health, development and well-being

Topic 6: Understanding meaningful activity

Topic 7: Planning and using meaningful activities

4.1 HOW PUBLIC HEALTH, SOCIAL CARE, CHILDCARE AND NHS WALES HAVE IMPROVED THE HEALTH AND WELL-BEING OF THE NATION
1 Improving health in Wales

Think about it

1. Make a list of three health or well-being services that are used by significant numbers of people in your area of Wales.

2. To what extent do you think individuals are responsible for ensuring that they are as healthy as they can be?

3. If you could get rid of one health problem in Wales, which one would you choose? Give your reasons why.

Tackling population health challenges in Wales

Unit 3 outlined health and well-being challenges faced by the population of Wales now and in the future. These included:

- an ageing population
- rising obesity levels
- increasing mental health needs
- sexual health issues
- growing child poverty.

Healthcare, social care and childcare organisations, agencies and practitioners have the task of tackling these health and well-being challenges. To make a significant difference to people's health and well-being experiences in Wales, service providers need to work together to deliver effective prevention, treatment and support strategies on these issues. This topic will focus on some of the ways in which this is happening.

▲ A wide range of NHS healthcare services is provided throughout Wales.

Ageing

Wales has an ageing population. By 2031, it is forecast that one in three people in the Welsh population will be over 65 years of age. The retirement age will have increased by then but some older people may still be able to enjoy a long period of retirement, support their own adult children and grandchildren and contribute to their local communities. However, as people age they are also at greater risk of falls due to physical **frailty**, may experience mental health problems due to isolation, loneliness or dementia, are at greater risk of poverty once retired and may feel frustrated at a lack of opportunities for development.

Ageing Well in Wales (www.ageingwellinwales.com) is a strategy designed to tackle the challenges presented by an ageing population. It involves public services, the **third sector**, the private sector, and national and local government working together to ensure that there is an improvement in the well-being of people aged 50+ in Wales. It recognises that older people are undervalued and that Welsh society must fundamentally change the way it thinks about older people and ageing.

Key terms

Frailty
Being weak, infirm and at greater risk of ill health and accidental injury.

Third sector
Another term for the voluntary sector, consisting of independent, not-for-profit organisations.

179

► Themes and aims of *Ageing Well in Wales*.

Theme	Aim
Age-friendly communities	To make Wales a nation of age-friendly communities.
Falls prevention	To support older people to reduce their risk of falling, reducing the number of falls amongst older people in Wales.
Dementia supportive communities	To make Wales a dementia supportive nation by building and promoting dementia supportive communities.
Opportunities for learning and employment	To ensure the experience of older people in Wales is optimised through continued learning and employment.
Loneliness and isolation	To reduce levels of loneliness and isolation and their negative impact on health and well-being as experienced by older people in Wales.

Ageing Well in Wales sets out to help older people to retain their independence and health for as long as possible. It has a preventative focus designed to allow older people to continue to be economically and socially active and to take personal responsibility for their health and well-being.

A range of public, private and voluntary sector services exists to meet the health, housing and well-being needs of older people in Wales. Some of these are national services, such as NHS Wales primary and secondary healthcare and local authority social work services. There are also examples of smaller, local services such as support groups, Dementia Friend initiatives and befriending services in local communities.

Obesity

Wales has an obesity problem affecting children and adults. Almost 12 per cent of children and 25 per cent of adults had a body mass index (BMI) that classified them as obese in 2015. This raises the risk of a range of health problems, including diabetes, heart disease and cancer. Adult obesity can also reduce a person's well-being, quality of life and ability to work and earn a living. Concern about rising obesity levels and their consequences has led to the development of a range of Welsh government anti-obesity initiatives and programmes, including:

- *Climbing Higher: Next Steps* (Welsh Assembly Government, 2006): resulting in a nutrition and physical activity network aiming to secure a better, fitter and healthier Wales.

- *Walking and Cycling Action plan* (Welsh Assembly Government, 2009): summarising the key steps to develop a walking and cycling culture in Wales.

There are two main strategies or approaches to tackling obesity in Wales: prevention and management.

Prevention of obesity	Delivered by
Health education initiatives	Schools
Health promotion campaigns	NHS Wales primary healthcare settings
Nutrition-related programmes	NHS Wales secondary healthcare settings
Fitness-related activities	Private sector providers

Management of obesity	Delivered by
Surgery	NHS Wales primary healthcare settings
Medication	NHS Wales secondary healthcare settings
Psychological therapies	Private sector providers

Social prescribing of exercise, sport and other physical activities by healthcare practitioners is also part of the preventative approach to obesity. Only the prevention strategy can influence the rising levels of obesity in Wales. Once a person has become obese, the strategy of managing that obesity through clinical treatments attempts to reduce the impact on the person.

Mental health

Awareness of mental health problems has grown in Wales and the rest of the United Kingdom over the last decade. A person's mental health is now seen as being equally as important to their physical health and well-being. In fact, it is now recognised that these two aspects of health and well-being are interlinked. Despite this, there are still high levels of **stigma** surrounding mental health issues. Many people avoid talking about their mental health difficulties and avoid seeking help because of this. Tackling the stigma associated with mental health difficulties and enabling people to access help and support early, and when they require it, is essential to improve the mental health of the Welsh population.

Time to Change Wales is a national campaign that aims to change attitudes to mental health problems in Wales. It does this through a range of mental health awareness campaigns, events and projects that encourage people to recognise, acknowledge and support people with mental health difficulties.

Many local groups and organisations run *Time to Change Wales* awareness-raising events across Wales and the campaign also works with schools, colleges and youth organisations to break down the stigma surrounding mental health difficulties. This kind of preventative, public health activity is complemented by a range of NHS Wales assessment and treatment services for people experiencing mental ill health as well as private and third sector social support services for people living with mental health difficulties.

Sexual health

The World Health Organisation (WHO) defines sexual health as '…a state of physical, emotional, mental and social well-being in relation to sexuality; it is not merely the absence of disease, dysfunction or infirmity'. The number of people attending sexual health clinics has doubled in Wales since 2012. Sexual health services, relating to contraception, abortion and sexually transmitted infections for example, are inconsistent across Wales.

Most sexual health services are provided by NHS Wales primary and secondary care organisations. There are some voluntary organisations, such as the Terrence Higgins Trust (https://www.tht.org.uk/our-work/our-campaigns/sexual-health-wales), that also provide sexual health education, counselling and testing services and support for people with sexual health issues. Sexual health education is also provided in schools and colleges.

Key terms

Social prescribing
A means of enabling GPs, nurses and other primary care professionals to refer people to a range of local, non-clinical services that have health and well-being benefits.

Stigma
Disapproval or discrimination against a person based on negative ideas about their social characteristics or personal qualities.

Did you know?

Public Health Wales provides information and advice about sexual health through the Frisky Wales website (http://www.friskywales.org/). It also publishes data and statistics about sexually transmitted infections on their website (www.wales.nhs.uk) every three months together with an annual report.

Tackling child poverty

Reducing the number of people who live in poverty is a priority for the Welsh government, local authorities and other public and third sector agencies in Wales. Poverty is a persistent problem in Wales and is difficult to tackle. The high level of child poverty in Wales is a problem that government and other health, education and social welfare agencies have been trying to address.

We saw in unit 3 that the Save the Children charity reported that approximately 1 in 3 children in Wales is living in poverty (see page 153). The Welsh government's *Flying Start* programme for families with children under four years of age living in disadvantaged areas of Wales is one way in which the causes and impact of child poverty are being tackled.

▶ The *Flying Start* programme.

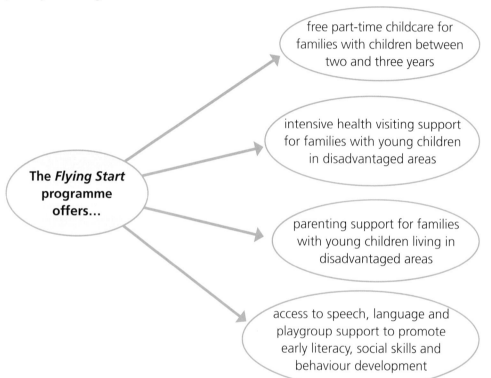

The *Flying Start* programme offers...

- free part-time childcare for families with children between two and three years
- intensive health visiting support for families with young children in disadvantaged areas
- parenting support for families with young children living in disadvantaged areas
- access to speech, language and playgroup support to promote early literacy, social skills and behaviour development

In addition to the *Flying Start* programme and the work of specialist public sector teams to deliver support to vulnerable families in disadvantaged areas of Wales, voluntary sector organisations such as Save the Children, Barnardo's and Children in Wales run campaigns and provide support services for children and families living in poverty. In addition, small local charities and faith groups often provide targeted support for members of their communities experiencing poverty.

Case study

Paula Thomas, aged 44, works as a carer in a nursing home for older people. She has recently been to see her GP about her general health problems. Paula's GP took some health measurements and asked about her lifestyle.

Height	– 1.63m
Weight	– 88.9kg
Resting pulse	– 125/minute
Blood pressure	– 200/135
Cigarettes	– 10 per day
Alcohol	– 40 units per week
Exercise	– None
Diet	– Eats a lot of burgers and chips

▼ How can Paula get help?

Paula also explained that she is having difficulty sleeping and has been feeling low in mood for the last six months. This is one of the reasons why she drinks alcohol every day. She has been too worried about what others would think to tell anybody about her mental health difficulties.

1. Which of Paula's health measures are a cause for concern?

2. Identify two health challenges that Paula has in common with many other Welsh people.

3. Describe two examples of initiatives, programmes or strategies that aim to help people such as Paula with their health challenges.

Check your understanding

1. List three ways in which the Welsh government's *Ageing Well in Wales* strategy aims to tackle the challenge of an ageing population.

2. Describe two examples of anti-obesity strategies that are being used in Wales to address this health and well-being problem.

3. Explain the term 'stigma' and describe how the *Time to Change Wales* programme is addressing this to improve mental health in Wales.

4. Explain what the *Flying Start* programme is and what its purpose or goal is in Wales.

▲ Foster carers such as Sarah and Bryn provide an alternative family environment for children like Daniel who cannot live with their own parents.

Think about it

1. List three local services that you have used and describe how they helped to meet your health and well-being needs.

2. Identify and describe two examples of services that are available to support pre-school children (and their parents) in your local area.

3. What health, social care and support services do you associate with the needs of older people?

Types of care and support

This topic builds upon your knowledge of health and social care, and childcare service provision gained in unit 1. You will develop your knowledge and understanding of the different types of care available within the services and how these types of care meet the needs of individuals across the life cycle.

Health, social care and childcare services are provided throughout Wales for people with physical and mental illnesses, physical disabilities and sensory impairments, as well as those with learning disabilities and developmental and social support needs. Some of these services are **statutory services**: national organisations, such as NHS Wales and local authorities (councils). Others are provided by small, local organisations that are part of the **private sector** or **voluntary sector**. You can probably think of health, social care and early years or childcare services in your local area. There may be a hospital, health centre, family doctor service, a playgroup, a nursery or a residential home near to where you live, for example.

Care and support for children in the early years

Infants and young children have a range of expected health, care and development needs. These include services that monitor and promote health, well-being and development. Some examples are shown in the table below.

Service	How does it provide help?
Health visitor services	Monitoring and providing support for growth and development, including feeding advice, assessing child growth and development needs, supporting young children with special needs
GP (family doctor) services	Health monitoring, diagnosis, treatment or specialist referral for more serious health problems
Nurseries and playgroups	Providing opportunities for play, early learning and language development
Child minders and crèches	Childcare for babies and younger children
Social work services	Assessing needs, investigating allegations of harm, abuse or neglect and referral to other agencies for intervention and support
Paediatric emergency and specialist services	Specialist healthcare services for babies and younger children who have medical problems or long-term healthcare needs

◄ Services available to promote the well-being of infants and young children.

Care and support for children and young people

Older children and young people (adolescents) have many similar health, care and development needs from younger children. As a result, primary healthcare services may be provided through GP (family doctor) practices and local hospitals that have a paediatric department.

Social work services are provided for children and young people in all local authority areas, focusing on safeguarding. Children and young people who are identified as 'at risk' of harm or abuse or who are unable to live with their parents or birth family for other reasons may be referred to **foster care** or **residential childcare** services following assessment by a specialist child protection social worker.

Key terms

Primary health care
Those parts of the health service, such as general practitioners, that deal with every day, nonemergency healthcare needs.

Secondary health care
Healthcare services that are generally provided for people with more complex or emergency care needs in hospital or residential settings.

Reablement
The active process of regaining skills, confidence and independence after a significant period of illness or a traumatic injury.

There are many local sports and activity-based clubs throughout Wales that aim to meet the health, development and well-being needs of children and young people. Examples in your local area might include football, rugby, swimming or other sports clubs. In addition, groups such as the Girl Guides and Scouts, Woodcraft Folk and Urdd Gobaith Cymru provide opportunities for children and young people to develop the physical, intellectual, social and emotional aspects of themselves whilst making a contribution to their communities.

Care and support for adults and older people

As we saw in unit 1, there are different types of healthcare services for adults and older people in Wales. These include:

- **primary care** services that diagnose and treat less serious, short-term health and illness issues or provide monitoring and treatment for **chronic**, longer-term health problems that can be managed outside of hospital. Primary healthcare services are provided in the community through local health centres, dental practices and opticians, for example.

- **secondary care** services that diagnose and treat **acute**, more complex and serious health and illness issues in larger, more specialist local and regional hospitals or specialist clinics.

Primary and secondary healthcare services also promote healthy lifestyles and provide health education services aimed at preventing people from developing illnesses or serious conditions in the first place. Information and advice about sexual health, stopping smoking, exercise and healthy eating are all examples of this.

Reablement services, staffed by healthcare support workers and occupational therapists, provide an important bridge between healthcare services and independent living. They support adults and older people to learn and re-learn mobility and daily living skills after experiencing a period of illness or injury. Reablement services are particularly important in helping and supporting older people and people who have long-term health problems and disabilities to leave hospital and return home so that they can regain independent living skills. They can involve providing personal care and hygiene, support with daily living activities such as shopping, cooking, feeding, and supporting the individual with general household tasks in the person's own home.

Adults and older people who are unable to live independently or who require ongoing support because of long-term health or social care needs may benefit from using community-based services such as:

- day care services that provide activity-based social care and opportunities to meet and spend time with others

- supported living in warden-controlled or sheltered accommodation where a person is able to live independently but with regular monitoring and support

- adult placement/shared lives services, which are a form of supported living but within the homes of individuals and families who are able to provide support for a vulnerable person

- residential care homes where an individual is supported and cared for in a group setting with other people over a relatively long period of time

- respite care.

People with long-term healthcare or **palliative care** needs are likely to require nursing care, either within a residential setting such as a **hospice**, nursing home or through a nursing service that visits them at home. People with degenerative, or worsening, conditions, such as dementia, tend to be cared for in nursing homes because they have a wide range of physical and mental health needs that can't usually be addressed in their own home.

Informal care

Informal care is care and support provided by partners, relatives and friends on a voluntary basis. A variety of informal care services are provided by a very large number of unpaid people in Wales. They look after their partners, children, relatives, friends or neighbours who have care needs. Because they are not trained, employed or paid to provide care, these people are known as informal carers.

Key terms

Palliative care
Care treatment and support for people with a life-limiting condition.

Hospice
A care setting providing palliative and supportive care to people in the final stages of life.

Case study

Stevie is 27 years of age and has Down's syndrome. Stevie's condition has affected his health and personal development throughout his life and will mean that he has lifelong care and support needs. Dr Hill is Stevie's GP. He works at a local NHS Wales health centre. Alison Rasheed is a learning disability social worker, employed by the local authority. Alison organises and monitors the special education and social care services that Stevie uses. Stevie attends the Stepping Stones day centre three days each week where he takes part in a range of education and leisure activities. The centre is run by MENCAP (Wales), a voluntary organisation. Stevie's parents also pay for him to attend a riding school that provides classes for people with learning disabilities. Stevie is still very reliant on his parents for day-to-day care and support. They provide practical and emotional support in a variety of ways to encourage Stevie to develop his daily living skills.

1. Which services and professionals look after Stevie's healthcare needs?

2. Which of Stevie's needs are met by attending Stepping Stones day centre?

3. Which of the services mentioned is part of the private sector?

4. What type of care do Stevie's parents provide for him?

▲ Stevie has access to a range of support services.

Check your understanding

1. Identify three examples of care or support services provided in Wales for infants and young children.

2. What is palliative care and where is it usually provided?

3. Explain what the main purpose of reablement care is.

4. Where are primary healthcare services usually provided – at a GP practice or at a local hospital?

3 Meeting individuals' needs

▼ Terry, aged 80, and his six-month-old great-grandson Oliver, both require help and support to meet their health and care needs.

► Different health and development needs.

Think about it

1. Make a list of the physical care and development needs a healthy six-month-old baby has.

2. Describe two examples of social or emotional support needs an older person such as Terry might have.

3. Apart from age, what other factors do you think affect a person's care and development needs?

Individuals' needs across the life cycle

Health, social care and childcare services in Wales are provided to meet the physical, intellectual, emotional and social needs of individuals in all life stages. Before we consider the types of services that are available to do this, it's important to understand the care, support and development needs that people have across the human life cycle.

Human needs across the life cycle

Human beings of all ages have a wide range of general health and development needs.

Type of needs	Examples of needs
Physical needs	• A balanced diet and sufficient fluids
	• Warmth
	• Shelter
	• Exercise
	• Sleep and rest
	• Good hygiene
	• Protection from harm, illness and injury
Intellectual needs	• Interesting and purposeful activities
	• Learning opportunities
	• Mental challenges and new experiences
Emotional needs	• Love, support and care
	• A sense of safety and security
	• Self-confidence and self-esteem
Social needs	• Attachment to a trusted carer
	• Relationships with other people
	• A sense of identity and belonging within a community

A person's physical needs must be satisfied in order for them to be physically healthy. A person's intellectual needs are the things they require to develop their knowledge, thinking skills and mental abilities. A person's emotional and social needs are the things they require to develop relationships and experience emotional well-being and good mental health.

In addition to these P.I.E.S needs, health, social care and childcare workers also recognise that at all stages of the life cycle, people have safety and spiritual needs. Safeguarding focuses on protecting and supporting children, young people and adults who are vulnerable to maltreatment or harm. An individual's spiritual needs are personal to them, focus on meaning (what is important) in their life and on any faith and beliefs they have. Spiritual needs are usually met through prayer, religious rituals (going to a church, mosque or synagogue, for example) or by possessing religious objects (for example, a crucifix) or wearing particular clothes (for example, a hijab).

Changing and overlapping needs

Whilst all human beings have a common range of P.I.E.S needs, a person's needs change and vary across the life cycle. This is because a person's needs, and their ability to meet them:

- change as people age and move from one life stage to another
- are affected by experiences of health, illness and disease
- are influenced by cultural issues and beliefs
- may differ according to gender
- are affected by an individual's living circumstances.

Health, social care and childcare workers recognise that the P.I.E.S, safety and spiritual needs people have are all interconnected and overlap. For example, an older person or a young child may have a safeguarding or safety need because they are unable to independently meet their basic physical need for nutrition. This could be because they also have unmet intellectual needs – for example, they haven't yet learnt how to make food or feed themselves, or have a form of dementia or confusion that means they have forgotten how to do so.

Focusing on client groups

Care organisations recognise that whilst everyone has physical, intellectual, emotional and social needs there are important similarities and differences between groups of people. These groups of people are referred to as **client groups**. For example, babies and children have similar health and development needs. However, these are quite different from the health and development needs of adolescents or older people, two other client groups in different life stages. As a result, care organisations tailor their services to meet the particular healthcare, social care and developmental needs of each client group.

Some of the services that are provided for a client group are **universal services**, such as general health care provided by GPs. These services are suitable for all members of the client group. However, care organisations such as the NHS also develop **targeted services**, such as child and adolescent mental health services and adult spinal rehabilitation services, for members of client groups who have particular care and development needs.

> ### Did you know?
> It is good practice for health, social care and childcare workers to adopt an holistic approach that sees the individual as a whole person with multiple needs.

> ### Key terms
>
> **Client groups**
> Groups of people who have the same types of problems or care needs.
>
> **Universal services**
> Health and welfare services provided for everybody within the population.
>
> **Targeted services**
> Services developed and provided for a group of people with specific care needs.

Personalising care and support

All care and support for people using health, social care and childcare services should be person-centred. This involves placing the individual at the centre of all decisions about their care and support. Any care or support should meet the particular needs of the individual rather than the service. In practice this involves:

- using an holistic approach to assessing the individual's needs
- supporting the individual to express their own needs and preferences
- co-producing a care plan or package of support with the individual
- supporting the active participation of the individual in their own care and support
- care and support staff working in ways that recognise the person's beliefs and preferences
- paying attention to the detail of the person's care and support.

Infants' care needs

Infants have a wide range of care needs because they are vulnerable and dependent on others for their survival and development.

▶ Care needs of healthy infants with normal development.

Care needs	Purpose of care	Ways of meeting care needs
Physical care	Provision of basic physical care and protection	• Assistance with feeding • Being washed/cleaned regularly • Having nappies changed • Being dressed • Receiving vaccinations to prevent infections • Having physical health monitored • Having personal safety monitored and safeguarded
Intellectual stimulation	Development of basic thinking and language skills	• Stimulating toys and books to play with • Being read stories or rhymes and sung to • Encouragement to babble and make sounds
Emotional support	Establishing basic attachment relationship	• Consistent, emotionally responsive relationship with a parent or carer • Reassuring, soothing and comforting response when upset
Social support	Development of relationship and interaction skills	• Attachment relationship with a parent or carer • Regular contact with parents or other carers • Opportunities and encouragement to play

Did you know?

A range of specialist health and early years practitioners are provided to meet the specific or additional care needs of infants. Examples of these are outlined in Unit 4, Topic 2.

Children's care needs

Compared with infants, children are more physically robust and have a range of physical skills that enable them to be more independent. As a result of physical, intellectual, emotional and social development, an individual's care needs change throughout childhood. The care needs of a five-year-old child are likely to be very different from those of a nine-year-old because of this ongoing development. Care in childhood focuses on encouraging development and increasing a child's capabilities.

Care needs	Purpose of care	Ways of meeting care needs
Physical care	Provision of physical care and protection to enable further development to occur	• Encouragement to eat a balanced diet • Provision of warmth and shelter • Help and encouragement to wash and dress • Opportunities and encouragement to exercise and develop physical skills • Regular rest and sleep • Protection from harm
Intellectual stimulation	Stimulation and support of intellectual abilities to develop knowledge, understanding and skills	• Play opportunities • Educational support and encouragement to learn basic reading, writing and numeracy skills • Books to read, television to watch, music to listen to • Friends and adults to learn from and talk to
Emotional support	Building self-confidence, emotional security and self-esteem	• Supportive parents or carers to provide love and affection • Respect and feeling of being valued by parents, friends and other adults • Opportunities to have fun, feel happy and express own feelings • Encouragement and positive feedback from parents, teachers and others, which boosts self-esteem
Social support	Supporting development of social skills and relationships	• Help and support to develop friendships with other children and safe relationships with adults outside of the family • Opportunities to play and learn alongside other children • Opportunities to experience a range of social activities and events • Development of basic organisational skills to deal with everyday activities

◄ Care needs of healthy children with normal development.

▶ Care needs of healthy adolescents with normal development.

A child may have additional or specific care needs because they experience:

- problems with their physical or mental health
- difficulties with learning, behaviour or relationships with others
- social or financial problems affecting their family.

Adolescents' care needs

Care in adolescence focuses less on directly meeting basic needs and more on providing opportunities, encouragement and support so that the individual can gradually take on the responsibility of meeting their needs independently.

Care needs	Purpose of care	Ways of meeting care needs
Physical care	Maintenance of good physical health and well-being to support growth and development through puberty	• Encouragement to eat a balanced diet • Shelter, physical security and warmth • Encouragement and facilities to ensure good personal hygiene • Opportunities and encouragement to be physically active and to exercise
Intellectual stimulation	Stimulation and extension of intellectual skills and abilities	• Education and learning opportunities • Opportunities to work and train in areas of interest • Stimulating books, music and television • Opportunities to talk and explore ideas and beliefs with others
Emotional support	Provision of supportive relationships to enable development of personal identity, self-confidence and self-esteem	• Supportive relationships with parents or carers to provide love and affection • Friendships that are supportive and stimulating • Respect and feeling of being valued as a capable person by parents, friends and other adults • Opportunities to have fun, feel happy and express own feelings • Encouragement and positive feedback from parents, teachers and others, which boosts self-esteem
Social support	To promote sense of belonging and social inclusion	• Active and supportive circle of friends • Opportunities to socialise with others • Opportunities to take part in leisure activities and meet new people

As in childhood, an adolescent may develop additional or specific care needs because they experience:

- problems with their physical or mental health
- difficulties with their learning, behaviour or relationships with others
- social or financial problems affecting their family.

Adults' care needs

Adults have largely completed their physical growth and developed many of the skills, abilities and attributes that they will make use of throughout the rest of their life. As a result, an adult's care needs tend to focus on maintaining and refining the different aspects of their health and well-being.

Care needs	Purpose of care	Ways of meeting care needs
Physical care	To maintain physical health and well-being and minimise effects of ill health	• A balanced diet and adequate fluids • A warm, safe place to live • Good hygiene • Opportunities to exercise • Sleep and rest • Access to health facilities
Intellectual stimulation	To provide a focus for using and developing intellectual abilities	• Stimulating work or other occupation • Stimulating relationships with others • Access to books, television, music, etc. • Learning opportunities and educational guidance and support
Emotional support	To achieve and maintain fulfilling and stable personal relationships, positive self-esteem and personal identity	• Love and support from close relationships (partner, family, children) • Respect from and feeling valued by others • A sense of personal identity • Independence and opportunities to make own decisions • Stable and fulfilling personal relationships
Social support	To establish and maintain a social network and an active social life	• An active and supportive circle of friends • Opportunities to take part in social activities • Opportunities to enjoy leisure activities

◄ Care needs of adults.

An adult may develop additional or specific care needs because they experience:

• problems with their physical or mental health

• difficulties in their personal or work relationships

• social or financial problems.

Older peoples' care needs

Later adulthood is the final stage in an individual's life. It is also a stage in which an individual's care needs are likely to increase. Many older people are very healthy and live active, enjoyable lives. However, the loss of physical and sensory abilities and the reduction in a person's social network as they retire from work and see less of old friends is a feature of many older people's lives. As a result, the care needs of older people tend to focus on using support, services and adaptations to maximise independence, maintain an active lifestyle and minimise the effects of illness and ageing.

▶ Care needs of older people.

Care needs	Purpose of care	Ways of meeting care needs
Physical care	To maximise physical health and well-being and minimise ill health and disabling effects of ageing	• Housing that provides warmth, shelter and safety • A balanced diet and adequate fluids • Provision of mobility support and assistance • Glasses / hearing aids / other **prostheses** • Opportunities to be physically active and to exercise • Access to health facilities
Intellectual stimulation	To maintain and use intellectual capabilities in ways that are stimulating and interesting	• Learning opportunities • Stimulating activities and hobbies • New experiences • Opportunities for reminiscence • Books, TV, magazines and newspapers • Conversation
Emotional support	Maintenance of supportive relationships, self-esteem and strong personal identity	• Supportive and loving relationships with partners, friends and family members • Being treated with respect and dignity by others • Being given opportunities to make choices and to be as independent as would wish • Stable relationships
Social support	To maintain social network and active social life	• Contact with friends and relatives • Opportunities to socialise • Participation in leisure activities

Key term

Prostheses
Artificial body parts that replace or supplement a missing or defective part.

Case study

Mrs Price is 80 years of age in March. She lives alone in a large house. She was married for 50 years until her husband Denis died two years ago. Since that time her physical and mental health and her memory have deteriorated. Mrs Price has no other family. She receives two home care visits each day to provide personal care and support at meal times. She really looks forward to seeing the home care workers each day as she rarely goes out and often doesn't see anybody else.

1. Identify three examples of physical care needs that Mrs Price requires help with.

2. Describe how the home care workers help to meet Mrs Price's physical, social and emotional care needs.

3. Explain how ageing is likely to have affected Mrs Price's care needs over the last 20 years.

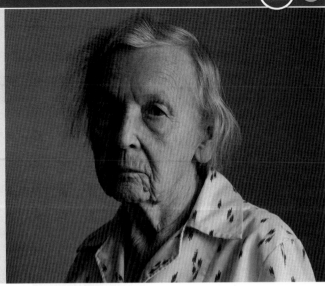

▲ Care needs can become more complex with age.

Check your understanding

1. List three examples of physical needs that all human beings have.

2. Describe how an infant's intellectual development needs could be supported by a parent or childcare worker.

3. How do the social development needs of children differ from those of adolescents?

4. Outline three ways the emotional support needs of older people can be met.

▲ Establishing a self-identity is one of the challenges of puberty and early adulthood.

Key terms

Self-identity
An individual's view of themselves, which is usually influenced by personal perceptions of their own abilities, flaws and status and by feedback received from others.

Self-worth
An individual's sense of their own value or worth as a person.

Self-image
A mental picture a person has of themselves, their abilities and attributes compared to those of others.

▶ Attachment relationships and bonding with parents lay the foundation for emotional security.

Think about it

1. Write five statements beginning with 'I am…' to express some things about your current self-identity.

2. How do you think your friends and classmates would describe you, as a person?

3. Describe the main influences on your sense of self-identity. Are these influences people or other factors?

What are self-identity and self-worth?

A person's **self-identity** is their view of who they are. It is continually developing during each life stage and is closely linked to emotional and social development. A person's self-identity expresses what they think and feel about themselves as an individual. It is important to have a clear sense of self-identity as this gives each of us a sense of our place in the world.

A person's self-identity is a combination of their **self-worth** and their **self-image**. Self-worth often comes from the way we compare ourselves to other people. People who think they are not as good, not as attractive or not as capable as others are more likely to have low self-worth. People who are confident but not arrogant, who accept that they have both strengths and weaknesses, and who feel encouraged, loved and wanted, tend not to undervalue themselves so much. Their self-worth is generally higher as a result.

Factors affecting self-identity and self-worth

A variety of factors influence self-identity and self-worth. Other people, particularly parents, siblings and friends, play a very important role in the way an individual's self-identity and self-worth develop during infancy, early childhood and adolescence, for example. Psychological processes, such as **attachment** and **bonding**, and social processes such as socialisation have been identified as important in shaping a person's self-identity and self-worth during these early life stages.

Age

The self-identity that you have today will not be the same self-identity that you reflect on when you are 40, 60 or 80 years old. The physical, intellectual, emotional and social changes that occur as you age and mature will affect your self-identity over time. For example, a person's self-image can be linked to the view that they have of their physical capabilities. Your physical capabilities will change as you experience health, fitness, illness and disability at different points in your life. The value that society attaches to you as an individual will also alter as you grow older. In Western societies, old age is generally viewed negatively and older people seem to be less valued than younger people. This is sometimes different for members of minority ethnic groups who may value old age more. The way that people of different ages are portrayed in the media confirms this and inevitably affects the self-identity of many older people.

Appearance

A person's physical features, their clothes and their non-verbal behaviour all influence and express aspects of their self-identity. How we present ourselves and how we believe others see us are particularly important influences on self-image and self-worth when we are adolescents and young adults. As we get older, physical appearance and the way that we present ourselves tend to have a smaller impact on our self-identity.

Gender

Gender refers to ideas about masculinity and femininity that are applied to men and women in our society. Wider social attitudes towards gender can shape a person's self-identity. In Western societies there are a number of **gender stereotypes** associated with male and female roles and behaviour. The images of men and women presented in the media question these stereotypes and the general social expectations of men and women in society.

Gender stereotypes do not reflect the reality of most people's lives in Wales, but they can still shape a person's self-image and self-worth. This can occur in a positive way where a person is able and wishes to conform to stereotypical roles, appearance and ways of behaving. On the other hand, gender stereotypes can have a negative effect on self-identity and self-worth where the person is unable or unwilling to match up to the expectations of men or women in a particular situation. Where this occurs, gender stereotyping can result in guilt, a sense of inadequacy and lack of self-confidence.

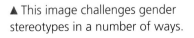
▲ This image challenges gender stereotypes in a number of ways.

Culture

A person's self-identity is shaped by their sense of belonging to an ethnic group as well as by the beliefs, values and way of life associated with their religion and culture. Culture and ethnic identity can, for example, strengthen a person's self-identity and give them a positive sense of self-worth where they are accepted and feel part of a community. However, it can also lead to people being treated differently, perhaps in an unfair and discriminatory way, where they are part of a religious, cultural or ethnic minority. This may then affect the person's sense of self-identity and self-worth if they feel they don't belong or are not fully accepted for who they are by members of the majority culture.

Emotional development

An individual will generally become more emotionally mature as they age. Growing maturity allows a person to become more reflective and accepting of themselves. This can mean that as people grow older they come to recognise both their personal strengths and their limitations. This is likely to occur from adolescence onwards as a person experiences puberty and develops emotionally and socially. For example, emotional maturity and self-knowledge play an important part in an individual's ability to establish and maintain close personal relationships, friendships as well as working relationships with others.

Education

Educational experiences can have a major impact on a person's self-identity. The things that teachers and fellow students say, and the way that they treat us, can affect our self-image and self-worth during childhood and adolescence. We are very open to suggestions about who and what we are during these life stages. For some people, educational success helps them to form a positive self-image and promotes self-worth. For others, school can be a more negative experience that leaves them feeling less capable than others, or with a negative view of themselves and their self-worth.

Relationships

The relationships that an individual has, especially within their family, during education and at work, will have a powerful effect on their self-identity. Family relationships, in particular, play a critical role in shaping our self-identity.

▶ There are many different types of relationship.

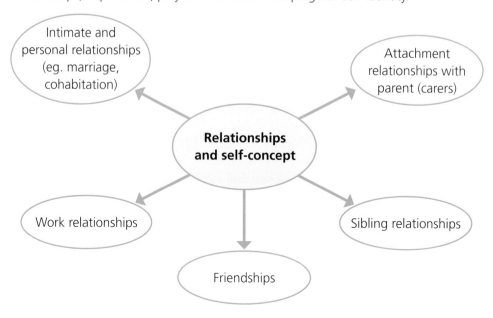

Early relationships are built on effective attachments to parents and close family members. The sense of security and feelings of being loved that can develop from these bonds are key ingredients in a positive self-identity. Poor family relationships, however, can do lasting damage to a person's self-identity and self-worth.

We go through a number of phases of emotional and sexual development during adolescence and adulthood, as we experience new friendships and more intimate relationships with non-family members. These experiences affect our self-identity. Simply because we grow older and become more emotionally mature, we also tend to adapt our outlook and behaviour towards others to take account of the thoughts and feelings that other people have. For example, a couple who may both have had a strong image of themselves as young, free and single individuals learn new things about themselves and have to adapt their self-identities when they form an intimate, long-term partnership or get married.

Sexual orientation

A person's sexual orientation refers to their preference for either a same-sex or opposite sex partner. Whilst some people identify themselves as heterosexual (attracted to the opposite sex), others identify themselves as lesbian or gay (attracted to the same sex), or bisexual (attracted to either sex). We tend to first become aware of our sexual orientation in adolescence, although many people remain uncertain about, experiment with or change their sexual orientation during adulthood. A person's sexual orientation will have a significant impact on their self-identity and on their social and emotional development.

Men's gay relationships were illegal in the United Kingdom until 1967. Lesbian relationships have never been illegal in the United Kingdom, although social disapproval and unfair discrimination against people who had same-sex partners, whether male or female, was widespread until the late 20th century. However, social attitudes have changed significantly, so a person's sexual orientation is now much less of an issue in most situations. This does not mean that prejudice and social disapproval about same-sex relationships has disappeared and many people still struggle to 'come out' about their homosexuality. Gay and lesbian adolescents and young people are particularly vulnerable to bullying and intimidation from peers if they declare their sexual orientation. Therefore, many choose not to 'come out' until they are older and are able to find support from a group or community of people who understand their interests, needs and concerns.

Life experiences

A person's self-identity develops over time, adapting and changing as the individual develops through different life stages, and experiences different life events and relationships with others. The way that you look at yourself and feel about your place in the world is affected by expected and unexpected life events. Some of these, such as finding a loving partner, being successful at your exams or growing up in a supportive family, are life experiences that shape self-identity and boost self-worth in a positive way. However, life experiences can also be negative and even traumatic, where a person is abused, experiences a serious disease or is bereaved when a loved one dies unexpectedly. These life events can also have a powerful influence on self-identity and self-worth. Life experiences, for many people, are a mixture of positive and negative events. It is the balance of these events, and the way the individual responds, that has a lasting effect on self-identity and self-worth.

▲ Natasha is struggling with her self-identity and self-worth.

Case study

Natasha Lloyd is 23 years old. She has been thinking about herself and her life recently. Natasha has worked in the same day centre since leaving school at 18, which she now regrets. In particular, she felt left behind when her school friends all moved away to start university. Natasha enjoys her job as a team leader but feels she should have achieved more in life. The long hours she works stop Natasha from socialising very often. In fact, she rarely sees people outside of work. Many of Natasha's friends have also got married over the last few years. She is disappointed that she hasn't found a partner yet but can't see why anyone would be attracted to her. Natasha thinks she looks 'plain and a bit overweight'. She has started to think that her life is not as good as those of other people her age, especially when she looks at her friends' social media pages. Natasha looks at herself in the mirror each morning, wondering how she got into this situation, wishing she could change the way that she feels about herself and her life.

1. How would you describe Natasha's self-identity?

2. How would you describe Natasha's self-worth?

3. Explain why Natasha's self-identity is likely to change as she moves through adulthood.

Check your understanding

1. Identify the two main elements or parts of self-identity.

2. Describe three factors that affect the development of an individual's self-identity during childhood and adolescence.

3. Explain how gender can influence a person's self-identity during adulthood.

4. Give two examples of negative life events that can have an impact on the development of an individual's self-identity.

5 Developing psychological security and resilience

What are psychological security and resilience?

A person's mental health and emotional well-being are an important part of their holistic health. To develop and function well, we all need to experience **psychological security**. This is a feeling of basic safety and confidence that you will be okay or are not threatened. It is something that most people do develop and then take for granted as feeling psychologically and emotionally secure becomes their 'normal' way of being. People who, for various reasons, are psychologically insecure, are likely to have difficulties with their mental health and emotional well-being.

Resilience is a psychological quality that helps a person to withstand stress and change in life, even though they may feel under a lot of pressure and struggle to cope. We all have some level of resilience. However, some people are more resilient than others and also make more use of the resilience they have when they experience a tragedy, **trauma**, natural disaster, health concern, relationship, work issue, or a problem at school. A person with good resilience can bounce back more quickly and with less **stress** than someone with less well-developed resilience.

▲ Calum has confidence in his ability to tackle challenges and any difficulties that occur at school and in his personal life.

Key terms

Psychological security
The absence of fear or distressing anxiety.

Resilience
The ability to adapt to and deal with a crisis or difficulty and return to normal afterwards again.

Trauma
A deeply distressing or disturbing experience.

Stress
Physical or mental tension caused by threats, difficulties or challenges to the person's coping skills.

▼ Resilience is needed to overcome personal difficulties and physical challenges.

Developing psychological security

We can all develop psychological security given the right circumstances and support. A person's early relationships in infancy and childhood are particularly important for this. Attachment to a parent or carer provides the foundation, or first building block, for the development of psychological security.

During infancy and childhood, we are vulnerable and dependent on the support, love and protection of others, particularly our parents or carers. To promote social and emotional development, the relationship we have with a parent or carer should be nurturing, secure and consistent. Importantly, this provides the right conditions for feelings of trust and security to develop. It is the beginning of a lifelong process of becoming aware of your 'self', developing self-identity and self-worth, and learning to trust others.

A person's emotional development, and sense of psychological security, also needs to be supported and promoted during childhood and adolescence. Parents, siblings, teachers and friends all play a part in this process by offering love, acceptance and respect. This boosts an individual's self-confidence and continues to shape and support their self-understanding and psychological security as their development progresses through puberty.

The effects of psychological insecurity

Unfortunately, not everyone is lucky enough to be brought up by caring, nurturing parents whom they learn to trust. There are various reasons why a person may feel insecure in their relationships with others, including lack of care, experiences of trauma and abuse, and being neglected by those who ought to be supporting them. This can damage a person's ability to form and maintain relationships, may result in anxiety and other mental health difficulties and can affect a person's emotional, social and intellectual development more generally.

Similarly, traumatic, unexpected life events such as serious illness, the death of a partner, parent or sibling, or being the victim of violent crime, for example, can damage a person's sense of psychological security. Events or experiences such as these can challenge and undermine the taken-for-granted assumptions a person made in their relationships with others. Instead of being able to automatically trust other people, they may become very cautious, anxious and avoidant of people they don't know or places and circumstances they are unfamiliar with.

◄ Insecurity can lead to loneliness, isolation and lack of self-confidence and has a long-term effect on social and emotional development.

Achieving security and resilience

Psychological security and resilience are qualities that can be learned and developed at any age, regardless of a person's circumstances, level of education or family background. It is beneficial to achieve and be able to maintain these qualities earlier rather than later in life, as they make dealing with life's challenges and difficulties easier.

Individuals of all ages can be supported to achieve and improve their sense of security and resilience, along with their self-identity and self-worth. These are all developed by active participation and involvement in physical activity, sport, hobbies and interests, and group activities, for example. Any activities that are meaningful to the person and which promote and empower the person's independence, self-help skills and decision-making will boost their sense of psychological security and levels of resilience. Successful participation in chosen activities and the achievement of personal goals will help the person to believe in their ability to influence and control important aspects of their everyday life and relationships.

> **Did you know?**
>
> The circumstances, experiences, and issues and challenges we face will all change over time and will, in turn, affect our levels of psychological security and resilience.

Case study

Kieran Goff, aged 42, is a solicitor. He has never been unemployed. Kieran worked part-time in shops and on building sites whilst he was studying to become a solicitor. He is very proud of his employment record and of the high status that his job gives him. This is particularly important for Kieran because he comes from an estate where very few people went to college or university, and where over half of the men are unemployed at any one time. Kieran was determined to escape from this situation. He believes that he has succeeded in life because he worked very hard, was very determined and never gave up on achieving his goals. Kieran still sets himself challenges and says that he is 'driven to succeed'. He believes that he can do most things if he sets his mind to it.

1. Does Kieran seem like a psychologically secure or insecure person? Explain your answer.

2. What evidence is there that Kieran is a resilient person?

3. What kinds of challenges did Kieran have to overcome to achieve his goals in life?

▲ Persistence, effort and taking on challenges builds resilience.

Check your understanding

1. List three personal characteristics that you think a psychologically secure person would have.

2. Using your own words, explain what 'being resilient' involves.

3. Briefly explain how a person can develop resilience.

4. How can psychological insecurity affect a person's health and well-being?

▲ Listening to music, dancing and having fun are all great ways to boost well-being.

Think about it

1. Give three reasons why you think people, like those in the picture above, enjoy dancing.

2. Describe two non-work activities or hobbies (other than dancing) that you like taking part in and the reasons you do them.

3. Suggest three leisure activities that an older person living in your part of Wales could take part in and benefit from.

Key term

Meaningful activity
Activity that enables a person to achieve a goal and meets one or more of their needs.

What are meaningful activities?

Activities are meaningful when they have a practical purpose or are chosen by an individual because they are fulfilling their needs in some way. Without us realising it, **meaningful activities** play an important part in our lives and our sense of identity.

When people are fit and healthy, they can usually carry out a range of meaningful activities (washing, dressing, shopping, cooking) to meet their everyday living needs. For example, you probably did a lot of different activities to get yourself ready for, and then go to, school or college this morning. You probably also choose to take part in activities that you find enjoyable, such as hobbies, sports or playing music.

The activities that we undertake as part of our everyday lives, both the practical, self-care and daily living activities and the ones we choose to take part in because we enjoy doing them, enable us to meet our physical, intellectual, emotional and social needs. As a result, being able to carry out and take part in meaningful activity is important for maintaining a person's health, development and well-being.

Using meaningful activities to help people

Health, social care and childcare workers often use meaningful activity as a way of promoting and supporting the development and well-being of the children, young people and adults they work with. Creative and **therapeutic** activities are used to meet a variety of physical, intellectual, emotional and social needs in different types of care setting, for example. In Wales, it is important that activities are used and provided in ways that follow the Social Services and Well-being (Wales) Act 2014. This requires that activities should:

- support individuals to achieve well-being
- allow individuals to have an equal say in the support they receive
- prevent escalating need.

The benefits of creative and therapeutic activity

Creative and therapeutic activities are used in health and social care settings to:

- help people to acquire, improve and practice a range of physical and intellectual skills and abilities
- enable people to explore and express feelings they may not be able to put into words
- provide opportunities for people to socialise and form relationships with others.

Creative and therapeutic activities can be used to meet an individual's physical, intellectual, emotional or social needs.

Did you know?

Health, social care and childcare workers need to have a good understanding of how a range of creative and therapeutic activities can be used as part of an individual's care.

Key term

Therapeutic
Another word for healing.

▼ Activities used in health and social care settings.

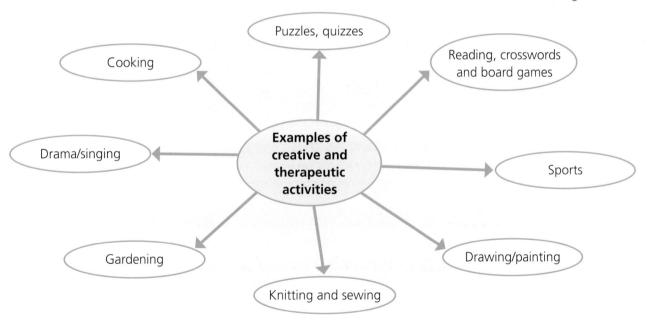

Key terms

Mobility
The ability to move freely in a coordinated way.

Dexterity
Skill in performing tasks, especially with the hands.

Stroke
The sudden death of brain cells due to a lack of blood flow (and oxygen) to the brain when an artery is blocked or ruptured. Loss of speech, weakness and loss of use of limbs on one side of the body may result.

► All of these activities have physical benefits.

Physical needs and benefits

People who use health and social care services often do so because they have physical health problems and physical care needs. These include, for example:

- **mobility** problems resulting from painful joints, fractures or conditions that cause physical weakness
- **dexterity** problems resulting from stiff or damaged muscles and inflamed tendons
- balance and coordination problems resulting from tremors and other involuntary muscle movements
- circulatory and respiratory problems that result in fatigue, breathlessness and lack of stamina
- weakness or paralysis of limbs as a result of **strokes**, brain injury or accidents
- loss of a limb as a result of an accident, infection or cancer, for example.

People who have physical needs may use creative and therapeutic activities as a way of:

- learning new physical skills (for example, the development of gross motor skills, the development or improvement of fine motor skills)
- reducing the symptoms of their physical or mental health problems (for example, reducing anxiety, improving cardiovascular health)
- maintaining, adapting or improving their existing physical skills (for example, dexterity) or movement abilities
- maintaining or improving their physical and hand–eye coordination
- maintaining or improving physical strength and fitness.

Cooking, movement, exercise, horse-riding and team games can all be used to help people learn new physical skills and promote their physical fitness, for example. People with learning disabilities or mental health problems are sometimes encouraged to take part in team games such as football or outdoor, adventure activities, such as long-distance walking, climbing and camping trips, to promote both their physical health and their social skills.

Exercise and movement programmes using a gym or a suitable outdoor area are increasingly being prescribed as treatment for people who have heart or respiratory problems. **Occupational therapists** and **physiotherapists** also use adapted equipment and exercise programmes to help stroke patients practise and relearn basic physical skills such as walking, going to the toilet and holding cutlery.

Intellectual needs and benefits

People who have learning disabilities or brain injuries caused by accidents, drug or alcohol misuse or by conditions such as Alzheimer's disease have **cognitive** problems and intellectual care needs. These include, for example:

- problems with confusion and memory loss

- learning difficulties that result from conditions such as Down's syndrome

- mental health problems that can cause distress, problems with decision-making, and difficulties with motivation, concentration and communication

- communication and language problems that can result from brain injuries caused by having a stroke, a head injury or by misuse of drugs and alcohol.

People who have intellectual care needs may use creative and therapeutic activities as a way of:

- learning new thinking, problem-solving or language skills

- regaining lost skills

- becoming more organised and independent

- maintaining, adapting or improving existing thinking, concentration and memory skills

- expressing their thoughts and imaginative ideas.

Playing computer games, card games and board games, reading and doing crosswords or other puzzles all help people to develop and use their cognitive skills and can help to meet an individual's intellectual needs.

Emotional needs and benefits

People who experience physical illness, mental distress or social problems are also likely to have a range of emotional needs. These can be the result of:

- relationship breakdown or the loss of loved ones

- loss of health, skills or abilities as a result of a condition, illness or negative life event

- low self-confidence and poor self-esteem as a result of being unwell or less capable than previous

- mood swings and marked changes in behaviour as an unwanted effect of medication or treatment

- hopelessness, depression or anger in response to the frustration of not getting better.

▲ Walking groups and 'green gym' activities are a sociable way of getting older people to take exercise.

Key terms

Occupational therapist
A care professional who helps people to take part as independently as possible in activities (occupations) that benefit their health and well-being.

Physiotherapist
A care professional who treats physical injury or movement problems with exercises and other physical treatments (such as massage).

Cognitive
Related to thinking, reasoning and remembering.

► Activities such as crosswords are easy to organise and can be intellectually stimulating and the focus of social activity in a care setting.

People who have emotional care needs may use creative and therapeutic activities as a way of:

- learning how to explore, control and express their feelings
- developing or boosting their self-esteem, self-concept and feelings of security
- maintaining, adapting or improving their motivation and coping strategies
- expressing distressing or troubling thoughts and feelings
- developing new interests, relaxation abilities and enjoyment of life.

Expressive art activities such as drawing and painting or playing with sand and water, making pottery, singing, performing music or taking part in drama are all activities that can be used to help people to release and express their feelings.

Social needs and benefits

People have social needs when they lack relationships, become isolated or don't have the skills needed to establish and maintain good relationships with others. People who use health and social care services may also have social needs because they:

- feel lonely, isolated and frightened when they are admitted to a care setting where they don't know anyone else
- have a poor or broken relationship with members of their family or they lack supportive friends
- have a mental health problem, learning difficulty or a condition such as Alzheimer's disease that makes trusting and communicating with other people difficult.

Creative and therapeutic activities such as drama, music, dance as well as taking part in group games and craft activities can be used to provide people with opportunities to:

- meet, cooperate and interact with others
- develop friendships and social relationships
- become part of supportive social networks.

▲ Activities can be used to bring people together and give them opportunities to use their social and emotional skills.

Which activities work best?

There are a lot of factors to take into account when assessing what type of activity might be beneficial for a person. For example, a health, social care or childcare worker would require a very good understanding of an individual's needs, strengths, abilities and preferences to work out the type of activities that would be meaningful and beneficial for the person. In addition, they would also need to consider whether:

- an individual or group activity would be most beneficial
- an indoor or outdoor activity would be preferred and be most beneficial
- the activity would need to focus on one of the individual's needs in particular or on multiple needs at the same time
- the activity is appropriate for the person's developmental life stage and age group.

Case study

Jayne Marshall is an occupational therapist working at Ty Arberth, a day centre for older people. Most of the people who use the day centre have a diagnosis of dementia or depression. Jayne and her colleagues use a variety of different creative activities in individual and group sessions with the people who attend Ty Arberth. The activities currently on offer include painting and drawing, pottery, knitting and making soft toys. Many of the people who attend also like to take part in cookery sessions, making cakes and lunchtime meals. Jayne also supervises a walk around the local park once a week. The people who come on the walk use this as an opportunity for exercise, take photographs of trees, birds and park scenes, and sometimes have a picnic if the weather is good. Jayne tries to encourage conversation and friendships between the people in all of the groups she runs. She has noticed that this has a positive effect on some people's confidence and can lift their mood if they are feeling down.

▲ Trying out a variety of different activities can have a beneficial impact on everyone.

1. Identify an example of the P.I.E.S benefits associated with three of the creative activities that are on offer at Ty Arberth.

2. Describe two important care values that Jayne should use when undertaking creative and therapeutic activities with the people who use Ty Arberth.

3. Explain how Jayne tries to support inclusion when she uses creative activities with people at Ty Arberth.

Check your understanding

1. Using your own words, explain what a 'meaningful' activity is.

2. Give an example of a meaningful activity that has physical benefits for the person taking part, briefly describing what these benefits are.

3. Explain how meaningful activities could help people experiencing mental health problems.

4. Describe a meaningful activity that could have multiple (physical, intellectual, emotional or social) benefits for participants.

7 Planning and using meaningful activities

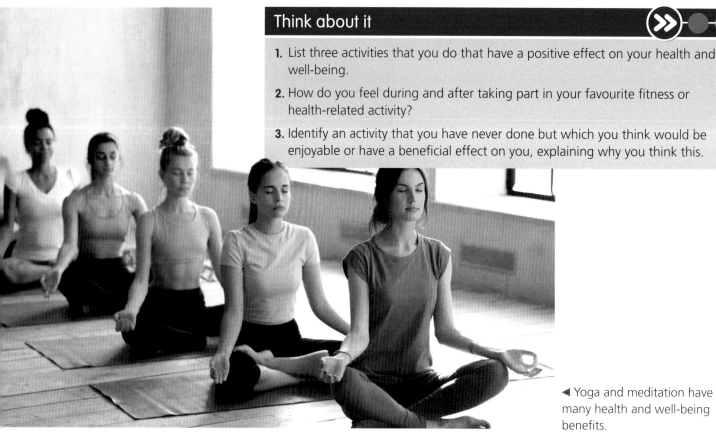

◀ Yoga and meditation have many health and well-being benefits.

Planning and using meaningful activities for health, development and well-being

Health, social care and childcare workers should have good reasons for using activities as part of a person's care, support or development plan. They should have a good understanding of what type of activity the person would like to try, for example. In addition, activity planning must take account of:

- legal and health and safety factors
- the needs of the individual or group involved.

Legal and health and safety issues

Recreational, creative and therapeutic activities have many potential benefits for people who use care services. However, there are also some **hazards** and **risks** involved in providing and taking part in these activities. Health, social care and childcare workers who use activities as part of people's care and support need to know about and work within a range of safety-related laws, **regulations** and guidelines that are designed to protect people from harm. These laws and regulations can affect, for example, the way that potentially **toxic** art and craft materials such as paints, glue and other chemicals, can be used and stored in a care or educational setting.

Key terms

Hazard
Anything that can cause harm.

Risk
Exposure to danger, harm or loss.

Regulations
Detailed legal rules.

Toxic
Poisonous.

Assessing individual and group needs

Health, social care and childcare workers who use activities in care and education settings have to plan this carefully. One of the first tasks is to assess the care, development or support needs of an individual to ensure that participating in particular activities is appropriate and beneficial for them. Health and social care workers should focus holistically, considering an individual's physical, cognitive (intellectual), social and emotional needs as well as the ways in which they are all linked.

▼ Assessment of the individual when planning meaningful activities.

Physical needs: stage of physical growth and development, fitness, mobility, balance problems, any requirements for assistance or support

Sensory needs: hearing or visual impairment, speech or communication problems, assistance, support or specialist equipment

Learning disabilities: will affect ability to make decisions, establish relationships, communicate and be independent

A care worker needs to assess

Developmental needs: may affect physical and communication skills and intellectual abilities

Social isolation: may be less able or willing to participate in some recreational or creative activities if there are few sources of support

Communication needs: speech or hearing problems; may not be using first language; any requirements for support

◄ Art activities can have social benefits when people meet regularly and feel part of a group.

Activities that meet an individual's needs, which help them to learn, maintain or regain skills or which improve their relationships or self-esteem, are likely to be beneficial and therapeutic for the person.

Choosing activities

In addition to assessing an individual's care, support or developmental needs, a health, social care or childcare worker should consider factors that are likely to have an impact on the person's preferences, and suitability, for different types of creative activity.

The type of setting

The type of care or education setting in which an individual lives (as an in-patient or resident) or attends during the day affects the types of activity that can be provided there. For example, general hospitals have few outdoor facilities. However, there may be specially designated rooms for art and craft or other creative activities and even a gym or fitness room where some forms of therapeutic exercise can take place. By contrast, a day centre, nursery school or children's playgroup centre may have specially designed and equipped rooms and safe outside spaces where activities ranging from cookery and art to woodwork and using physical equipment can take place.

Potential benefits

In the previous topic we saw how meaningful activities can have physical, intellectual (cognitive), emotional and social benefits for an individual. A health, social care or childcare worker should analyse both the individual's needs and the potential benefits of an activity before they suggest or select it as part of a person's care, support or learning. There will be a clear benefit to the individual if the activity enables them to develop, improve or regain any physical, intellectual, emotional or social skills or abilities.

Co-production and active participation

People should be involved in choosing, creating and actively participating in activities to ensure that they are meaningful and beneficial. Co-production is about involving people impacted by services in the design and delivery of those services. This requires an equal partnership that values the skills, strengths and expertise of both parties.

An individual's interests and preferences for taking part in particular activities are probably the most important factors affecting choice. It is bad practice to choose activities for an individual without consulting or fully involving them. Ignoring what the individual would like to do in favour of what you would like them to do is also likely to be counter-productive as they may not wish to participate in or be motivated by *your* choice of activities. The person has to be genuinely motivated for the activity to have any benefit for them. This means that they:

- have to want to do it

- can see the benefits for themselves

- are likely to enjoy the activity and are capable of actively taking part.

Health, social care and childcare workers often have to provide information and sometimes offer encouragement and support before people have enough confidence and motivation to suggest and take part in recreational, creative and therapeutic activities that are meaningful to them.

Age

An individual's age may affect their interests, skills and abilities. Younger children and older adults who have dexterity or mobility problems may find certain activities (such as yoga, cookery or horse-riding) difficult. However, they may be more interested in other activities because they better match their age and stage of development. Many activities, such as music, cookery and art, can be adapted and presented in age-specific ways so that they are appropriate for an individual's age-related level of ability, knowledge and interest.

Abilities

An individual's physical and intellectual abilities may affect their opportunities and motivation to take part in some creative and therapeutic activities. For some people, this occurs because they have not yet developed the abilities that are needed to read, play music or use computers, for example. However, other people who have physical disabilities or learning difficulties may find it difficult to participate in creative activities because of their specific physical or intellectual needs. In these circumstances, activities and equipment may need to be adapted to enable an individual to participate. An assessment of an individual's abilities should be carried out before any activities are suggested or used as part of their treatment plan.

▲ Wheelchair basketball is a demanding and tiring sport that requires and develops physical abilities as well as other thinking and teamwork skills.

Communication skills

Communication skills are essential to establish good relationships and enable interaction between people. An individual's age, intellectual ability, sensory impairment or cultural background could affect their ability to communicate with others. Children and people with learning disabilities tend to have less well-developed communication skills than adults, for example. A person who is not using their first language may also require communication support in order to participate fully in some creative activities that rely on speech and the use of language.

Culture

A person's cultural background affects their values, lifestyle and beliefs. A person's gender can affect how they think about and manage physical contact with other people. Culture and gender may influence, for example, the way a person uses or reveals their body, and their expectations about touch and proximity. Massages from someone of the opposite sex, swimming or exercise classes may be unsuitable for men and women who hold certain religious beliefs, for example. Similarly, cooking may be a therapeutic activity if it enables an individual to prepare, cook and eat food that expresses their cultural identity. It is always important to assess whether an activity, or the way it is presented and run, could offend an individual because of their gender or cultural background.

Gender

How is a person's gender likely to influence the types of activities in which they are interested and feel motivated to take part? It is important not to **stereotype** men and women, but males are more likely to want to participate in football than flower arranging, for example. Similarly, many girls and women may be drawn to art, cooking and yoga in a way that many (but not all) men are not. It is important to get to know an individual's needs and preferences for different types of activities because it is possible that they may not conform to expected gender patterns. Nevertheless, the way an activity is presented or carried out should take account of gender differences so that one gender isn't put off or excluded from taking part.

Health and fitness

Some recreational, creative and therapeutic activities require a higher level of health and fitness than others. Many people who are frail or unwell can carry out activities that require little physical strength or stamina, such as listening to music, watching television or reading a book. However, more strenuous activities such as taking part in sport, swimming or even walking around a local park may be too difficult and not advisable for people who have mobility and physical health problems. Assessing the physical demands of an activity is an important part of the **risk assessment** process.

Key terms

Stereotype
Apply a simplified, over-generalised expectation.

Risk assessment
A careful examination of what could cause harm to people.

Resources and facilities

The nature of a care setting is likely to affect the resources and facilities that are available for activities. Some care settings allocate rooms and staff time, and purchase equipment and other resources to support recreational, creative and therapeutic activities. In other settings, such as residential homes and hospitals, areas of the care setting (such as a lounge or kitchen area) may need to be adapted or used occasionally for these activities. It is important to find out what resources and facilities are available before discussing or planning any activities for people.

Time and cost

The amount of time needed to participate in a creative or therapeutic activity may affect how appealing it is to people. Activities that fit into people's everyday routines (for example, knitting, crochet) or which are relatively short (for example, playing cards, chess) are usually more appealing than those that require a lot of preparation (for example, pottery, dress-making) or which disrupt everyday life (for example, long walks, visiting the theatre). Similarly, activities that are free or low cost are more accessible than those that require people to spend money to participate (for example, buying tickets to watch plays or films).

Did you know?

Health and social care organisations will often only have a very small budget for activities, so it is important to think about cost early in the planning process.

Key term

Implement
Put something into practice.

▼ The steps to a successful meaningful activity.

Step 1 – Matching an individual with an activity

- Identify an individual and describe their needs.
- Identify a creative or therapeutic activity for them.
- Describe the benefits to the individual of participating in the activity.

Using meaningful activities in practice

The best way to learn how to plan using meaningful activities as part of a care or learning plan is to actually do it! To demonstrate that you are able to select, plan and **implement** activities for an individual or group you will need to undertake several linked tasks. These include:

- carrying out a risk assessment to identify and minimise potential hazards and risks to those who will participate in the proposed activity
- planning and explaining how you would carry out the creative activity in a health or social care environment, including identifying any equipment or assistance required
- evaluating the effectiveness of your planned activity in terms of how well it met the needs of the individual or group involved and recommending any improvements that could be made.

You should consider a range of issues. It is best to work through the tasks identified above in stages so that your preparation is thorough, person-centred and considered. Avoid trying to plan or carry out activities that are very ambitious, require specialist or expensive equipment or depend on participants having a lot of time or a high level of skill or ability. Remember that the aim of any recreational, creative or therapeutic activity is always to meet the participants' health, well-being or development needs.

Step 2 – Planning the activity

- Outline how you will carry out the activity.
- Identify any materials or resources needed.
- Decide when and for how long the activity will run.
- Identify and deal with any health and safety issues.

Step 3 – Carrying out the activity

- Obtain tutor and workplace consent to run the activity.
- Implement your planned activity.

Step 4 – Evaluating the activity

- Describe what went well and what didn't.
- Explain how well the activity met the individual's needs.
- Describe how you would change or improve the activity or your approach to it.

Case study

Edward is three years old. He attends the Stepping Stones pre-school nursery for two and a half hours twice a week. Edward's mum was reluctant to enrol him at first but was persuaded by a neighbour that Edward would benefit from attending. Edward really loves going to the nursery and looks forward to meeting his new friends, playing with a variety of different toys and games, and painting. He particularly likes listening to stories read by the nursery teacher or one of the nursery nurses. Since starting at the nursery six months ago, Edward has become more self-confident, talks a lot more and has learnt a lot of different things. When asked what he likes best about the nursery, Edward always says, 'my friends who play with me'.

1. Identify two creative or therapeutic activities that Edward takes part in at the nursery.

2. Analyse one of these activities and explain, using P.I.E.S, the benefits this could have for Edward.

3. What have been the main social benefits of attending the nursery for Edward?

▲ Edward enjoys going to pre-school and experiencing a variety of activities.

Check your understanding

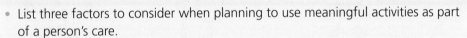

- List three factors to consider when planning to use meaningful activities as part of a person's care.

- Describe factors that should be taken into account when assessing an individual's needs as part of activity planning.

- Explain what co-production means and how this makes using meaningful activities more effective in care settings.

- Explain why it is important to carry out a risk assessment when planning to use meaningful activities as part of care.

4.1 How public health, social care, childcare and NHS Wales have improved the health and well-being of the nation

Population health challenges in Wales

An ageing population

Rising obesity levels

Increasing mental health needs

Sexual health issues

Growing child poverty

4.2 How types of care can support individuals to achieve positive outcomes

Types of care provision

Health, social care and childcare services are provided throughout Wales by statutory, voluntary and private sector organisations and agencies.

Services are designed to meet the health, social care and childcare needs of different client groups.

Client groups include infants, children and young people, adults and older people.

Primary, secondary and specialist care services are provided across Wales to meet a wide range of everyday and specialist healthcare needs.

Informal care is care and support provided by partners, relatives and friends on a voluntary basis.

Meeting individual care needs

 A person's physical, intellectual, emotional and social needs change across the lifespan.

 Changing healthcare needs are influenced by age, gender, culture and beliefs, circumstances and a person's previous health experiences.

 Services that are provided for a client group may be universal or targeted services.

 Care provision should always be personalised and holistic.

4.3 Supporting self-identity, self-worth, sense of security and resilience across the life cycle

Population health challenges in Wales

Self-identity refers to an individual's view of themselves whilst self-worth refers to the sense they have of their own value or worth as a person.

Factors that influence self-identity and self-worth include age, appearance, gender, culture, emotional development, education, relationships, sexual orientation and life experiences.

Psychological (attachment and bonding) and social (socialisation) processes play an important part in shaping self-identity and self-worth in early life.

Self-identity and self-worth continue to develop and change throughout life.

Psychological security

- Psychological security is a feeling of basic safety and confidence that you will be okay or are not threatened.
- People who are psychologically insecure are likely to experience difficulties with their mental health and emotional well-being.
- Resilience is a psychological quality that helps a person to withstand stress and change in life.
- Psychological security and resilience are qualities that can be learned and developed at any age.

4.4 Meaningful activities to support and promote health, development and well-being

Understanding meaningful activity

Meaningful activities enable a person to achieve a goal and meet one or more of their needs.

Meaningful activities play an important part in our lives and our sense of identity.

Health, social care and childcare workers often use meaningful activities as a way of promoting and supporting an individual's development and well-being.

Creative and therapeutic activities are used to meet a variety of physical, intellectual, emotional and social needs in different types of care setting.

Using activities in care settings

Health, social care and childcare workers should have good reasons for using activities as part of a person's care, support or development plan.

Activity planning must take account of legal and health and safety factors and the needs of the individual or group involved.

A range of factors affect the choice of meaningful activities for an individual including the type of care setting, the person's age, gender, culture and communication skills, and the potential benefits to the person from taking part.

References

Bongard, V., McDermott, A.Y., Dallal, G.E. & Schaefer, E.J. (2007), 'Effects of age and gender on physical performance', *Journal of Age*, Sept; 29 (2–3): 77–85.

Census (2011) https://www.ons.gov.uk/census

Emmerson, C. & Smith, J. (2016) *Piecing the Puzzle: The annual profile for substance misuse*, Public Health Wales

Gartner, A., Francis, I., Hickey, D., Hughes, R. & May, L. (2014) *Alcohol and Health in Wales 2014*, Public Health Wales Observatory

National Survey for Wales 2017–18, https://gov.wales/statistics-and-research/national-survey

Office for National Statistics (2016) www.ons.gov.uk/peoplepopulationandcommunity/birthsdeathsandmarriages/livebirths/bulletins/birthsummarytablesenglandandwales/2016

Oppenheim, C. & Harker, L. (1996) *Poverty: the facts*, 3rd edn, Child Poverty Action Group

Riordan, P. (2014), 'Improving the Health of Everyone in Wales – the Public Health Challenge of Prudent Healthcare', http://www.prudenthealthcare.org.uk/wp-content/uploads/2014/10/Improving-thehealth-of-everyone-in-Wales---thepublic-health-challenge-of-prudenthealthcare.pdf

Save the Children (2014) *Child Poverty Snapshots: The local picture in Wales*

Smith, J. (2017) *Data mining Wales: The annual profile for substance misuse 2016–17*, Public Health Wales

Smith, J. & Turner, D. (2017) *Drug deaths in Wales 2016*, Public Health Wales

StatsWales (2016, 2018) https://statswales.gov.wales/Catalogue

Welsh Assembly Government (2006),
Climbing Higher: Next Steps. http://sport.wales/media/119237/climbing_higher_e[1].pdf

Welsh Assembly Government (2009), *Walking and Cycling Action Plan*

Welsh Health Survey (2012) https://gweddill.gov.wales/docs/statistics/2013/130911-welsh-health-survey-2012-en.pdf

Welsh Health Survey (2015) *Health Status, Illnesses, and Other Conditions*, https://gweddill.gov.wales/docs/statistics/2016/160622-welsh-health-survey-2015-healthstatus-illnesses-other-conditions-en.pdf

World Health Organisation (1946)

Glossary

Absolute poverty Lacking the minimum amount of income needed to meet basic living needs for food, shelter or housing.

Abstract thinking The ability to think about objects, principles, and ideas that are not physically present.

Accountable When a person or organisation is required or expected to justify their actions.

Active participation Direct, influential involvement in planning, making decisions about or meeting care and support needs.

Acute Severe, lasting a short time.

Advocate A person who supports, promotes the best interests of or speaks on behalf of another person.

Associative play Children take part in similar or identical activities as part of a group but there is no definite goal or organisation to their play.

Attachment An emotionally close, secure relationship with a parent or carer.

Attachment relationship A deep and lasting emotional bond that connects one person to another over time, such as a parent–child relationship.

Autism A lifelong condition that affects how an individual communicates with, and relates to, other people and the world around them.

Balanced diet A diet consisting of a variety of different types of food and providing adequate amounts of the nutrients necessary for good health.

Bereavement The feeling of loss and grief following the death of a loved one.

Bonding The formation of an emotionally close human relationship.

Bronchitis An infection of the main airways of the lungs (bronchi) resulting in them being irritated and inflamed and producing mucus.

Carbohydrates A nutrient found in bread, pasta and potatoes, for example, that provides the body with energy.

Cardiovascular disease A diseases that involves the heart or blood vessels.

Carotid artery Either of the two large arteries, one on each side of the head, that carry blood to the head and which can be felt in the neck.

Challenging behaviour Behaviour that is seen as socially unacceptable and which challenges the coping ability of others (parents, teachers, care workers).

Childcare Services that safeguard or promote the development of children.

Chlamydia A curable bacterial infection spread through unprotected sex that can damage a woman's reproductive system.

Chromosomes Chemical structures found in most living cells that carry genetic information in the form of genes.

Chronic condition A long-term, constantly recurring and incurable condition.

Chronic health problems Long-term or ongoing health conditions that a person will always have.

Cilia The small hairs lining the lungs.

Client groups Groups of people who have the same types of problems or care needs.

Cognitive Relating to mental processes involved in knowing, learning and understanding.

Communication skills The ability to convey information and ideas to others.

Confidentiality Keeping information private, or restricting access only to those authorised to know.

Consultation A meeting with a doctor or another health professional to diagnose and discuss health problems or treatments.

Cooperative play Organised play activity that has a goal and through which children interact.

Co-production Involves care professionals and users of services jointly planning and delivering public services in an equal relationship.

Coronary heart disease A disease in which a waxy substance called plaque gradually builds up inside the arteries that supply oxygen-rich blood to your heart muscle.

Culture The way of life, especially the beliefs, customs and practices, of a particular group of people at a particular time.

Cystic fibrosis An inherited disorder that affects the cell membranes, causing the production of thick and sticky mucus in the lungs.

Dementia-related illnesses Brain conditions that cause a gradual decrease in the ability to think and remember which affect a person's daily functioning.

Demographic data Information about the size and structure of the population.

Development The emergence (appearance) and increase in sophistication of skills, abilities and emotions.

Developmental norms Standards by which the progress of a child's development can be measured.

Dexterity Skill in performing tasks, especially with the hands.

Diagnosis The process of identifying an illness or disease.

Diastolic blood pressure The minimum pressure on the arteries when the chambers of the heart fill with blood.

Disabilities Impairments of physical, mental or sensory functions that affect a person's abilities or activities.

Disabling Limiting a person's movements, senses or activities.

Discriminate Act in an unfair and unequal way because of prejudice.

Disease An abnormal condition that negatively affects part of a person's body.

Diversity A range of different and varied things.

Domiciliary services Non-medical welfare services, such as meals-on-wheels and home help, provided in a person's home.

Economic Money-related.

Eligibility criteria The rules governing access to a service.

Emotions A state of mind resulting from mood, relationships with others or the circumstances a person is in.

Equality Having equal status, rights and opportunities.

Ethnicity People with the same ethnicity have a shared way of life or culture, a common geographical origin, a similar skin colour or a common language or religion.

Fats An essential nutrient that stores energy, absorbs vitamins and maintains core body temperature.

Fine motor skills Movements of the hands, wrists, fingers, feet and toes that rely on control over smaller muscles.

Food poverty The inability to obtain healthy, affordable food.

Foster care Full-time substitute care of children, not in their own home, by people who are not their biological or adoptive parents.

Frailty Being weak, infirm and at greater risk of ill health and accidental injury.

Funding Finance or money to pay for services.

Gender A term used to describe the social and cultural expectations of males and females.

Gender stereotypes Simplified, over-generalised expectations of male and female roles.

Genes Small sections of DNA on a chromosome, that are the basic units of heredity, and may be copied and passed on to the next generation.

Gross motor skills Whole body movements that depend on a person being able to control the large muscles in their arms and legs.

Growth mind-set The belief that skills and abilities can be improved, and that their development is the purpose of the work you do.

Growth spurt A period of accelerated physical change that occurs in mid-childhood and during puberty.

Haemoglobin The substance in blood that carries oxygen.

Hazard Anything that can cause harm.

Health inequalities Differences in the health status or the influences on health between groups in the population.

Health messages Focused information about health issues or actions that a person can take to improve an aspect of their health and well-being.

Health promotion The process of enabling people to increase control over, and to improve, their health.

Health Visitor A qualified and registered nurse or midwife with additional training who assesses the health needs of individuals, children and their families.

Holistic Focusing on the whole person, physically, intellectually, emotionally and socially.

Hospice A care setting providing palliative and supportive care to people in the final stages of life.

Hydration The process of making your body absorb water or other liquid.

Illness A form of sickness affecting the person's body or mind.

Immunisation Making people immune to infection.

Immunity Protection against an infectious disease.

Implement Put something into practice.

Inclusion Being included in a group, not left out.

Income The money a person receives usually from work.

Independent healthcare provider A non-government organisation or private practitioner.

Informal care Care that is provided by family, friends and neighbours rather than by trained professionals.

Insecurity A lack of confidence, uncertainty or anxiety.

Inspection Looking at or examining something carefully.

Integrated Another term for linked or coordinated.

Intellectual Refers to a person's ability to think and understand ideas and information.

Interventions Actions or activities designed to improve health and well-being.

Learning difficulty An impaired or reduced ability to learn.

Legislation Written laws, such as Acts of Parliament.

Legislative framework A set of laws.

Life expectancy The average period a person may expect to live.

Life span The time between a person's birth and their death.

Life stages A stage, phase or period of the human life cycle.

Local authority An organisation that is officially responsible for public services and facilities in a particular area.

Looked after children Children who are in the care of their local authority (rather than their parents) for more than 24 hours.

Maturity The state of being fully developed or adult.

Meaningful activity Activity that enables a person to achieve a goal and meets one or more of their needs.

Menopause The ceasing of menstruation and loss of fertility in women.

Mental capacity The awareness and ability to make informed decisions or choices.

Migration Movement of people from one place to another with the intention of settling.

Mindfulness Maintaining a moment-by-moment awareness of our thoughts, feelings, bodily sensations and surrounding environment, through a gentle, nurturing focus.

Minerals Micronutrients such as calcium and iron that are needed in small amounts to allow the human body to function.

Mobility The ability to move freely in a coordinated way.

Moral judgement The process of making decisions about the right course of action or an acceptable way to behave.

Multi-agency working A cooperative arrangement between several agencies or organisations to work together towards a shared goal.

Multi-disciplinary team A group of care practitioners with different specialisms (doctors, nurses, social workers) working together to meet people's care needs.

Normal ageing Natural physical changes that happen over a person's life.

Nutrients Substances found in food that are essential for growth and the maintenance of life. The five main nutrients are protein, carbohydrates, vitamins, minerals and fats.

Obese Having excess body fat that may have a negative effect on health.

Osteoporosis A medical condition in which the bones become brittle.

Palliative care Care treatment and support for people with a life-limiting condition.

Parallel play Children play independently in similar activities, alongside each other, without sharing or influencing each other's activity.

Parkour The sport of moving rapidly through an area, typically in a town or city, negotiating obstacles by running, jumping, and climbing.

Partnership working Collaboration and cooperation between different organisations to achieve a common aim.

Peer group A group of people about the same age, who see themselves (or are seen by others) as belonging together in some way.

Percentile chart A way of monitoring and recording a child's growth by comparing it to a certain percentage of the population.

Personal identity A person's view of their qualities, beliefs, personality and sense of belonging.

Person-centred approach An holistic approach that puts the needs of the individual first.

Physical growth An increase in physical size (mass and height).

Physiotherapist A care professional who treats physical injury or movement problems with exercises and other physical treatments (such as massage).

Postcode lottery The idea that access to health, social care and childcare services is affected by where a person lives.

Prejudice A strongly-held negative belief or attitude relating to a particular individual or group of people.

Prescription A doctor's written instructions to dispense medication.

Primary health care Those parts of the health service, such as general practitioners, that deal with every day, nonemergency healthcare needs.

Primary socialisation The first stage of socialisation when a child is taught by family members to interact, behave and talk in socially acceptable ways.

Private sector Care businesses and private practitioners who charge for their services.

Proportionate assessment A simpler, person-centred assessment of need that focuses on what matters to the individual.

Prostheses Artificial body parts that replace or supplement a missing or defective part.

Protected characteristics A characteristic or feature of a person that may not be used as a basis for decision-making as, if used, this might result in unlawful discrimination.

Proteins Nutrients found in meat, eggs and milk that are needed for human growth.

Prudent healthcare Doing less in a cautious way, to achieve better outcomes for patients in greatest need.

Psychoactive A substance that has a major effect on mental (brain) processes.

Psychological security The absence of fear or distressing anxiety.

Puberty The process of physical change through which a child's body matures into an adult body capable of sexual reproduction.

Public health The health of the population as a whole, and the strategies used to prevent disease and promote health in a society.

Radial artery An artery that begins at the elbow and extends down the forearm.

Reablement The active process of regaining skills, confidence and independence after a significant period of illness or a traumatic injury.

Redundancy The loss of a job because an employer no longer needs a person to do it.

Registered nurse A nurse who has met the standards of practice and achieved a qualification that allows them to register with the Nursing and Midwifery Council.

Regulatory body An independent organisation, such as the Nursing and Midwifery Council, that makes rules and sets standards for a profession such as registered nursing.

Relative poverty Having a household income that is 50 per cent less than the median (average) income.

Residential childcare Long-term care given to young adults or children in a residential setting that is not their own family home.

Resilience The ability to adapt to and deal with a crisis or difficulty and return to normal afterwards again.

Respiratory disorders A disease or condition affecting the respiratory (breathing) system such as pneumonia or asthma.

Resuscitate Bring back to life.

Risk Exposure to danger, harm or loss.

Safeguarding Protecting children and vulnerable adults from abuse or neglect and educating those around them to recognise the signs and dangers.

Screening A strategy used with a population to identify the possible presence of as yet unidentified disease in those without signs or symptoms.

Secondary health care Healthcare services that are generally provided for people with more complex or emergency care needs in hospital or residential settings.

Self A person's sense of 'who' they are.

Self-concept The beliefs, ideas or mental image a person has about themselves, including their strengths, weaknesses and how others view them.

Self-confidence A feeling of trust that a person has in their abilities, qualities and judgement.

Self-esteem Confidence in your own worth or abilities, closely linked to self-respect.

Self-identity An individual's view of themselves, which is usually influenced by personal perceptions of their own abilities, flaws and status and by feedback received from others.

Self-image A mental picture a person has of themselves, their abilities and attributes compared to those of others.

Self-worth An individual's sense of their own value or worth as a person.

Sensory impairment A defect in one or more of a person's senses (sight, hearing, touch, smell, taste).

Sexual maturity The point at which a person is biologically capable of sexual reproduction.

Sexuality The ability to experience and express sexual feelings.

Sexually transmitted infection An infection transmitted through the exchange of semen, blood or other bodily fluids during sex.

Sibling A brother or sister.

Social care Social work, personal care, protection or social support services to children or adults in need or at risk.

Social exclusion Being isolated and lacking the rights, benefits and resources normally available to members of society.

Social prescribing A means of enabling GPs, nurses and other primary care professionals to refer people to a range of local, non-clinical services that have health and well-being benefits.

Social services departments The departments of a local authority that deal with non-medical social work, social care and safeguarding needs of children and adults.

Socialisation The process of learning to behave in a way that is acceptable to society.

Solo play Children play independently, focusing on their own activity, without interacting with each other.

Statutory sector Care services that are provided on behalf of the state (government) because of a legal duty.

Statutory services Services that are funded and run by the government (state).

Stigma Disapproval or discrimination against a person based on negative ideas about their social characteristics or personal qualities.

Stress Physical or mental tension caused by threats, difficulties or challenges to a person's coping skills.

Stroke The sudden death of brain cells due to a lack of blood flow (and oxygen) to the brain when an artery is blocked or ruptured. Loss of speech, weakness and paralysis on one side of the body may result.

Substance misuse A term to describe illegal or unauthorised drug abuse or excessive use of alcohol that is damaging to health.

Sustainability The ability to continue something over time.

Sustainable Able to be supported, maintained or kept going over time (for example, a service).

Symptom A physical or mental indicator of a condition or disease.

Systolic blood pressure The blood pressure on the artery walls when the heart is contracting or pushing blood out.

Target groups The groups of people health promotion campaigns are trying to influence.

Targeted services Services developed and provided for a group of people with specific care needs.

Therapeutic Another word for healing.

Third sector Another term for the voluntary sector, consisting of independent, not-for-profit organisations.

Trauma A deeply distressing or disturbing experience.

Universal services Health and welfare services provided for everybody within the population.

Vaccinations Treatment with a vaccine to produce immunity against a particular infectious disease, virus or tropical disease.

Vitamins Micronutrients such as vitamin C that are needed in small amounts to keep the body healthy and functioning well.

Voluntary sector Registered charities and not-for-profit organisations.

Well-being A state characterised by health, happiness and prosperity.

Index

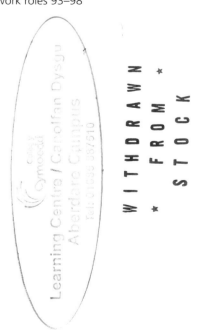